Modern Health Administration

George R. Wren

MODERN HEALTH ADMINISTRATION

University of Georgia Press, Athens

Library of Congress Catalog Card Number: 72-91995
International Standard Book Number: 0-8203-0268-6

The University of Georgia Press, Athens 30602

Printed in the United States of America

To Hope Leech

CONTENTS

List of Figures   x

Foreword   xi

Preface   xiii

Section One: **Management**   **1**

Chapter One.   Management: An Introduction to Formal
                 Considerations   3

I.   What Is Management?   3
II.   The Universality of Management   4
III.   Management as an Art and a Science   6
IV.   The Functions of Management   6
V.   Carrying Out the Functions of Management   8
VI.   Conclusion   17

Chapter Two.   The Behavioral Science Approach to
                 Management   19

I.   Introduction   19
II.   Some Early Behavioral Scientists   20
III.   Human Relations   21
IV.   Some Findings of the Behavioral Scientists
        Looking At Management   23

Chapter Three.   Decision-Making in Management   50

I.   Introduction   50
II.   Characteristics of Decisions   51
III.   Classification of Decisions   54
IV.   Theories of Decision-Making   56
V.   Psychology in Decision-Making   59
VI.   Creativity in Decision-Making   61
VII.   Steps in Decision-Making   64
VIII.   Who Should Make Decisions   66
IX.   Decision-Making as an Art   68

X.	Improving Decision-Making	69
XI.	Conclusion	71

Section Two: **Systems—The Scientific Approach to Management** **73**

Chapter Four.	Systems	75
I.	The History of Management Thought	75
II.	Systems: The Scientific Method Applied to Management	79
III.	General Systems Theory	80
IV.	Definitions	81
V.	Designing a System	85
VI.	Systems Controls	87
VII.	Components of a System	90
VIII.	Systems and Human Relations	95
IX.	Conclusion	97

Section Three: **Modern Management in Production** **99**

Chapter Five.	Automation	101
Chapter Six.	Work Simplification	107
I.	Time and Motion Study	108
II.	Tool and Machine Design	108
III.	Physical Plant Design	109
IV.	Work Standardization	110
V.	Production Control	110
Chapter Seven.	Value Analysis	116

Section Four: **Modern Decision Methods; Operations Research** **123**

Chapter Eight.	Operations Research and Models	125
I.	Operations Research	125
II.	Mathematics in Management	127
III.	Models	129
Chapter Nine	Linear Programming	130
I.	Definition	130
II.	History	130
III.	What Is Linear Programming?	131
IV.	Examples of Linear Programming	131
V.	Advantages of Linear Programming	133
VI.	Disadvantages of Linear Programming	135
Chapter Ten.	Non-Linear and Dynamic Programming	137
Chapter Eleven.	Queuing Theory	141
I.	Introduction	141
II.	General Queuing Theory	143
III.	General Queuing Characteristics	143
IV.	The Poisson Function	146

V.	Health Applications of Queuing Theory	147
VI.	Queuing Theory and the Emergency Room	150
VII.	Conclusion	151
Chapter Twelve.	Simulation	153
I.	Introduction	153
II.	What is Simulation?	153
III.	How Can Simulation Be Used?	155
IV.	Advantages of Simulation	156
V.	Disadvantages of Simulation	159
VI.	Some Examples of Simulation Used in the Health Field	159
VII.	Conclusion	162
Chapter Thirteen.	Gaming	163

Section Five: Other Modern Decision Methods — **169**

Chapter Fourteen.	Program Evaluation and Review Technique (PERT)	171
I.	Introduction	171
II.	What is PERT?	171
III.	History of PERT	176
IV.	Critical Path Method (CPM)	178
V.	PERT-COST	179
VI.	An Example of PERT	180
VII.	Health Examples of PERT-CPM	182
VIII.	Conclusion	185
Chapter Fifteen.	Payoff Tables and Decision Trees	188
I.	Introduction	188
II.	Payoff Tables	188
III.	Decision Trees	192
IV.	Conclusion	196
Chapter Sixteen.	Decision-Making under Risk or Uncertainty	197
I.	Introduction	197
II.	Decision-Making under Certainty	198
III.	Decision-Making under Risk	199
IV.	Decision-Making under Uncertainty	200
V.	Monte Carlo	202
VI.	Game Theory	203
VII.	Conclusion	206

Section Six: Conclusion — **209**

Notes	214
Author Index	227
Subject Index	230

LIST OF FIGURES

1.1	The Total Process of Management	9
1.2	Interpersonal Relationships and Number of Sub-ordinates	10
4.1	A Hierarchy of Systems	81
4.2	A Typical System	82
4.3	A Typical Systems Control	88
4.4	A Non-electronic Systems Control Panel	89
14.1	A Simple PERT Network for Construction of a Physicians' Clinic	174–175
15.1	Payoff Table for Location of Cocktail Party in Face of Overcast Skies	189
15.2	Payoff Table for Location of Cocktail Party in Face of Overcast Skies and 75 Percent Chance of Rain	190
15.3	Payoff Table on Expenditure of Different Amounts on Student Nurse Recruitment	191
15.4	A Decision Tree	193
15.5	Payoff Table Giving Results of First Decision	195
16.1	Payoff Matrix	206

Foreword

The health and hospital field has had great need for a book on the application of systems theory and quantitative management to health institutions and organizations. This book fills that need very nicely. While health and hospital administration is more than just the interpretation of computer printouts and the application of mathematics to management, today's health administrator must become more familiar with the application of these modern theories and methods in management. They are no longer something to be left to the expert but are now very much an everyday part of the management process.

Since these are necessarily complicated subjects, books and articles which have been written on them are also very complicated. In addition, since the applications of systems theory and quantitative management have been developed primarily in industry, the examples in existing books and articles are drawn from industry and therefore do not aid the health administrator much in his understanding of the use of the complex subject matter in his own work.

That is why this book should fill a very real need in the health field. It explains these complicated topics in relatively simple language and yet, at the same time, does not sacrifice accuracy for simplicity. The illustrative examples are drawn from health administration and should greatly aid the reader's understanding of their role and use in his work.

I can think of no one better qualified to write such a book. George Wren received his master's degree in hospital administration from the University of Chicago and then had sixteen years of experience as the administrator of three large hospitals. He then decided to return to school in order to obtain a Ph. D. in business. Fortunately he did so at a time when graduate education in business had already taken on its systems and quantitative orientation.

George Wren's education and experience in hospital administration, his experience in writing, and his recent doctoral education all blend together so that he has produced a needed, useful, and readable book.

Ray E. Brown

McGaw-Northwestern
University Medical Center
Chicago, Illinois

Preface

In recent years all the modern management methods developed by systems analysis, operations research, industrial engineering, and quantitative management science have swept over administration like a tidal wave. Health administration is no exception. While health administrators are well aware of the existence and importance of these modern management methods their understanding is often limited by a lack of background in quantitative administration. This confusion is compounded by the fact that the field of quantitative management has grown so rapidly that overlap and duplication of terminology and concepts are common.

It is the purpose of this book to help the ordinary health administrator understand the methods of modern management by providing as simple an explanation as is possible for the most common of these. This is not intended to qualify the reader to use these methods—only to permit him to know what they are so that he may be better able to function in his relationships with specialized assistants and consultants who are experts. To help the health administrator understand modern management methods, this book clarifies the relationships between the various modern management methods by providing an outline or model of relationships and by limiting each term to a single usage.

Since there are some health administrators who have entered the field from a professional and not an administrative background, the first section of this volume provides an introduction to administration, including chapters on management theory, on the behavioral science approach to management, and on managerial decision-making.

Handling subject matter such as this so as to present it in a relatively non-technical manner—understandable to the ordinary health administrator without sacrificing accuracy and scope—is not an easy task. This work was made easier for me, however, by the conviction that the subject matter is important and that there is a need for a book of this type.

George R. Wren

Georgia State University
Atlanta, Georgia

Section One: Management

The three chapters in this section are intended to give a brief introduction to management. Chapter 1 provides a general overall look at management as an art and a science—as a total process divided into functions. Organizations as social groups and personnel as human beings, with some of the implications of this for management, are the subjects for Chapter 2. Managerial decision-making is the subject of the third chapter in this section.

Chapter One

Management: An Introduction to Formal Considerations

I. What Is Management?

Like many other very familiar things, management seems to be a difficult concept to define. The following are some examples of definitions of management.

"Management is the function of getting things done through people and directing the efforts of individuals towards a common objective."[1]

"Management is the basic, integrating process of the business activity that surrounds our daily life."[2]

"Management consists of all activities undertaken to secure the accomplishment of work through the efforts of other people."[3]

"Management is defined here as the accomplishment of desired objectives by establishing an environment favorable to performance by people operating in organized groups."[4]

"Management has been defined in very simple terms as getting things done through the efforts of other people."[5]

"Management may be defined as a technique by means of which the purposes and objectives of a particular human group are determined, clarified and effectuated."[6]

"Management may be defined as the process by which the execution of a given purpose is put into operation and supervised. The combined output of various types and grades of human effort by which the process is effected is again known as management, in the human sense. Again, the combination of those persons who together put forth this effect in any given enterprise is known as the management of the enterprise."[7]

One of the best and most comprehensive definitions of management is that given by Mee who says that management is "securing maximum results with a minimum of effort so as to secure maximum prosperity and happiness for both employer and employee, and give the public the best possible service."[8] This definition includes efficency of operations (securing maximum results with a minimum of effort); profit-making (maximum prosperity for both employer and employee); job satisfaction (maximum happiness for both employer and employee); social values and public responsibility (give the public the best possible service).

II. The Universality of Management

The widely-accepted "universality of management concept" means that the basic task of management and fundamental principles of administration exist, regardless of what is being managed. As McFarland puts it, "Management is a universal process in all organized living. . . . [It is] a basic operative force in all complex, purposive organizations. . . ."[9] R. C. Davis writes: "Management is the function of executive leadership anywhere."[10] Thus it follows that an executive who is successful in managing one type of organization or business could be successful in managing another type. As McFarland says, "An interesting implication of management as a fundamental process with universal characteristics and principles is that management skills are transferable."[11]

Is this true, however? It is easy to agree that the successful manager of an A&P supermarket could move over and become the successful manager of a Kroger supermarket. Moreover, that this same successful A&P manager could probably be a success in managing a J. C. Penney department store. On the other hand, could this successful manager of a supermarket become a successful bank president? For that matter, could a successful bank president be a success as a supermarket manager? Can a successful physician or accountant or high school principal be a success as a public health administrator? We are not so sure of this. Therefore is the universality of management true after all?

This same doubt has bothered Drucker who says that management is not universal since there are fundamental differences between managing an economic unit like a business and non-economic organizations.[12] Dale has also taken issue with the universality of management principle on the basis that no one person can encompass all the widely differing philosophies underlying religious, academic, military, and business institutions in both communist and democratic countries. He adds that the universality of management principle is contradicted by observed examples of the difficulties encountered by managers who shift into a widely different type of organization from the one in which they were initially successful.[13]

These two apparently opposing points of view can be reconciled and the universality of management principle can be accepted, if it is noted that while management may be universal, the environments within which management takes place may differ greatly. The physical facilities, the products, the type of customer, the type of personnel, and even the philosophy and objectives are greatly different when one considers a food store, a bank, a high school, or a hospital.

A successful manager must know the basic principles and the basic job of management, and he also must know and thoroughly understand the environment in which these principles are applied. Both are vital to the success of any manager. Therefore we can say that the universality of management concept is true but that is not enough.

Large modern business corporations expect the student graduating from a collegiate school of business to have learned principles of management. The corporation then provides the required knowledge of the environment through executive training programs over a period of years.

Such executive training programs are not common in the health field, probably because of the small size of the basic health organization units. Even the hospital industry, said to be one of the largest industries in the country, is made up of over seven-thousand small units. Only a few of these units are large enough to provide an executive training program for young hospital administrators. Therefore the field of hospital administration depends upon graduate programs to provide both the principles of management and a background in their application to the hospital environment, the latter in the administrative residency. The existence of these administrative residencies as an integral part of the graduate education of hospital administrators demonstrates an awareness that management of hospitals requires both a knowledge of management principles and of the special hospital environment (both internal and external) in which these principles are practiced.

III. Management as an Art and a Science

Is management an art or a science? Some authorities have favored one point of view (e.g., Ordway Tead whose widely-read book is entitled *The Art of Administration*)[14] and others the differing viewpoint (e.g., Starr,[15] Veinott,[16] Nord,[17] and Teichroew,[18] all of whose books are entitled "Management Science"). However, the scientific approach to management does appear to be receiving the bulk of attention these days.

Management is *both* an art and a science. It is an art based on a scientific foundation. The science of management can be learned through formal education. Organization theory is a good example of the science of management. It can be learned as basic principles. The art, however, can be only partly acquired in that manner. Part must be obtained by experience, by trial and error, by individual preference. An example of the art of management is timing, an all important ingredient of managerial decision-making.

IV. The Functions of Management

Management is a process which has been broken down into various functions. Different authors have divided the process of management into a number of functions. We find that Clough[19] gives only two—making decisions and providing leadership. R. C. Davis[20] has three—creative planning, organizing, and controlling. Four seems to be the most common number, with Newman, Summer and Warren[21] listing organizing, planning, leading, and controlling. Harbinson and Myers[22] have the undertaking of risk and the handling of uncertainty; planning and innovation; coordination, administration and control; and routine supervision. Broom and Longenecker[23] give planning, organizing and staffing, actuating work accomplishment, and controlling. Terry[24] notes planning, organizing, actuating, and controlling.

Koontz and O'Donnell[25] find management divided into five functions: planning, organizing, staffing, direction, and control. Hicks[26] expands this to six: creating; planning, organizing, motivating, communicating, and controlling. Dale[27] goes one step further with seven management functions—planning, organizing, staffing, direction, control, innovation, and representation.

Since management is a total process, no one can say that any of the authors cited, or the many others who have dealt with this subject, are either right or wrong. It is a question of taking the whole pie and dividing it into some definite number of pieces. Since Terry's four functions of management are well known and since they provide a simple conceptual framework, they will be the ones used here. They are:

A. Planning. The most basic function of management, planning, may extend from initial planning of a new organization through the hour-to-hour planning of a department's activities. Planning may also involve the activities of one department or subdepartment or may be for the entire organization or may even be correlated with community-wide or industry plans.

Planning may also be divided into long range and short range. An example of long-range planning from the health field would be a regional health plan for the next twenty-five years. An example of short-range planning would be next week's staffing pattern for a hospital nursing unit.

B. Organizing. Having decided through planning what he wishes his organization to do, the executive is now responsible for mobilizing and organizing his resources—human, material, and financial—in order to carry out the plans and get the job done. An organizational chart of a health agency is a good example of one way that this function is carried out by management.

C. Actuating. Having decided what his institution or agency should do and having organized it accordingly, the manager must now set the organization into motion to achieve the planned objectives. Most of the everyday activities of the organization come under the actuating function. Examples would be the in-service education of auxiliary health personnel, the hiring and firing of personnel, and the actual treatment rendered patients.

D. Controlling. Although planned objectives are established and the organization is functioning, the manager still cannot sit back and consider his job done. An integral part of management is control, seeing that the functioning organization is really working as planned. Internal accounting controls provide an excellent example of management exercising its control function. So does a medical or professional audit.

E. Management as a total process. Even this presentation of a simple model of management, may tend to obscure the fact that management is a total process. It cannot actually be broken down as neatly into separate functions as might be supposed. For example, in planning, consideration must be given to organizing and actuating or else the plan may not be capable of achievement. Controls must be also built into the plan at the time it is originated.

Overemphasis on the organizational function of management is a bureaucratic disease. No organization can function without planning and, of course, an organizational chart is dead until people, working through the actuating function, bring it to life. These people going about day-to-day tasks would achieve little without an organizational framework and planned objectives.

Finally, controls can only come into existence as a part of the planning and organizing functions and since control must be operated by people, controls are thus a part of the actuating function too.

Figure 1.1 gives a simple model of the management process, divided into these four functions and presented in a way intended to emphasize the interrelationships of the functions.

V. Carrying Out the Functions of Management

What are some of the methods managers use to carry out their functions? How do they work within the special organizational environment?

A. Formal organization. In order to be a success, every institution and agency must have a formal organization. Origi-

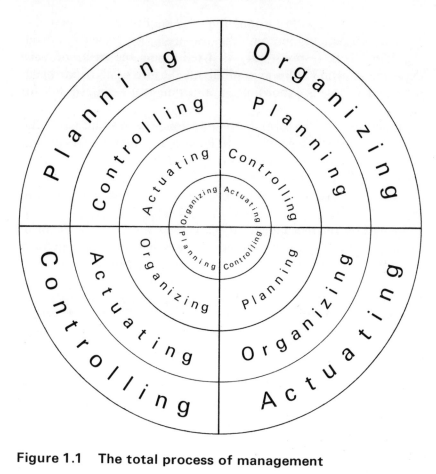

Figure 1.1　The total process of management

nating and maintaining this organization is one of the important
jobs of management leaders.

In setting up this organization, the manager first divides the
total job for which he is held responsible into various departmental or unit functions. In doing so, he must be certain that
no jobs are omitted: that is, each and every job must be assigned
to a department. However, it is just as important to be certain
that there is no duplication or overlap of jobs. If there is such
overlap and duplication, organizational friction is bound to
develop.

Now, having divided his total organization into departments
and having assigned all of the functions of the organization to

the departments, with no omissions and no overlap, the manager is in a position to pinpoint the responsibility for carrying out the jobs. This responsibility is fixed upon the head of each department, who in turn may subdivide the jobs of his department, assign them to his subordinates, and pinpoint responsibility for them.

In setting up his formal organization, the manager is faced with an interesting problem. If he has too many subordinates reporting to him or to one of the department heads, he will be unable to do his job properly. In management terms, too many people reporting to one superior is said to "exceed the span of control."

In writing on the dangers of exceeding the executive span of control, Graicunas has computed mathematically the number of interpersonal relationships involved and their increase in a geometric fashion, as the number of subordinates reporting to one superior increases.[28] When one supervisor (S) supervised one worker (A), the only relationship involved is S to A. When another worker (B) is added, then the number of relationships is increased to six which can be expressed as S to A; S to B; S to A and B together; A to S and B; B to S and A; and A to B. When more workers are added under this one supervisor, the number of relationships increase as shown in figure 1.2. Obviously

Number of subordinates	Number of relationships
1	1
2	6
4	44
8	1,080
12	24,708

Figure 1.2   Interpersonal relationships and number of subordinates

no one executive can cope with that many relationships, but the answer seems deceptively simple. Just set up the organization so that no one executive has over a certain number of subordinates reporting to him. (Graicunas suggested four or five.) Then each superior will be able to deal adequately with this small number of subordinates.

The difficulty with this type of organization is that the number of levels of the organization will necessarily then be exceptionally large, thus hampering organizational communication. As Dale says, there should be as few levels of management as possible between the top manager and the worker.[29] This is called the "short chain of command" principle.

As can be seen, the principle of the "small span of control" is in direct conflict with the "short chain of command" principle. If the number of subordinates reporting to a single superior is maintained at five, then an organization cannot have over 781 total workers and managers without exceeding five levels in the chain of command. What is the answer? It lies in the principle of organizational balance. That is, the top manager must set up his organization to meet its special characteristics and needs, with due balance between the width of the spans of control and the length of the chain of command.

The conflict between these two principles may be more apparent and intuitive than real. Suojanen[30] shows that successful companies almost universally violate the span of control principle with no apparent ill effects. He states that Graicunas's mathematical model of the increase of relationships fails to take account of (1) the fact that all of the relationships are not vital nor of constant occurrence and (2) the subordinates form informal groups and thus all the executive's subordinates do not report to him directly in reality, but the contact is through a small number of informal group leaders. The formal organizational chart is therefore misleading. (Suojanen's work is a good example of the contributions of behavioral scientists to management.) While the dangers of an overly extended span of control are still recognized, the tendency in organizations is now to make them "flat" (i.e., fewer levels and wider span of control).

Having set up the formal organization, with due regard for proper balance, the manager then must see that the organization is implemented by written policies, rules and procedures, which thus become a part of the formal organization.

B. Management by exception. Frederick W. Taylor has been credited with advocating a very valuable and valid principle for use by managers in carrying out their functions.[31] This is the principle of "management by exception." In this principle it is the responsibility of the executive to set up policies, rules, and procedures to handle those types of decisions which recur frequently, so that he himself is not called upon each time to make the decision. The executive need only be called upon to handle the exceptions to the "patterned decisions" he has previously made in setting up the policies, rules, and procedures. Of course, recognizing when the exception exists does call for some judgment on the part of the subordinates. Still the small amount of risk that an exception may be handled routinely and not recognized as such is worthwhile in the saving of time for the executive. The application of management by exception is an example of the control aspect of systems which will be discussed later in this book.

C. Delegation. The assumption that job tasks will be delegated is implicit in the idea of formal organization. The question of what can be delegated has been an interesting subject in management.

Authority is the power the manager possesses to get the job done. Responsibility is his accountability to his superiors for the job. It has sometimes been said that authority may be delegated but responsibility may not (e.g., Newman[32]). This is based on the fact that an executive may obviously invest a subordinate with authority over lower levels of an organization. Therefore authority can clearly be delegated. However, when the superior attempts to delegate his responsibility for the functions of a lower level of the organization to a subordinate, the superior will find that his superiors still hold him responsible for the total operation. They will not accept the excuse that the superior delegated his responsibility to a subordinate. Therefore responsibility cannot be delegated. As Urwick says, "A member does not, by delegation, divest himself of responsibility."[33]

In reality neither authority or responsibility can be delegated. What actually occurs is that each superior can create new authority and responsibility on to his subordinates. At the same time the superior does not relinquish in any way his own previous authority and responsibility.

For example, a nursing home administrator delegates the authority over housekeeping maids to the housekeeping supervisor.

However, the fact that the administrator has created new authority in the housekeeping supervisor without losing any of his own authority is shown when the administrator upon seeing a dangerous puddle of water on the floor, orders a maid to mop up the puddle of water and is not questioned. In other words the administrator still has the authority even though he has created new and similar authority in his housekeeping supervisor. In a like way responsibility is created; it can never be delegated.

One of the major principles which must be remembered when considering delegation is that authority must be commensurate with responsibility. Some authors state that "authority must be equal with responsibility" (e.g., Dale[34]) but this is obviously impossible because authority and responsibility are two different things. To say that authority must be equal with responsibility is like saying that apples must be equal with oranges in a basket of fruit. Regardless of how it is stated, the principle is of great importance. If anyone in an organization is held responsible for the successful completion of a job, the individual must be given at the same time enough authority to carry it out. A manager cannot be given the responsibility for doing a job and then have his hands tied so that it is impossible for him to do the job.

As an example, if the dean of a nursing school has been assigned the responsibility of having the school of nursing fully accredited, she must at the same time be given authority over the hiring and dismissal of the faculty, as well as over the total educational program of the school and the admission and dismissal of students. Her position would be untenable if she were held responsible for full accreditation for the nursing school but at the same time told that the school must continue to employ three faculty members whose educational qualifications, experience, and attitudes made it impossible for the school to offer an academic program which could be accredited. The dean would first become frustrated and unhappy, and then she might resign. She had not been given authority commensurate with her assigned responsibilities.

Hospital administrators often find themselves in a similar situation. For example, the board of trustees may hold the hospital administrator responsible for the hospital's accreditation but at the same time, it may not delegate to the administrator requisite authority over the practice of medicine at that hospital. In other words the administrator does not have authority commensurate with his responsibility, because obviously the quality of medical care is the primary criterion on which hospital accreditation is based. One answer to that situation would be to give the hospital administrator authority over the medical staff including appointment of physicians, dismissal of physicians from the medical staff, and suspension of physician privileges. This solution is not recommended. A more logical solution would be to continue to delegate this authority to the medical staff but to remove the responsibility for that aspect of hospital administration from the administrator and instead to delegate that to the medical staff so that its responsibility is commensurate with its authority.

D. Line and staff organization. In setting up this formal organization, the manager will establish two types of subordinate executives—line executives and staff executives.

A line executive is one who has authority over people within the organization. He will probably also have authority over money, equipment, materials, and certain jobs; but he very clearly will have authority over the people under him. An example would be a laboratory director who has full authority over all laboratory personnel. Staff authority is advisory in nature only. That is, a staff executive is an advisor to a line executive. This simple definition suffers from the fact that it is obviously not true in all cases. Certainly most staff executives have some authority other than being a mere counselor to a line executive.

Actually the term "staff authority" applies to a variety of different executive relationships. Executives who are in an advisory capacity only are staff. An example of such an individual would be an attorney for a state licensing agency. His function is to give legal advice to line executives.

Other executives have their major authority over a function instead of over people. An example would be the hospital personnel director whose only line authority is over the few workers in his own department. His primary authority is over the personnel function. He therefore is a staff executive. Staff executives are also those persons whose primary authority is over things instead of over people. The hospital engineer does have authority over the workers in his department, but his primary authority is over the engineering and maintenance functions and over things (i.e., buildings and equipment). Since the purchasing agent is in the same situation, he too is a staff executive.

Finally another type of staff executive is the "administrative assistant." When these people function as a special assistant to a line officer, they clearly are to be defined as staff. Even when these special assistants are given a temporary line function, as for example when an administrative assistant would be put in charge of a branch office during a temporary three-month absence of the chief executive of the branch, he would still probably be considered as a staff executive on temporary line assignment.

Probably the best definition of line authority is that it is authority over people, while staff authority is all other types of authority other than line authority. The increase in size and complexity of health organizations has been accompanied by a sharp increase in the use of staff executives who serve as extensions of the line officers and line organization.

E. Motivation. In order to carry out his job as a manager, the administrator must get people to do work and assume responsibility in the organization. How this is done is obviously a very important subject in management.

Financial incentives and fringe benefits have a primary place because not only do people work because they need money to live but in addition money as the medium of exchange in our society is the one element in every organization to which all else can be equated and compared. Therefore the status and prestige aspects of salary have important motivating functions.

The managerial concept that compensation should be geared to contribution is widely accepted but little applied in the health field, primarily due to the difficulty of establishing performance standards and of measuring comparative contributions by different types and levels of professional, technical, and non-professional health workers. Public and governmental resistance to rising health care costs, plus organized group pressure for higher wages from health personnel on all levels, have focused increasing attention on wage and salary administration, of which this is a part.

Fringe benefits, both those which appear to the worker as rewards for a job well done and those which add to workers security and organizational stability, are also prime motivating factors. The motivation of workers, beyond the mere financial and fringe benefit level, has been the subject of much work by behavioral scientists. Some of their findings are given in the next chapter.

F. Communications. In order for people within an organization to work in a logical manner, it is important that they be in possession of facts concerning their jobs as well as what is expected of them. The establishment of policies, rules, and procedures when the manager sets up the formal organization is a recognition of the importance of communications. So is the consideration of the number of levels existing in the organization, because the chain of command also serves as one means of communication.

The manager is primarily concerned with formal channels of communication. He does also know that informal channels of communication (the grapevine) exist and he must take cognizance of these in his job. Some managers make the mistake of thinking that their formal organizational chart establishes rigid lines of communication as well as lines of authority. Nothing could be or should be further from the truth! In order for everyone in the organization on all levels to be in possession of the facts he needs, communication within the organization must work up, down, and sideways.

G. Finances. Even though health institutions and agencies may be "non-profit organizations," they exist within a society which uses money as a medium of exchange. Therefore the health administrator has the same job in the financial area as do all other managers. He must obtain adequate money for the current operations of his institution or agency and, in addition, he must obtain finances for continued growth and expansion, for the financial stability of the organization is a prime management responsibility.

H. Creative Innovation. The world is constantly changing, especially in the health field. As the environment in which his health institution or agency changes, the manager is responsible for creative planning and innovation to meet these demands.

While management has no monopoly on creativity (as well-run suggestion plans have demonstrated), the primary responsibility in this area does fall on top management. No one really expects the workers to provide the creative ideas needed to meet changing conditions nor is much expected of the foremen, supervisors, and department heads in this regard. (As a matter of fact, we probably expect too little!) If the top manager cannot come up with new ideas to solve new problems and meet new conditions, it is obvious that he has failed to meet one of his responsibilities.

I. Leadership. Finally, in carrying out the functions of management, the manager is expected to provide leadership. Leadership is a general *concept* which embraces many areas. Different types of leadership are needed in different situations. Whether it is leadership based on respect for superior ability or on proven past successes, whether it is leadership based on the fact that everybody likes the boss because he is a "good guy," or whether leadership is based on pure charisma or on some other factor, the leadership responsibility is unquestioned. The administrator must be the leader of the organization.

As the symbol of his institution or agency when he participates in community affairs and other outside activities, as the final authority to be consulted in the most difficult situations, and as a personal example to all of his followers, the manager is the organization's leader. Management is leadership and leadership is management.

VI. Conclusion

The major purpose of this chapter has been to present an introduction to the formal consideration of management. Management is defined and presented as being based on universal principles but requiring a special knowledge of the environment in which it is practiced.

Management is presented as an art based on a scientific foundation and as a total process divided into a number of functions. Management tools in carrying out these functions are briefly presented including formal organization, management by exception, delegation, line and staff authority, worker motivation, communications, finances, creative innovation and managerial leadership.

Chapter Two

The Behavioral Science Approach to Management

I. Introduction

The preceding chapter presented an introduction to the formal considerations of management. This view is exemplified by the "scientific management" of Frederick W. Taylor and others, in which the worker is seen as a kind of machine to be motivated by rewards and punishment. We also considered the pure organization theory of management, in which the solutions to the proper functioning of the organization are arrived at through the application of organization principles, including efficency, delegation, proper balance between span of control and chain of command, unity of command, and job classification, among other concepts.

As Dale writes, "the classicists [i.e., the scientific management school and the organization theorists] seem to assume that top management need only (1) know what it wants done, (2) arrange for an organization in which the various tasks are exactly dovetailed, (3) issue the necessary orders down through the chain of command, and (4) hold each person accountable for his part of the work. If this is done, the classicists seem to believe, the organization will function harmoniously and effectively, each person in it being spurred on by the hope of reward (in the form of raises or promotions) and the fear of penalties (denial of advancement or dismissal)."[1]

The major objection to the scientific management and organization theory approaches to management is that their authors seem to ignore the fact that organizations are made up of people.

People do the work, people do the supervision, people *are* the organization. In the study of management people just cannot be ignored or treated as machines or pawns. Bringing to managers an understanding of how people function in work and organizational situations has been the contribution of the behavioral scientists.

The work of Suojanen is a good example of the contribution of these behavioral scientists (sociologists, psychologists, social anthropologists, economists, and political scientists) to the study and understanding of management. Graicunas's mathematical model of the proliferation of relationships beyond any manageable level "proved" the validity of the "span of control" principle. But the observed facts clearly demonstrated that reality was in conflict with the model and that there were no apparent seriously disruptive organizational effects when the recommended span of control was exceeded. Suojanen postulated some explanations for this based on observed behavior of people in work situations.

II. Some Early Behavioral Scientists

While often criticized for regarding workers as mere machines, Frederick W. Taylor, the father of scientific management, actually was well aware that workers were people. It was his intent to increase worker productivity and to *ease the worker's tasks* by breaking down jobs into their components for scientific analysis and by financial incentives. Then the company *and the worker* would each benefit financially from the resultant savings.

At an earlier time enlightened managers had recognized that increased productivity might be obtained by more humane treatment of workers. Robert Owen (1771–1858) achieved remarkable commercial success at his Scottish mills with his humane treatment of the workers. Andrew Ure added the human factor to the mechanical and commercial aspects of manufacturing in his book[2] and provided his workers with mechanical ventilation, hot tea, medical treatment, and sick pay.

One of the first modern exponents of the behavioral science approach to management theory was Chester I. Barnard. Barnard, who wrote his significant book in 1938,[3] was not a behavioral scientist himself but an executive who had been the president of New

Jersey Bell Telephone Company. His major contributions include the recognition of psychological and social factors in the functioning of an organization, especially his observation that authority is delegated upward from subordinates to superiors and not downward. Barnard wrote that the superior had only that amount of authority his subordinates were willing to accord him—no more.

III. Human Relations

Following the then-current interest in improving worker productivity through "scientific management," the Hawthorne, Illinois, plant of the Western Electric Company began a series of experiments in 1924 to study the relation between worker productivity and plant lighting. Because both an increase and a decrease in the intensity of lighting caused an increase in production in both t' test and control groups, the experiments were considered a fail re.

Intrigued with these results, which were in strong contradic on to what was expected under the theories of the "scientific manag ment" school, Elton Mayo, Fritz Roethlisberger, and others conducted the now-famous "Hawthorne Experiments" in the 1930s. Mayo was an industrial sociologist and Roethlisberger an engineer. Results of the continued lighting experiments made no sense until a totally new hypothesis was formed: that the workers were human beings who wanted, needed, and appreciated management attention and who responded to this management attention by increasing production.

Continuation of the experiments along this line gave results which indicated that workers did respond to humane treatment and recognition by increased productivity and higher morale. Workers were found to respond to the total work situation, including social and group contacts, and not just to the actual job itself. The worker is not a mere machine: he is a person with personal and group needs which affect his work activities.

These findings were published in 1939, giving rise to a wave of interest in worker motivation and to the "human relations" school of management.[4] As commonly happens, these new discoveries were looked upon by many people as one key that would unlock all doors. Human relations was too often taught as a series of gimmicks for management to pick up practically and use to get more production from the workers. The "happiness school of management" was born: its creed was "just keep 'em happy and they'll work harder." A story from that time gives an indication of how human relations were used.

A personnel director had just returned to the plant after attending an institute on human relations. He observed that one of the foremen was reprimanding one of his workers, a young woman, before all the other workers. The poor woman was crying as the foreman shouted at the top of his voice, "Mary, you are so stupid! How many times do I have to tell you how to do the easiest job? I should have fired you long ago! You are the dumbest person I have ever met!" The personnel director thought that here was someone who needed to learn about human relations, so he had the foreman sent to the next institute on that subject. A few days after the foreman had returned from the institute, the personnel director walked over to his work area to see how he was doing. There was the same foreman berating the same poor weeping woman before the same workers in the same loud voice. He was shouting, "Mary, you are so stupid! How many times do I have to tell you how to do the easiest job? I should have fired you long ago! You are the dumbest person I have ever met!—By the way, how's your mother?"

After the initial widespread enthusiastic acceptance of the theory growing out of the Hawthorne experiments, other researchers in the same area became more cautious. It became popular to criticize the Hawthorne findings. Major criticisms were that Mayo and Roethlisberger seemed to think workers existed in a confused and senseless world from which they could derive meaning only out of the work situation, that they seem to assume too easily an acceptance by the workers of management goals, and that they failed to include the role of unions and collective bargaining in their considerations.[5] These criticisms and some answers to them were presented by Landsberger in 1960,[6] and it now seems that Mayo and Roethlisberger had paved the way for a better understanding of management theory even though their initial findings were perhaps too broadly interpreted and too easily manipulated by others.

Good managers have learned from human relations that gimmicks or simulated interest in the worker are not a lasting way to manage. Even the more current "enlightened self-interest" approach of management is now considered only a temporary solution to management problems. It is soon seen by the worker for what it is—just another management device to get more production from workers, a way to use some things that have been discovered about workers to achieve management ends.

On the other hand, genuine interest by management in the worker, in their needs and goals, and in the implementation of ways that the workers can achieve these within the organizational framework has been one of the answers to better management-worker relations. When management has honestly tried to fuse the workers' needs and goals with those of the organization—to set up the organization in a way to meet both worker and management goals—better total organizational patterns and functions seem to have been created.

So human relations was a key. Not a key to all of management functions but a key that opened doors leading to other research and further findings.

IV. Some Findings of the Behavioral Scientists Looking at Management

While all the authors presented so far in this chapter could be called behavioral scientists from some points of view, this term will be reserved for those people who have applied scientific methodology utilized by the social sciences (observation, collecting facts, hypothesis formation, experimentation, theory construction, and prediction) to the area of management. Using this scientific methodology in work situations, the behavioral scientists go beyond formal management theory to explain, interpret, and even supplant the theories and findings of the "scientific management" school and the organization theorists.

In seeking a theory or theories to explain worker behavior and management functions, the approach of the behavioral scientists is much more rigid than earlier management theorists. It is based on research and, in some cases, even on experimentation. Several examples will now be presented in order to acquaint the reader with the way the behavioral scientist approaches the study of various aspects of management.

A. Informal groups.   Small groups of three or four or up to a dozen or more people apparently spring up spontaneously within all formal organizations. These informal groups tend to polarize for one of many possible factors. A group may consist of all the nursing personnel in one nursing unit or all those personnel who ride to work in one car pool or all the employees of one organization who belong to one minority group—these are examples of factors leading to the formation of a small group.

Most of the work in the Hawthorne experiments was on small group behavior. The findings of these experiments provided the foundation for the human relations school of management and for much of the behavioral science research in succeeding years. The best accounts of these experiments are to be found in Roethlisberger and Dickson[7] and in Whitehead.[8] Extracts and shorter summaries of the work are to be found in many volumes. A good example is in Lawrence and Seiler.[9]

It is difficult to cite adequately and comprehensively the findings of the research on small informal work groups because of the great amount of work that has been done and the extensive nature of the findings and resultant theory. Instead some of the representative findings will be given briefly.

Once formed, small groups produce one or more informal group leaders who have power and influence over other group members even though their leadership position is nowhere to be found in the organizational chart. These informal leaders can work with or against the formal organization and the formal leaders. They owe their position to personal characteristics and to meeting the group's needs. Attempts to utilize the leadership qualities of the informal leaders by appointing them to formal leadership positions in an attempt to fuse the goals of the formal and informal organizations have been almost uniformly unsuccessful since the qualities of informal leadership are not necessarily those of formal leadership (e.g., skill in blocking change by informal leaders) and because the group will find a new informal leader.

Small informal groups may provide many or most of the everyday rewards and satisfactions for most people. These include a sense of belonging, aid on the job, and protection from outside forces like the boss.[10] These objectives are accomplished in many ways: by establishing and enforcing informal work and production quotas, by group pressures to conform, including a system of rewards and punishments, and by resistance to change.

Probably because they were the first small groups studied, and for reasons of investigative convenience, most of the small group findings have been based on industrial production workers. This does not mean that similar informal group behavior does not exist at all levels in the organization. French found similar manifestations of group behavior among furniture salesmen, for example.[11] Informal group sales norms were established and so were informal sanctions against "snitching" on fellow salesmen.

In a well-known study Whyte analyzed informal group behavior in twelve restaurants.[12] Similar studies have been carried out in hospitals, which have become a favorite hunting ground for sociologists. An example of such a study is that by Argyris.[13] Even management itself has its own informal groups and informal leaders. However, the study of informal management groups has lagged behind that of worker groups. Miller and Form give a number of reasons for this: the studies are initiated by management who are more likely to study the workers than themselves since they conceive of the workers' behavior as irrational and in need of study while their own behavior seems logical and easy to understand; management jobs are not as physically circumscribed as are production jobs and hence are more difficult to study; and with the more conservative, restrained, and reserved behavior of upper-middle and upper-class people like managers it is more difficult to observe deviations from anticipated organizational behavior while the overt physical activities, swearing, razzing, and horseplay of the worker are more easily seen, especially by the usual middle-class observer.[14]

By way of summarizing the behavioral science research on informal small groups, it should be said that these exist within all formal organizations. They spring up spontaneously in response to individual social needs and are polarized about some aspect or aspects of the job situation. Informal leaders arise within the small groups. These informal groups and the relationships the members derive from them provide most of the satisfactions that make work bearable and life worthwhile. Small groups establish informally a group social culture (including a special language, norms of conduct, standards of production, myths, group rituals) and attempt to perpetuate this culture, thus providing a major source of resistance to management change. Informal groups compete with other informal groups and with the formal management organization.

B. Worker Motivation. Motivation can be defined as that internal drive which moves a person toward a goal of meeting a personal need. So if management is to understand and perhaps utilize worker motivation, there must be an understanding of the basic needs of the worker.

A conceptual framework to help understand the human needs of the worker is provided by Maslow,[15] who postulates a hierarchy of human needs:

> 5. Self-actualization
> 4. Self-esteem
> 3. Social needs
> 2. Safety and security
> 1. Physiological needs

He suggests that all people begin on the lowest level of physiological need: a requirement for water, air, and food. Until these are satisfied the person is not interested in other needs. When the physiological needs are satisfied, then the person turns his motivation towards achieving his needs on the safety and security level, but not until the physiological needs are first substantially met.

In turn, as each level of human need is met, the person turns his attention towards achieving his needs on the next higher level and so on up through the hierarchy of human needs. Level 3 includes the need to be loved, accepted, and to belong to groups. Level 4 includes self-esteem based on the evaluation of others (reputation) and that based on one's own acceptance of himself (self-respect, confidence, adequacy, and self-acceptance). Level 5 is rarely achieved—primarily because few people succeed in achieving their other needs satisfactorily enough to climb up to level 5. It is the desire for total self-fulfillments—to be everything that one could be. Perhaps the term "creativity" best describes this level of need.

Inherent in Maslow's hierarchy of human needs is the idea that needs on a lower level must be met before a person exhibits much interest in needs on a higher level. A person who is starving is not very interested in love. Troops dying of thirst after a long march through a desert will rush to drink from a river (meeting their physiological need) with no regard for being surprised at that moment by the enemy (a safety need). People who lack adequate human relationships and affection are unable to attain adequate self-respect and confidence. Until these are obtained a person finds it difficult or impossible to be very creative. All this verifies Maslow's theory and shows that motivation for human action must be approached on the level where that person currently exists. Therefore hungry nations must be fed before we can expect their people to be concerned about defending themselves against totalitarian aggression. Health workers must be adequately compensated so that they can meet their needs on levels 1 and 2 before we can expect them to feel themselves a part of the health care team (level 3).

Maslow's theory goes beyond this. Inherent in his concept is the idea that when a need is met, it is no longer important in motivating behavior. People will do things to obtain air, water, and food. When they have obtained enough, however, then they can use no more, and air, water, and food can no longer serve as motivators. Therefore motivation must be provided from the next highest level in the hierarchy. So it is important to determine where a worker stands in the hierarchy in order to motivate him correctly. Actually no professional nurses are starving, although many lack adequate financial reserves for emergencies and for retirement. This is a security level need. What they do seem to complain about most is that the physicians do not accept them as full-fledged members of the patient-care team. To motivate nurses these days, one should concentrate on meeting their needs at levels 2 and 3 and less on merely providing higher salaries, a need which has already been met at level 1.

In a like manner, when the top administrator of a health institution or agency has expressed his desire to resign, it is usually ineffective for his governing body to offer him a salary raise in an attempt to make him change his mind and stay. The administrator is already beyond levels 1 and 2 where money is most effective. An analysis using Maslow's concepts would probably show that he is already on level 4 (i.e., he thinks himself important) but is having difficulty reaching level 5. He feels that he is not being permitted to be all he could be—he is not permitted by his governing body or by circumstances to make his greatest possible contribution. So offering him more money is no real solution. If it does make him stay longer, he will still be unhappy because he cannot meet his needs on level 5. What the governing body should do is save the money and solve the problem by aiding its administrator to make the contribution he feels himself capable of making.

It should be noted that in a materialistic, profit-making society such as ours, people tend to equate many things with money. Hence people who find themselves frustrated by failure to meet their needs at any specific level of this hierarchy will complain that they are not getting paid enough. A salary increase may solve the problem very briefly by removing the immediate focus of discontent. It does not remove the basic source of the discontent; the frustration remains, to simmer a while, and then boil over again; and the money given in the pay increase has been wasted.

Maslow's theory should not be considered as all-or-nothing. It is not necessary to satisfy a person's physiological needs completely in order for him to become interested in and motivated by needs on the safety and security level. Rather the satisfaction of needs should be seen as existing in a decreasing percentage of unmet needs as the hierarchy is ascended. Thus the director of a state health department might have his unmet needs existing as follows:

On level 5—95% unmet needs
On level 4—60% unmet needs
On level 3—40% unmet needs
On level 2—25% unmet needs
On level 1— 5% unmet needs

This still means that attention to meeting the director's needs and reducing his frustrations as well as motivating him towards desired organizational goals must be focused on the greatest areas of his unmet needs to be most effective.

Maslow's contribution is primarily theoretical, and it is not based on extensive collection of data or on experimentation.

Others have collected data and done experimentation based on Maslow's model and have modified the original concepts, based on both confirming and conflicting findings.

Another important motivational model is that of Herzberg.[16] His contribution is based on interviews of engineers and accountants, during which the interviewees were asked to tell of some time when they felt particularly good or bad about their job and what led to these feelings at that time. It was found that different things led to good and bad feelings and that these were not merely opposite sides of the same coin.

Job satisfaction was found to be based on job factors themselves—promotion, pay raises, recognition, responsibility. Job dissatisfaction was focused on conditions related to the job—working conditions, quality of supervision, and interpersonal relations on the job. When the employees were unhappy with their jobs, the only way to remove this unhappiness was to attack the job-dissatisfaction factors. Adding to the job-satisfaction factors did not help. In other words promotions, pay increase, added recognition, or added responsibility would not solve the problem.

Herzberg postulated the existence of two kinds of conditions necessary to provide satisfied employees. First are the "maintenance factors": adequate salary, good working conditions, job security, good supervision, pleasant interpersonal relations, equitable company policies. These provide a healthy environment in which job satisfaction can grow but in themselves do not create job satisfaction.

The motivational factors are those such as advancement, recognition, added responsibility, and pay raises. In themselves, without the proper "maintenance factors," they do not lead to job satisfaction but when the maintenance factors are present, then the motivational factors leading towards job satisfaction will grow and bear fruit. Therefore higher salaries and better fringe benefits will not, in themselves, bring about happy employees. These can only work when the maintenance factors of an adequate salary level, good working conditions, job security, good supervision, pleasant interpersonal relations, and equitable company policies already exist. This is why the nurses in some hospitals who have achieved signficant pay raises through mass "sickouts" are still not as happy as are lower-paid nurses in other hospitals which have better maintenance factors.

Worker morale has been studied extensively, since it is related to different types of leadership and to worker motivation and productivity. Leadership style has been found to influence both worker morale and worker productivity. The concept that high morale would produce high productivity is an attractive one for managers, and such a cause-and-effect relationship has been sought repeatedly. But no consistent correlation between morale and productivity has been found. Kahn and Katz[17] have summarized the results of many such studies. In some cases high morale is found associated with high productivity, but in others low morale and high productivity occur together and even (though rarely) high morale and low productivity. It is obvious that morale, motivation, and productivity are complex relationships.

The conclusion is that organizational motivation is based on personal and social needs of individuals, needs which can be analyzed and understood in terms of conceptual models. The failure of management to understand these conceptions will result in failure to solve motivational problems and a waste of organizational resources.

C. Leadership. Keith Davis has defined leadership as the ability to persuade others to seek defined objectives enthusiastically and as the human factor which binds organizations together and encourages them toward goals.[18] Because of the obvious importance of such qualities, leadership has been the subject of much behavioral science inquiry, including attempts to find out what is leadership and how to develop and use it.

Early studies, reviewed by Stogdill,[19] focused on collecting and classifying physical and mental traits of recognized leaders (e.g., intelligence level, height, weight, appearance, among others) in attempts to obtain identifiable leadership factors for use in selection and prediction of leadership potential. As might be expected, no correlation was found to exist. Gouldner sums this up and leads into a more sophisticated concept of leadership, denying the concept that there are some traits common to all leaders and asserting that leadership is a position which an individual occupies in a given group at a given time.[20] In other words leadership is both a function of the leader and of those led. Applewhite[21] classified studies on leadership into the following categories: leadership traits, leaders and their followers, leadership roles and functions, leadership attempts, leadership under stress, leadership and communication, assessment of leadership, and leadership styles.

A good example and one of the more interesting and revealing of these leadership studies is one by White and Lippitt.[22] In this study ten-year-old boys were engaged in a project of making masks. They were divided into four groups, "equated on patterns of interpersonal relationships, intellectual, physical, socio-economic status and personality characteristics so that one group's response to leadership would be expected to be similar to another's." Then the leaders were instructed in three different styles of leadership: autocratic, democratic, and laissez-faire. The leaders were rotated every six weeks so that each group spent some time under different styles of adult leadership given by different leaders.

The findings show that the greatest production of masks was obtained under autocratic leadership, the least under laissez-faire. Evaluation of group behavior and the attainment of certain social goals showed that there was more aggressive behavior and displayed hostility and less achievement of "desirable social goals" under the autocratic leadership although some individual boys seemed to achieve their greatest personal satisfaction under that type of leadership. Democratic leadership showed the greatest attainment of desired social goals—i.e., group-mindedness and friendliness.

Baumgartel[23] studied twenty research laboratories and classified them according to the leadership style of the lab director: six were laissez-faire, seven democratic, five autocratic (i.e., highly directive), and the other two did not fit into these categories. In the democratic labs (in which there was a high degree of scientist participation in the lab direction) questionnaires revealed a greater overall satisfaction with organizational leadership, a higher feeling of research orientation and freedom of originality, and a greater sense of progress towards organizational research goals. The highly-directed scientists rated their labs lowest on those characteristics.

A summary of the behavioral science findings concerning leadership is that it is complex in nature, clearly dependent on the relationship of the leader and the group being led, dependent also on the particular situation and group needs at that time, that there are differing styles of leadership and these different styles do have a differential effect on the achievement of group goals—both production and social.

D. The Management of Change. It is obvious that change is universal. Everything changes including organizations—their pattern, needs, philosophies, goals, and personnel. Change is rarely welcomed by those affected by or participating in it. Usually it is opposed. Because of the necessity of organizational changes to meet changing situations, the innovation, control, and management of change is one of management's major responsibilities.

It is not surprising that changes and its effects on organizations has been an area of interest to behavioral scientists. People's attitudes towards change, resistance to change, how to initiate and carry through change successfully have all been the subject of interesting research work.

A good example of such experimentation related to change is a study by Coch and French of a pajama factory.[24] The authors found that despite good personnel relations, when it was necessary to transfer a worker from one job to another the transferred worker seemed unable to achieve regular standards of production, even after the completion of a training program and a subsequent adjustment period.

Postulating that this was a worker defense mechanism of resistance to change, Coch and French formed workers into four groups. The first was the control group, and hence job changes among these workers were handled the same as previously—i.e., by management fiat without worker participation. The second group was permitted to choose representatives to discuss job changes with management while any job changes involving the third and fourth groups were first discussed by management with *all* the workers in that group. Then changes in job assignments were made for all groups.

Group 1 (the control group consisting of hand pressers) were called together and told that due to competitive conditions a new piece-rate had been set. Production immediately went down and stayed there. Marked hostility appeared toward the supervisor and methods engineer. Grievances were filed about the new piece-rate. Seventeen percent of the workers quit their jobs within forty days of the introduction of the new rate.

For group 2, consisting of thirteen pajama folders, a meeting was held between management and the special operators whose work and piece-rate was to be changed. The need for new rates, which was based on competition, was explained as well as new methods of production. Then the special operators were asked about the new rate and methods, and these were approved. The special operators were then trained in the new methods and, in turn, they trained the other operators. Their relearning curve was very good and within fourteen days their new rate had exceeded the old. Their relations with the methods engineer and the supervisor (who incidentally was the same one who was in charge of the control group) were friendly and there were no resignations in forty days.

Group 3 consisted of eight pajama examiners, and group 4 was made up of seven pajama examiners. Management held meetings with all members of each group, explaining the need for new methods and rates due to competition. In this case new methods of clipping threads and examining seams were required. Both groups approved of the new methods and plans. Their recovery to the same or higher production standards was much more rapid than group 2; they reached the old level after only a single day under the new methods and rates. No additional training was needed for them after the second day, no acts of hostility developed, and there were no resignations in the forty-day test period.

Coch and French continued these experiments with various additions and refinements and concluded that it is possible for mangement to control resistance to change by use of democratic group meetings and worker participation in the decision-making process.

A general summary of behavioral science findings on organizational change is that individual and informal group resistance to any change should be expected. The worker's security is being threatened and so are the cultural patterns and norms of the group as well as, perhaps, its very existence. Hence a strong individual and group resistance to change will appear as defense mechanisms. Since probably the primary function of small informal groups is to provide social relationships among the members, the threat of disturbance of these established social relationships by the impending change provides its greatest threat to the members and will elicit strong, often extreme, resistance from them. People must accept change, and they will accept it. Research has shown that change is most acceptable when those affected by the change participate in bringing it about.

E. Participative Management. Findings on overcoming resistance to change are also applicable to what is called "participative management." While this is sometimes erroneously described as permitting the worker to make the company decisions, obviously this is not what is meant, for that would be abdication from management's proper role and prerogative. Neither does participative management mean the manipulation of subordinates by superiors in an attempt to give the impression that the subordinates are making the decision—a type of human relations "confidence game." Participative management simply means that members of an organization who are involved in or who will be affected by decisions are permitted, even required, to participate in the deliberations leading up to the decision. More importantly the members must have a meaningful involvement in the decision-making.

There has been a great amount of research and interest in participative management. Likert[25] has given the following hypothesis about which the study and practice of participative management can be built. "If it is desired to bring about a change in the behavior of an organization and to get effective acceptance, it is necessary to secure the active participation of those persons who will be affected by the change."

One of the early studies in this area, demonstrating a higher rate of acceptance if people are permitted to participate in group discussions concerning new ideas, was Lewin's.[26] During World War II the government was interested in having people eat some of the less popular parts of meat such as beef hearts and sweetbreads. Six groups of women (of thirteen to seventeen women each) who were taking a Red Cross home nursing course were included in the experiment. Three of the groups were lectured on the subject, and the other three had the same lecture followed by discussion groups covering the points of the lectures. Later, when both sets of groups were checked, 32 percent of the members of the discussion groups had used the unpopular meats while only 3 percent of the lecture groups had done so. A rather dramatic demonstration, particularly when it comes to changing something as deeply ingrained as people's dietary habits. Other experiments by Lewin revealed similar results, which he felt demonstrated that participation in a discussion group requires a higher degree of member involvement than listening to a lecture and that involvement leads to action.

Pennington and others[27] organized groups of college students and had them perform a decision-making activity. Some of the groups just discussed the situation presented but were not permitted to make a decision; some of the groups were asked to make the decision but were permitted no opportunity to discuss it; while the third set of groups were permitted to discuss the situation presented and to then make a decision. Measurement of individual consensus with the group decision was found to be greatest when both discussion and decision-making were permitted.

Many other researchers have reported similar results and participative management is now widely practiced in industry with many examples of excellent results obtained in reducing costs, absenteeism, and labor strife. Among the ways in which industry practices participative management are employee suggestion systems, profit-sharing plans, production committees, and consultative supervision (in which the manager consults with his employees before making decisions).

Participative management has the following advantages: (1) It aids implementation of the decision because those who participate in the decision feel a strong commitment to carry it out. (2) It helps assure a better decision by bringing more people into the decision-making process. "Several heads are better than one." (3) It creates greater acceptance of change by those who participate in bringing it about. (4) It raises general organizational morale because members of the organization feel wanted—they feel that they belong, that they are really part of the organization.

On the other hand there has been much criticism of participative management. One such critic, Strauss, says: "Considering the rather limited amount of research done, there is too much loose talk about the 'proven' superiority of group decisions and participative methods."[28] Most of this criticism has been of the use of democratic techniques such as mere management gimmicks, but some has been criticism of the basic philosophy itself. Long ago Barnard[29] pointed out some of the dilemmas which arise when democratic concepts are applied to organizations within which authoritarian concepts and management are necessary for proper functioning. Jennings[30] has pointed out some of the problems which arise when group participation is over-emphasized in an organization. Replacement of the decision-making function of management by organizational group decision-making has been widely criticized as a surrender of the essence of management itself. Leavitt[31] admits that group decision-making may raise morale and increase acceptance and implementation of the decision, but he asks whether the group decision itself is better than one which would have been made by management alone.

The unlimited application of the concepts of participative management in health organizations also raises serious doubts. Traditionally these organizations are very authoritarian and often necessarily so. For example, how far can hospitals go in use of time consuming participative decision-making when human life is at stake?

Probably the answer to the use of participative management in the health field is that it should be confined to those areas of management in which time is not crucial—areas nevertheless of great importance like planning. Then the advantages of participative management can be obtained without jeopardizing the swift decision-making essential in crisis situations.

The use of committees is an example of participative management. Their widespread use indicates a recognition of their importance: the many jokes about committees (for example, "a camel is a horse designed by a committee," or "a committee is a group of people who keep minutes and waste hours") show an awareness of some of their disadvantages. All the advantages of participative management previously listed plus others apply also to committees. The advantages of committees are outlined in an excellent way by Hicks who gives this list.[32]

1. Creating. Committees can produce large numbers of ideas through such techniques as "brain storming."

2. Communicating. By having many interested people together during the discussions, communication problems are minimized.

3. Motivating. Those who participate in decision-making have strong motivation to carry it out.

4. Democratizing. A committee can be used to reduce the unbridled authority of an executive when this is desirable. A good example of this is the "advise and consent" powers of Congress in relation to the president of the United States.

5. Consolidating power and authority. When individual committee members do not have enough power and authority to make or implement a particular decision, their combined power and authority on the committee may be enough to do the job.

6. Combining abilities. "Several heads are better than one."

7. Avoiding action. While too often committees fail to take action when it is truly needed and too often items needing decision are referred to a committee as a ruse to avoid taking action, there truly are times when it is in the best interest of the organization and perhaps all parties concerned to delay or avoid a definite decision or action. Moreover referring the matter to a committee can be a positive and valuable executive action that may save face for all concerned.

8. Blurring responsibility. Executives should not be permitted to avoid a clear-cut responsibility by assigning the matter to a committee. On the other hand there are some decisions which should be the subject of group action and for which the group, not any individual, should be held responsible. A verdict rendered by a jury is a good example of this. (Hicks credits the identification of this advantage of a committee to Moore.[33])

9. Advising. No one person can know everything, so the advisory function of a committee is one of its most valuable uses.

10. Representing. A committee can be a mechanism to insure that all sides of a question are discussed, and that differences are resolved so compromises may be reached.

To these may be added a further advantage in that committees permit efficent use of executive time since meetings can be scheduled and thus provide a known time when certain interested people will be getting together to discuss certain matters. Thus interruptions of executives in their other duties can be minimized.

Advance preparation for committee meetings can make for more efficent use of time during the meeting.

Hicks gives the disadvantages of committees as follows:

1. Cost. By wasting time, requiring the attendance of many people (some of whom may not be concerned about the issue under discussion), and generating travel expenses for attending meetings.

2. Least common denominator. Sometimes the committee decision is so scaled down that no one on the committee is happy with it.

3. Indecision. Sometimes issues cannot be resolved nor a decision made because of the democratic nature of a committee.

4. Split accountability. It is difficult to fix accountability upon any member of the committee. Each member can retreat behind the statement that it was not his decision, it was that of the committee. (Author's note: This disadvantage of committees is a good example of the other side of the management principle that authority must be commensurate with responsibility, as described in Chapter 1. Although this principle is much more rarely seen, responsibility must also be commensurate with authority. To permit a committee to have decision-making authority without assigning responsibility for those decisions is a violation of this principle.)

5. Tyranny of a minority. This is a danger in any democracy that a very cohesive, aggressive, and verbal minority may block majority action and prevent consensus on decisions from being reached.

6. Self-perpetuation. If care is not taken, committees, even when appointed for only one specific matter, have a way of staying in existence.

Another disadvantage of committees is that they tend to reduce the authority of executives by making them appear to be figureheads. This could be especially true of an organization's chief executive officer when there is a strong executive committee with wide decision-making powers. Certainly the existence of such strong decision-making executive committees as part of the governing boards and medical staffs of hospitals often has the effect of weakening the authority of the hospital administrator in the eyes of all who deal with him. The addition of the hospital administrator as a voting member of the board of trustees executive committee may have some effect in overcoming that problem.

Ray E. Brown, who has probably written the most significant book on administration ever produced by a hospital administrator, has recognized the value of committees but is highly critical of their overuse and misuse. He writes:

> This time honored device for bringing to bear on a particular problem the best judgment of these best informed has become increasingly utilized as a homeopathic application of democratic administration and an exercise in group therapy. Because it is being used as a means to let people sound off rather than as a means to let the administrator sound out, it has become in many instances a vehicle of expression for the most voluble rather than for the most valuable. It has also become an escape mechanism for those administrators who can't take the organizational heat and who resort to presiding in order to avoid the personal responsibility of deciding.[34]

In spite of the disadvantages and dangers of committees, their uses and advantages require that management learn how to use them. If the Du Pont Company can have its top management decisions made by its president and nine vice-presidents, each with a single vote on the "Ex Committee,"[35] certainly health administrators can learn to utilize the advantages of committees and to avoid or reduce the disadvantages.

F. Communications. All writers on the subject agree on the importance of communication to management. As Terry says, "success in management is conditioned to a great degree by the ability of the manager to understand other people and of others to understand the manager. The success of a manager probably depends as much on his ability to communicate as upon any other skill."[36]

A great deal has been written on the subject of communications in management. Brown writes: "Much has been written in recent years about communications in administration. Perhaps too much has been written, for it has become a fashion in administration to bend the employees' ears with a mass of canned information not worth the bending. Still, failure to communicate represents one of the major sins of most administrators."[37]

Moore says: "So much has been written about the part communication plays in delegation that you would think that is all there is to managing. There is so much truth to this, yet so much that is not true, that it is hard to put communication in its right place. You can't make a company succeed by good communication alone, but you can fail from a poor communication."[38] Dale and Michelon point out that "since World War II, management has been deluged with books and articles on communication. It has also spent a great deal of money on communication tools: employee publications, newsletters, and meetings of various kinds. Yet communication in industry is as serious a problem as it ever was, and there are good reasons to believe that the situation may get worse."[39]

Because of the mass of written material, it is difficult to deal with this subject in a brief, yet thorough manner appropriate to this book. Interested readers should pursue the subject by reading about basic concepts in books on semantics, formal aspects of organizational communication in volumes on the science of management and organizational theory, informal communications in works written by behavioral scientists, and practical hints on management communications in the writings of those concentrating on the art and practice of administration.

1. Semantics. It is the basic science underlying communication. It concerns the meaning of words and the relationship between signs and symbols and what these denote. Semanticists point out that words are not the things they represent: they are only symbolic abstractions. As abstractions they are very useful, but they also have some drawbacks, the most important of which is that the meaning of a word may not be the same for all people.

Numerous models of message transmission by means of words have been postulated. A very primitive model is described by Aristotle who said that every speech has three ingredients—the speaker, the speech, and the audience.[40] Shannon and Weaver expand this to five elements in communication: a source, a transmitter, a signal, a receiver, and a destination.[41] Berlo has seven parts of his communication model: source, encoder, message, channel, receiver, decoder, and meaning.[42] Noise, in his model, is any external interference with communication, and feedback from meaning to source shows fidelity of message transmission.

The special contribution of semantics to management is to point out that the words one person says may not be interpreted as having the same meaning by the listener. That is, the word symbol may denote one thing to the speaker and another to the listener. The "noise" giving rise to that interference may come from many different sources—different cultural backgrounds of the speaker and listener, for example, or differences in knowledge or in attitudes.

A good example of this barrier to communication is called "loaded words." These are certain words which are so "loaded" with emotional meaning that they serve as barriers to communication instead of facilitating it. When one of these loaded words is used in a conversation, the listener reacts mentally in such a way that a curtain falls in his mind, blocking any possible interpretation by him of that word except his preconceived, emotion-laden meanings, and perhaps even blocking any further communication between that listener and that speaker at that time or later.

Obvious examples of such loaded words are ones used to refer to minority groups in a disparaging way. Such expressions as kike, wop, nigger, sheeny, or hunky, when used in a conversation with a member of such a group, or someone who feels very strongly against the use of such words, will probably color the entire conversation and the relationship between the speaker and the listener, not only at that time but perhaps from then on.

Words may be loaded for only the listener and not the speaker. Language is in a constant state of change and so new words are constantly being loaded with emotional barriers to communication. In recent years the perfectly good word "integrate" and its derivatives (the harmless meaning being merely to bring parts together into the whole) has become a barrier to communication when used with some listeners. Knowledge of such concepts pointed out by semanticists is obviously vital to those whose success as managers depends on the ability to communicate adequately.

2. Formal Communications. This includes the relationship of communications to the organizational structure. The organizational chart establishes both the lines of authority and the formal channels of communication. It is obvious that all communication is two way—between the speaker and the listener.

If we assume this, formal communication within the organization is expected to take place both up and down—down so that superiors may give orders to their subordinates, up so that the subordinates may provide the information upon which the superiors base their orders.

Downward communication is in the form of orders and requests for information. It is therefore highly directive in nature. Distortion in downward communication occurs primarily through misunderstanding of the order due to many causes. Such opportunities for distortion are amplified as the channels of downward communication become longer. This is one reason why larger organizations rely more on written communications than do smaller ones.

"Administrative resistance" is a term used to describe the responsibility of a subordinate to resist taking an order when he knows or feels strongly that the boss is incorrect. Carried to an extreme it can be pure negativism, but properly used it can protect the superior against serious errors and make the subordinate invaluable.

Upward communication occurs as reports, recommendations, and suggestions. It too may suffer from distortion as the information is conveyed from one person upward to another. It also is subject to the distortion of "sweetening"—that is, changing the information to provide the superior with the information the subordinate thinks the boss wants to hear.

The most common fault in organizational communication is that too little information is passed on to those who need it for decision-making and other purposes. However, in spite of what is commonly said (e.g., Foegen, who writes, "Too much communication is impossible"[43]), overcommunication also exists. As an organizational disease its symptoms are the waste of executive time spent in issuing and reading masses of unnecessary communications and especially the partial or total immobilization of the decision-making function, as the managers attempt to sort out the pertinent from the unneeded information before they make a decision. As Ray Brown writes, "drowning problems in an ocean of information is not the same as solving them."[44]

Formal communication can be both written and verbal. The most formal of all written communications are the organizational charter, bylaws, and written policies. Other means of formal written communication include employee newspapers, handbooks, bulletin board notices, written rules and procedures. These are all downward communication. Examples of formal written upward communication instruments would be employee suggestion system forms, written grievances, and written reports.

Formal channels and means of communication, especially written, are more than merely a means of transmitting information from one person to another—orders down and reports up. Such formal communications also provide the cement which holds the formal organization together.

3. Informal Communications. Whereas formal communication is up and down, informal communication is up, down, and lateral. All organizations have informal channels of communication which taken together are known as the grapevine.

The grapevine is commonly looked upon as something mysterious and well beyond the control, or even the understanding, of management. As Hicks says: "The grapevine, as the informal communications within an organization have been labeled, is very difficult to isolate; hence, managers have often looked upon the grapevine as something undesirable."[45] However, because of the work of many behavioral scientists, much has been learned about informal channels of communication.

While the grapevine is commonly thought of as existing only among the workers, this is not true. Informal channels of communication are as common among executives as among workers. Simpson in his study of communications in a textile mill, found that 40 percent of the communication among foremen was horizontal.[46]

Keith Davis[47] has studies how information is transmitted by the grapevine. He has postulated four different ways in which the grapevine could operate:

1. As a single strand chain: one person passes on information to a second person, who in turn passes it on to a third person, and so on. Each person passes his information on to only a single person. This is the way the grapevine is usually visualized as operating. This would provide the greatest amount of information distortion. It is the way the game of "rumor" is played, in which a large number of people sit in a circle, number one person thinks up a brief piece of information to pass on, he writes it down secretly on a piece of paper and then whispers the information to number two who whispers it to number three and so on in turn until the last person repeats aloud what he has heard. Then number one reads what he originally whispered and the variance between that and the final result usually causes much amusement. Showing how much misinformation is accepted about grapevines, Davis found that this means of communication was the least common of the four patterns, although it is thought to be the usual way that grapevines function.

2. As a gossip chain: one person, the gossiper, is the source of all of the information, as he seeks out and tells everyone else who then keeps the information to himself. As almost everyone knows from experience, this is not likely to happen, and so this too is an uncommon way for a grapevine to function.

3. As a probability chain: one person communicates at random with some other people who then also communicate at random with some others and so on, in a random manner according to the laws of probability—i.e., each communicates with whomever he runs into while the information is on his mind. Davis found that this means of communication was also not a common way for grapevines to operate.

4. As a cluster chain: the original person has certain selected other people with whom he shares information and these in turn have their own selected few and so on. Davis found that this was the most common way for the grapevine to function. Hallberg has provided an example of this cluster function of the grapevine among executives.[48]

> The president and general manager of the radio station planned to make a change that would affect all the personnel. This plan was supposed to be a secret until it was consummated. However, the program director was taken into their confidence. The president then told the studio engineer and the station attorney about the plan and pledged them to secrecy. While the general manager was confiding the secret to the secretary, the accountant dropped in and overheard it. He did not realize the full significance of the secret. In the meantime, the program director confided in the operations director, who told the secretary, who already knew. The studio engineer also told the secretary, who later reported it to the participant observer.

From the work of Keith Davis and others it can be seen that the grapevine is not mysterious after all. It follows a pattern which can be determined, studied, predicted, and perhaps even utilized. Jacobson and Seashore have shown the existence of distinct roles among grapevine participants.[49] First, there are those individuals who have frequent, reciprocal, and important contacts with a small number of other individuals and few important contacts outside that group. Second, there are those people who have few contacts with any of the groups: they are outside of the grapevine. Third, there are those people who tie the groups together in that they act as liaison in spreading information from one group to another. The first people form the clusters; the second are outside the grapevine, while the third bind the clusters together.

Kelley has written of an interesting piece of research performed by the University of Michigan Center for Group Dynamics in which rumors were planted within an organization and their spread subsequently recorded by members of the organization who recorded all rumors they heard and the sources.[50] It had been generally accepted that the spread of information via the grapevine was mostly downward (when a subordinate picked up a tidbit of information from a superior) and especially lateral. This study showed clearly however, that most of the informal communication was upward. Nineteen rumor transmissions were recorded in the study. Thirteen were directed upward, four to individuals on the same level, and only two downward. The researchers suggest that perhaps informal communication makes the conveyor of it feel important and thus serves as a substitute for "upward mobility." (Of course, as Applewhite has pointed out, communication with a superior may often be done merely to ensure that the superior knows of the existence of the subordinate, thus increasing the latter's chance of success within the organization.[51])

Probably out of a lack of understanding of the grapevine, managers generally fear or distrust it and hence view it as something bad and undesirable. In reality the grapevine serves many useful functions. Because of the importance to the organization of the widespread dissemination of information, entrusting this solely to one channel of communication—the formal—is dangerous and unwise. The grapevine serves a useful purpose in providing an additional channel of information dispersal which is rapid and inexpensive. As a matter of fact the grapevine may even transmit useful information that cannot be conveyed through other channels and may explain management orders and directives in a language that all employees can understand, as Longenecker has pointed out.[52] There may even be information which management wishes to reach the worker but which it may not desire to transmit formally. The grapevine provides a mechanism for this, according to Keith Davis.[53] Of course, the inaccuracy of the grapevine must be guarded against.

The grapevine also functions exactly as do formal communication channels—as a means of binding the organization together. Its role in providing a feeling of importance to workers who have little other source of status also provides a mechanism for relieving personal feelings of frustration which otherwise might be dysfunctional for the organization.

The necessity of possessing a store of information, both to aid in making correct decisions and to establish one's importance within the organization, is as vital a requisite of leadership to informal organization leaders as it is to the formal managers. Blau[54] found that the person who is at the center of information gains status in the eyes of his group.

Leaders are well aware of the indispensability which comes with being the sole possessor of needed information. The author saw an amusing example of this when he entered the U.S. Army in January 1941. Because of the unprepared state of the military at that time, no recruit reception centers existed and the first draftees were therefore assigned to regular army units in which many of the newly promoted noncommissioned officers were of marginal leadership quality. One of these men became the author's platoon sergeant. A group of privates asked this sergeant whether there were going to be weekend passes the next Saturday. The sergeant first said he did not know. When pressed with the fact that he obviously knew, he admitted this but said he wouldn't tell. When asked why not, the sergeant answered that if he told the men whether or not there were going to be any passes that weekend, they would know as much as he did and pretty soon one of them would have his job.

Informal channels of communication within organizations do make constructive and valuable contributions. The grapevine does exist. It is a normal part of all human group relationships. Wishing it were not there or taking steps to stamp it out will not eliminate it. Management must learn how to live with it. This can be done by knowing of the existence of the grapevine as well as its characteristics, its faults, and its contributions. The major fault of the grapevine is that it is highly inaccurate in information transmission. Management can handle this by speedy correction of incorrect rumors and earn a reputation for telling the truth and for sharing important information with all concerned through regular formal management channels.

Most good managers have a source through which they can tune in on the grapevine and keep up with what it is saying. While managers are foolish to think that they can know all that is being spread on the grapevine, a good contact or two may be very helpful, and it will make the informant feel important as well.

Using the grapevine for spreading desired information for which the formal channels is inappropriate is a good management technique. As Newman, Summer, and Warren say, "For instance, a key executive may have 'resigned' suddenly; his associates are naturally curious why. Management may not want to state publicly the explanation—perhaps insubordination, incompetence, or drunkenness—but may want other employees to know that it will not tolerate such behavior and that the discharge was not capricious or unfair. In such a situation, the actual reasons for dismissal can be revealed to active members of the grapevine in the expectation that they will spread the news."[55]

The author made use of the hospital grapevine once for such a purpose. Union activities were occurring among the non-professional employees, centered around the legitimate grievance of low wages. A lengthy study had been made of the situation, including an area wage study, and the administrator's recommendation for a package wage and salary program, including sizeable salary increases financed by the largest patient service-rate increases in the history of the hospital, had already been approved by the board of trustees. By agreement with the other hospitals in the city, official announcement of this was being withheld for two weeks to permit the other hospitals to approve similar wage and rate increases through their normal channels, which extended beyond the immediate hospital. Yet the union activities were proceeding at such a rate that they would make much headway within that two weeks and might reach a point where they could not be halted by the already approved wage increase.

So the administrator held a "confidential" conference with the department heads in which he indicated the strong possibility of there being a sizeable wage increase within two weeks. As he expected, two of the department heads performed their usual informal function of adding to their feelings of importance by spreading this information on the hospital grapevine. The employees adopted a watch and wait attitude for the next two weeks and union activities came to a virtual halt. Two weeks later the official announcement of the wage increase may not have surprised many employees, but the grapevine had done its job well and the administrator's objective was accomplished.

G. Conclusion.   The reader has been introduced to some of the formal aspects of management and to organization theory. That is, to how an organization is supposed to be set up and how people are supposed to act in work and other organizational situations. This chapter is an introduction to how people actually do function in such situations. Thus the behavioral science approach to management not only complements but goes beyond the formal aspects of management and of organization theory.

The behavioral science contribution to management was traced historically as starting on a social level in the nineteenth century from the desire of some individuals to improve the lot of the worker. Growing out of this was increased productivity and better personnel relations.

The human relations school of management was the next major behavioral science development in management. Pioneered by the Hawthorne studies and experiments, the human relations school was pragmatic, based on observable though not accurately measured results in the improvement of worker morale and output—at least on a short term basis. Human relations as a school of management theory reached its peak in the late 1940s and the early 1950s. Its demise was hastened by the human relations "experts" whose gimmicks soon became obvious and ineffectual.

Out of the ashes of the human relations school of management rose the behavioral science school of management. Borrowing from all of the behavioral sciences, this school of management has its theory firmly founded on scientific methodology. Therefore management based on behavioral science findings is not a collection of simple devices but upon proven—or, at least, observed—human individual and group behavior. It is as much dedicated to meeting the workers' needs as those of management, and the ideal objective is to achieve congruence of both as far as this is possible. The behavioral science school of management is still in a relative stage of infancy, and it shows much promise as it continues its development alongside the newer systems and quantitative approaches to management.

Chapter Three

Decision-Making in Management

I. Introduction

Because of the obvious importance of decision-making to management and because all managers make decisions, it is not strange that nearly all managers consider themselves experts on this subject. Yet, as Dale[1] says: "Most executives themselves do not know how they make decisions." This, as well as a consideration of decision-making being a logical lead-in to consideration of the systems approach to management and quantitative management tools and techniques, justifies some special attention to the subject of decision-making.

Since decision-making is such a common function in life and even more in management, it would seem easy to obtain a simple, agreed-upon definition. Such is not the case. Definitions of decision-making in management range from simple ones such as Applewhite's[2] "Decision-making merely involves making a choice among alternatives," to one by Shackle[3] describing decision-making as "the focal creative psychic event where knowledge, thought, feeling and imagination are fused into action." Usually falling somewhere between these two, good definitions of managerial decision-making take into account two factors—the choice among alternatives and that decision-making is a mental process of managers. Therefore, in this book, decision-making by managers will be defined as a *choice among alternatives where the outcome is uncertain based upon rational mental processes.*

The importance of decision-making in management has even led to the formation of an entire school of management theory. Given weight and impetus by the writings of Simon,[4] the decision theory school of management emerged in the late 1950s. Simon expanded the theories of Barnard and focused on managerial decision-making as the most important function of management —the key to management theory. He even suggested that organizations be constructed about the decision-making process—that is, around the points where decisions are to be made and around the sources of information supplied to the decision-makers.

There is no doubt that decision-making is one of the most important things a manager must do. A manager who has difficulty making decisions is not a very good manager. A manager who will not make decisions is not a manager at all! However, management is more than just decision-making. Decision-making must be rationally related to many things—to plans, philosophies, needs of the organization, management, and workers. Managerial decision-making must take place within the functional framework of management. The manager is not some sort of queen termite, situated within an inner sanctum office, giving birth to multitudes of decisions which are then carried away by his attendants and put to use. Managerial decisions must pertain to planning, organizing, actuating, and controlling. Thus management is the art and science of making decisions pertaining to the functions of management. All this constitutes the management process.

II. Characteristics of Decisions

The definition just given includes several of the characteristics of decision-making. Certainly decision-making involves a choice among alternatives. If only one possibility exists, then this is not decision-making. There is no need of an executive to decide what to do when only one possibility exists. If a professor's old-model car finally stops running and is completely beyond repair, and he must have a car with which to continue to function in his profession, and he only has enough money to purchase a Volkswagen, then the alternatives of purchasing a Rolls Royce or a Porsche are not open to him, so his acquisition of the Volkswagen is not a decision in our sense.

This points out an important aspect of decision-making. There really are always at least two alternatives open to the decision-maker because he can always choose the possibility or he can do nothing at all. The professor thus actually need not have purchased the Volkswagen—he could have bought no car at all, taking a teaching appointment or some other job within walking distance of his home. Often the wise decision by the executive is to choose not to make a decision at all. This in itself is a decision of course, especially when it is considered as one of the alternative courses of action and is rationally and knowingly chosen.

This is not the same as the inadequate executive who is indecisive and puts off decisions by not making any choice of alternatives at all. But this inaction in itself is a type of decision, whether or not the executive realizes it, for life within the organization moves on and things proceed—perhaps poorly or with difficulty—in spite of the unmade decision. So even indecision or failure to make a decision is a type of decision: it is an unwitting choice between alternatives. The executive is a decision-maker by virtue of his position—he cannot avoid this function.

Another important characteristic of decisions is that the results are uncertain, in spite of all the data collecting and manipulation which may proceed the decision. If the decision-making always took place under conditions of absolute certainty, then there would be no need to have managers. A clerk in the bookkeeping office could add up the certain returns on each alternative, and everyone would then follow the alternative with the greatest return. As Ray Brown says,[5] "The administrator can never be sure. He can only know the uncertain and reacting environment imperfectly, and even his most informed decisions represent educated guesses. A decision is a prediction of the future. No matter how high the pile of facts on which he stands, the pile will always be too thin to permit the administrator to see precisely and exactly into the future. His function begins only where the clearly verifiable ends."

Efforts to reduce this uncertainty or, at least, to define where it exists are the major contribution of the quantitative techniques to managerial decision-making. These techniques will be the principal subject of this book.

Decision-making is not a purely mechanical, routine, step-by-step process, in spite of the analysis of decision-making into logical steps. It is a mental activity, involving creativity, which is itself little understood. Information reception, assimilation, storage, retrieval, organization, and manipulation are essential functions of the human brain in decision making. All this, since it takes place within human beings, is affected by the decision-maker's previous experience, his feelings, his temperament, his subconscious and unconscious mind, his state of physical and mental health—to mention some of the factors which can have an effect on decision-making as a mental process.

The necessity of an executive to make decisions so as to resolve *organization conflict* is well known. For example, suppose two nurses both want vacations at the same time. Both have an equal claim to that vacation time. Neither will budge from her desire. So their supervisor makes the decision. One nurse gets the vacation period she desires, the other does not. One is unhappy, the other probably accepts this as her due. The important point is that the conflict was resolved, an important characteristic of decision-making.

Gross and others[6] have presented another dimension of conflict as a characteristic of decision-making. This is the resolution of *personal internal conflict* of the executive who is faced with the necessity of making a decision. In such a situation the executive has four alternatives open to him. He can make decision A (in the case above, he can give the desired vacation time to Nurse Jones); he can make decision B (that is, decide in favor of Nurse Smith); he can attempt to work out a compromise; or he can avoid the decision altogether.

Gross says that the choice made will depend upon three social factors: legitimacy, sanctions, and personal orientation. Legitimacy is the decision-maker's perception of what others expect of him in the situation. Sanctions are the rewards and penalties which will accrue to the decision-maker depending on the choice he makes. Personal orientation refers to the weight the decision maker places on the legitimacy and sanction dimensions of the decision. It is a function of his own personal executive philosophy. The morally-oriented person will place more weight on legitimacy than upon sanctions in his decision-making. That is, he is primarily concerned about what others will think and so he makes the decision accordingly. Some executives, on the other hand, will be primarily concerned with the personal rewards and punishments which will result from the decision. They are expedient-oriented. Finally some executives will give equal weight to legitimacy and sanctions—these are the moral-expedient persons.

Miller and Shull[7] have worked out a model of managerial approaches to decision-making based on legitimacy and penalties involved which they have tested on 115 decision-makers. These executives were first asked questions which established their views concerning the legitimacy and sanctions of a situation. Then they were asked to make the decision in the situation. Since these findings were based on each individual's feelings concerning the legitimacy of group expectations about the decision and about the individual's perception of the penalties and rewards attached, Miller and Shull were able to predict with 71 percent accuracy what decision each individual of the 115 would make. This was a statistically significant result.

Everyone is constantly faced with the resolution of his own personal internal conflicts. Managerial decision-making is an example. The resolution of such internal conflict is undoubtedly an essential characteristic of decision-making.

III. Classification of Decisions

Classification is one of the major steps in the scientific process and since management has a scientific foundation, it is only logical to anticipate that management and its divisions such as decision-making have been classified.

Dale[8] classifies decisions in three groups: policy decisions, administrative decisions, and executive or ad hoc decisions. Policy decisions are very broad and underlie most of the other decisions. The nature of the organization, its personnel policies, the main outlines of the organizational structure—these are some examples of policy decisions. Administrative decisions are those broad decisions on implementation of policy. Personnel rules would be an example of an administrative policy. Finally the decisions which executives make on a day-to-day basis are classified as executive decisions by Dale. How a certain personnel rule is to be applied to a certain worker in a specific situation may require an executive decision.

Terry[9] has classified decisions in a number of ways. From a functional point of view he has given one classification: production decisions, sales decisions, finance decisions, and personnel decisions. Considering the amount of uncertainty involved, he says that decisions can be classified into "routine," those with a "fair amount of uncertainty," those with "considerable uncertainty," and those with "great uncertainty." Finally he also points out another broad classification—that of individual decision versus group decision.

McFarland[10] also presents different types of decision classifications. He cites Barnard's organization and personal decisions[11] —the former made by a manager in his executive role and the latter involving merely the executive's own actions which cannot be delegated, even though they may have an effect on the organization. McFarland's second classification divides decisions into basic and routine—basic being policy and policy implementation while routine refers to those decisions made on a day-to-day basis. Finally McFarland presents Simon's[12] classification of decisions as either programmed or non-programmed. Programmed decisions are those which are routine and repetitive and based on previously set policies, rules and procedures—e.g., a medical social worker deciding into which payment categories to place outpatients. Non-programmed decisions are of a policy nature— e.g., the decision by the hospital governing board and administrator on what income limits place outpatients into certain payment categories. Simon, in the same book, also divides decision-making into traditional (based on habit, clerical routine, organizational structure, judgment, intuition, rule of thumb, and executive selection) and modern (operations research, electronic data processing, and heuristic problem-solving such as training decision-makers).

It can be seen from these examples that decisions can be classified in many ways, depending upon the criteria used and the results desired. Yet classification in science is merely a means to an end—the end being the construction of a general theory that will explain observations and enable the prediction of results of alternative actions. Hence the classification of decisions has the same objectives, as well as the training of decision-makers and the improvement of executive decision-making. More important than mere classification is the theory behind it.

IV. Theories of Decision-Making

To aid in understanding of managerial decision-making, authorities have sought a general theory underlying that process. Among the most important theories of managerial decision-making are the marginal, the scientific method, the psychological, and the mathematical.

A. The marginal theory.   This is derived primarily from the work of economists. It assumes that there is an optimum point for every situation—a place where all of the many factors are properly balanced and the best possible results are achieved. According to this theory, the task of the decision-maker is to weigh all important factors, to determine the optimum point, and attempt to reach it through his decision. For instance, how many registered nurses should be assigned to a hospital emergency room? Too few may result in loss of life but too many will result in excessively high costs, the waste of valuable RN time and skills vitally needed elsewhere in the hospital, and perhaps even the resignation of the best nurses who see their skills wasted in the overstaffed emergency room. It is the job of the administrator to determine what is too many and what is too few. To do so, he may—and probably does to a considerable extent even without realizing it—use marginal analysis. Therefore the marginal analysis theory of decision-making is a valid category. However, it suffers from certain defects which reduce its value as a theory of decision-making with practical managerial applications.

Marginal theory assumes certain things such as the rationality of the decision-maker and those affected by the decision, the predictability of pertinent factors, and finally the assumption that it is possible to isolate and deal with the pertinent factors, holding all others at least relatively equal—the famous *ceteris paribus* of the economists. Unfortunately for the more widespread application of the marginal theory of decision-making, all three assumptions are open to question. The behavioral scientists have shown us much about the non-rationality—even the irrationality —of all human beings, including the executive decision-makers themselves. To understand decision-makers, decision-making, and the results and conditions surrounding decisions and their implementation, the apparently non-rational and irrational psychological and sociological factors cannot be ignored.

This applies also to the predictability of the factors involved in decision-making. It is an axiom of decision-making that all the facts are never available. This is recognized by the quantitative theory of decision-making, even though this theory is based on eliminating as much as possible uncertainty and unpredictability. To assume that all the pertinent factors in a decision are predictable is to weaken marginal decision-making theory.

Finally decision-making takes place within extremely complicated social situations and structures, especially in the health field; therefore any theory such as the marginal theory of decision-making which requires an assumption that any factor can be constant is doomed to fail, at least in its practical contributions and applications.

The foregoing criticisms of the marginal theory of decision-making are not intended to say that it has made no contribution to managerial thought. This is not so. Undoubtedly every manager in considering a decision does seek to reach an optimum point through more or less unconscious marginal analysis. He is dealing with non-rational and irrational approaches by himself and others, with factors of dubious accuracy and predictability, and with a real world in which very little reliance can be placed on a decision reached by the assumption that all else is held constant.

B. The scientific theory. This theory assumes that there is a correct, step-by-step way to make decisions and that executives do go through these steps more or less consciously when they make decisions—or, at least that they should go through these steps. Closely related to scientific problem-solving, this theory of decision-making offers a cookbook approach to making right decisions and one which can be learned by executives and students.

Unfortunately there are drawbacks to this theory also. Like the marginal theory it ignores the human element—the lack of perfect rationality in the decision-maker and in others. It also assumes the availability and accuracy of needed facts—certainly an incorrect assumption that weakens this as a general theory of decision-making. Useful as a guide to decision-making, the primary contribution of the scientific method school seems to be less in its general theory than in its practical application to teaching the decision-making process, especially as this relates to the solving of definite management problems. It has also led to a better understanding of the decision-making process.

C. The psychological theory. While other theories of decision-making assume that the executive is rational and scientific in his approach, observation has demonstrated that such is not always the case. The psychological theory of decision-making (which perhaps should better be named the behavioral science theory) takes this into account. The decision-maker is viewed as a human being—a total of his heredity, his life conditioning, his basic desires and wants, and his reactions to all of the group pressures to which he is subject. Not only is he not always rational and scientific, but he may not even know why he acts as he does in his decision-making, although he can usually "rationalize" his decision in one way or another.

The behavioral scientists still say that there is method in decision-making and that this method can be determined and used as a general theory of decision-making based on psychological and sociological principles. Decisions are made and executives act in accordance with their own personalities and group pressures. Decision-making to resolve personal internal conflict of the decision-maker would fit into this theory.

In this psychological theory, to understand decision-making, one must understand the decision-maker as a total individual and social human being. Therein lies its major weakness as a general theory of decision-making, for how can even one human being be totally understood? This theory has much to contribute to decision theory, but it is not the whole answer. Executives are also rational and scientific as well as irrational. Facts and figures are at least as important to decision-making as the feelings of the decision-maker.

D. The mathematical theory. Closely related to the scientific decision-making theory, this theory is also called the quantitative theory of decision-making. Assuming that decision-making is based on facts, this theory emphasizes obtaining the facts as accurately, as completely, and as quickly as possible. The more accurate, comprehensive, and current the facts, the better will be the decision.

There is no doubt that facts are important in decision-making and that incorrect, too few, or too late facts can result in wrong decisions. There is also no doubt that mathematical facts obtained by means of electronic computers are the most accurate, the most complete, and the most current. The contribution of mathematics to decision-making has been highly significant. In some cases, it has even eliminated the need for human choice. No wonder quantitative management has assumed such importance in decision theory. While the purely mathematical approach to management has had its critics, one wonders if some of its critics are people who had their administrative education before the recent emphasis on quantitative methods and whose reaction is to devaluate the very real contribution of mathematics to management.

To be sure, the mathematical approach also has its weaknesses. It tends to ignore the art of management in its focus on the science. As Ray Brown[13] has written, "Administration is not a numbers game." Mathematics provides the tools and the facts for decision-making, but it also does much more than that. It also provides the decision-maker with a better understanding of the total picture, for the mathematical approach provides not only the facts that are available but it also shows which facts are not available and which are hazy. Sometimes this knowledge is more valuable to the executive than are the available facts themselves. So the mathematical approach to decision-making is more than just a tool—it makes theoretical contributions. Of course, like the other decision theories it is not complete in itself but, combined with the other approaches described in this section, it adds to our understanding of the theory underlying decision-making and to its teaching and improvement.

V. Psychology in Decision-Making

This subject was introduced previously when one of the characteristics of decisions—the resolution of individual conflict within the decision-maker—was discussed. It was shown that it is possible to predict what a decision will be based on the proportionate weights the decision-maker gives to legitimacy and sanction (defined as expectations of others and potential reward or punishment).

It is not only the decision itself that can be predicted from an analysis of the decision-maker's perception of the proportionate legitimacy and sanction weights of that individual decision. Since decisions are made by people, decisions themselves cannot really be separated from the personality of the executive who makes the decision. Decision-makers themselves fall into predictable types, and their individual approaches to decision-making can thus be anticipated. The effect of the different personality postulated by Fromm[14] has been studied by Dale[15] who has classified five types of decision-makers based on Fromm's personality types.

1. The defensive type, who leans heavily on his assistants and associates and who delegates authority and responsibility freely because he believes that the correct answers are in sources outside of himself. Insecure as a decision-maker, this type will push decisions off onto other people.

2. The exploitive type, who also feels that the correct answers are in sources outside of himself. Unwilling to delegate or to give credit to others, this type "steals" the ideas and decisions of others and presents them as his own.

3. The hoarding type, who believes that all of the correct answers are within himself, makes all the decisions himself, not even accepting advice from others.

4. The marketing type, who is constantly trying to sell himself so that he can get ahead, believes that the correct answers are to be found in the approval of others. So he makes his decisions based on how pleasing they will be to others, especially his superiors. He is the typical "organization man."

5. The productive type, who has a mature balance of believing that the correct answers are sometimes to be found in others, sometimes within himself, but usually in a combination of what he and others have to combine, is the "ideal" executive who uses the ideas of others but gives them credit for this. He helps others to get ahead.

Of course, there are artificial types and many executives would be combinations of these. However, the fact that everyone recognizes one or more people he knows who fit into each type shows that these categories are very real, that they are based on the personalities of the decision-makers, and that decisions can be predicted with a fair accuracy based on the personality type of the executive. It suggests also that executives can be selected by type depending on what sort of decision-making is required for that position at that time and with regard to the personal decision-making characteristics of their associates.

VI. Creativity in Decision-Making

In our present world of rapid change, innovation and creativity are essential and highly rewarded. New problems demand new solutions and the executives who can see beyond the usual alternatives in their decision-making and come up with new possibilities are highly prized. New ideas and the creative executives who can provide them are so essential that there has been much examination of creativity to determine how it can be strengthened and developed. From these studies the following things have been learned.

The creative process is often thought of as consisting of a moment of blinding revelation—the new idea just suddenly appearing in someone's mind. While it is true that even creators of new innovations may think that ideas occur in this manner, study has shown that there are distinct stages in the creative process. Newman[16] gives these as follows:

1. Saturation: becoming thoroughly familiar with the problem and everything connected with it.

2. Deliberation: mulling over the problem, considering alternate solutions, and constantly rearranging all aspects of the situation in the mind.

3. Incubation: relaxing, forgetting about the problem, letting the subconscious mind work on the problem.

4. Illumination: getting the new idea and sensing that it may work even though it does seem perhaps inappropriate.

5. Accommodation: refining and working out the new idea so that it is a practical solution to the problem.

Hicks[17] makes an interesting addition to the above. While admitting that many creative ideas are obtained in such a step-by-step process, he says that other discoveries arise from only a single element of the process and that further, there are creative individuals who are skilled in only a single type of creativity. He gives as the different types of creativity:

1. Innovation: instead of being the sum total of the creative process, Hicks says that innovation (defined here as the ability to think up totally new ideas) is merely one type of creativity and that there are individuals whose creativity is limited to that alone.

2. Synthesis: this is the ability to absorb, combine and use ideas from many varied sources, thus creating something new.

3. Extension: a type of creativity involving thinking up added or new uses for old or new ideas.

4. Duplication: the use of successful ideas of others for one's own purpose. While usually not thought of as creativity per se, Hicks suggests that it takes a special type of creative wisdom to recognize and use other people's good ideas and that one view of the educational process is that students are being taught to duplicate the successful experiences of others.

In addition to the development of creativity in executives and students by discovering what it is, barriers to creativity have also been recognized. Since creativity is a mental process, the most important barriers are psychological. Among these barriers to creativity are cultural blocks and perceptual blocks. The former is an inability to obtain or recognize new ideas because of having been pushed into rigid patterns of thought and behavior by pressure toward social conformity. Perceptual blocks are the sheer inability to see or visualize new ways of doing things—an inability to rise above our ordinary ways of viewing people, ideas, and objects.

In the search for creativity two paths have been followed. One is the attempt to develop creativity in executives and students. The preceding analysis of the creative process and blocks to creativity have arisen from efforts to develop creativity. The second approach consists of attempts to determine who are the creative individuals so that their gifts can be utilized. This has led to development of tests of creativity. An example of such are the tests developed for this purpose by the Institute of Personality Assessment and Research in Berkeley, California. As described in an article by Barron,[18] these consist of unusual uses test, consequences test, plot titles test, ink blot test, anagrams test, thematic perception test, and word rearrangement test.

An interesting approach to the stimulation of creativity through group participation aroused a great deal of attention a number of years ago under the name of "brainstorming." As developed by Osborn,[19] the essentials of brainstorming are the high rate of production of ideas regardless of their merits and also of deferred judgment on the ideas. A group of people, more or less knowledgeable on a subject, meet together to consider a problem. They are encouraged to present as many ideas concerning solutions as may occur to them and these are recorded by a non-participating secretary. No criticism of anyone's ideas is permitted, but building upon and modifying the ideas of others are encouraged.

The ideas thus collected in the session, which lasts from ten minutes to one hour, are then presented to the executive who is responsible for solving the problem. It is his responsibility to assess, sift out, choose, and implement any ideas which appear good to him. Thus brainstorming utilizes the stimulated creativity of many people without violating any of the principles of authority delegation and fixing of executive responsibility.

Brainstorming is a very appealing concept and its production of new ideas in large numbers led to its widespread use in the 1950s. It obviously produces more ideas than does a single executive alone, and the ideas have been shown to be of as high or higher quality than those produced by the individual. However, studies such as those by Dunnette and others[20] and by Taylor and others[21] have shown that this is true only when comparing the brainstorming group with one executive working alone. When a comparison is made with the production of a brainstorming group and with the production of the same people working individually, more ideas of equal or higher quality were produced by the individuals working by themselves. Apparently several heads are better than one, but they need not work together to be better.

VII. Steps in Decision-Making

One of the major contributions of the scientific theory of decision making is its presentation of a step-by-step approach to the subject. The intent of such a presentation is to understand the decision-making process better and to be able to improve decision-making by executives and to teach it to management students. As might be expected, various authorities present the subject differently. For example, Newman and others[22] give these four phases for rational decision-making: (1) making a diagnosis, (2) finding alternative solutions, (3) analyzing and comparing alternatives, and (4) selecting the plan to follow.

Haynes and Massie[23] add one more important step: (1) consciousness of the problem-provoking situation, (2) recognition of the problem and its definition, (3) search for and analysis of available alternatives and their probable consequences, (4) selection of the best solution, and (5) implementing the decision.

Dale and Michelon[24] give these steps: (1) determine the objective, (2) analyze the situation in light of the objective, (3) consider possible alternatives, (4) consider the alternatives in light of the situation and weigh them against their possible consequences, (5) make the decision, and (6) implement the decision.

Young[25] gives a sophisticated ten-step approach to decision making: (1) define organizational objectives, (2) raise the problem of how these goals can be achieved, (3) the nature of the problem must be investigated, (4) search for alternative solutions, (5) after full evaluation select the best alternative, (6) organizational consensus must be achieved, (7) the solution must be authorized, (8) the solution must be implemented, (9) non-decision-makers must be instructed in the use of the decision, and (10) an audit must be conducted for evaluating the effectiveness of the decision.

The author of this book teaches the following step-by-step approach to decision-making, primarily so that the students may grasp the totality of the process involved:

1. Become aware of the problem. This may seem simple enough, but sometimes the executive is told that or thinks that there is a problem when in reality none exists. Certainly health administrators have enough real problems without dealing with non-existent imaginary ones.

2. Investigate the nature of the problem. Why is it a problem? Why has it just become a problem demanding solution now? What are its ramifications? Who is involved in and affected by the problem?

3. Determine the objective of the solution desired in light of total organizational objectives.

4. Determine alternative solutions which will solve the problem while being consistent with organizational objectives and without creating other problems through solving one.

5. Weigh the consequences and the relative efficiency of each alternative solution. If no solution seems acceptable, creatively seek other solutions. Don't just use one solution which seems the best of a bad lot but which will not solve the problem. Seek a better answer.

6. Try out various alternatives—either in discussion with other people or possibly in trial-run experimental situations.

7. Select the best alternative solution.

8. Implement the decision by communicating it, training those who must carry it out, and seeing that it is being correctly carried out.

9. Check up on the solution at intervals to be certain that it is solving the problem and that it was the best solution.

10. Finally change, correct, or even withdraw the solution if evaluation shows that it is not working or was not the best answer. Most step-by-step approaches to decision-making seem to assume that once a decision is made, it is as if it were carved into a stone tablet—immutable and irreversible. Actually few executive decisions are that unchangeable. The lapse of time or the experience gained may indicate that the decision should be reversed or modified. If so, then this should be done. Anyone can make a wrong decision, but only a fool persists in one when the mistake is proven to him.

From the foregoing presentation of several step-by-step approaches, it should be obvious that decision-making is closely linked to problem-solving methodology. Its relationship to the creative process is evident. This should not be unexpected because all three are merely somewhat different applications of the general scientific method, which Dewey[26] has given as: (1) state the problem, (2) list the alternatives, and (3) select the best alternative. Somewhat expanded, the same idea appears in Johnson's[27] scientific methodology, the steps of which follow: (1) define the problem, (2) state objectives, (3) formulate hypotheses, (4) collect data (empirical observation and verification), (5) classify, analyze and interpret, and (6) draw conclusions, generalize, restate, or develop new hypotheses.

While decision-making and problem-solving are closely related through the scientific method, McFarland[28] warns against confusing the two as synonymous. He quotes Drucker[29] who has said that an overemphasis on problem solving leads to exaggerating the need for getting answers, whereas, in reality, it may be more important to find the right question than to find the right answer. Drucker believes that problem-solving should deal with unimportant, routine, or tactical matters, with decision-making being reserved for the more important policy and strategy. Identifying and defining the right problems is the key to successful decision-making. Such an important and clean-cut distinction between decision-making and problem-solving has not been observed by many writers on the subject.

VIII. Who Should Make Decisions

In discussing the functions of committees I urged that committees not have decision-making powers since this is a violation of the basic management principle that responsibility and authority must be commensurate so that the responsibility for the results of a decision can be fixed definitely. Earlier we have seen the findings of researchers showing that the same number of individuals working alone can come up with more creative solutions to problems than when working together. This points out strongly that decision-making is to be performed by individuals. It is an individual executive function.

This does not mean, however, that the top executive need make all the decisions. Decision-making can and should be delegated. As a matter of fact it should be delegated down the organizational line to the "lowest competent level." The lowest competent level in the organization is where the decision-maker can see the effect of that decision on the total organization.

For example, it is logical to let a two-year-old child make the decision as to which color balloon he wishes his father to buy him on a trip to the zoo. The consequences of that decision, which are slight, are apparent to the child, therefore he should be allowed to make the decision. On the other hand the same child should not be permitted to decide whether to ride his tricycle on the sidewalk or in a busy street. The two-year-old child cannot foresee the consequences of such a decision—possible long hospitalization in a fracture frame or even death if the decision is to ride in the street. Since the child is below the lowest competent decision-making level, his mother makes the decision that he should stay on the sidewalk.

Similarly the decision as to individual patient assignments for nurses is one that should be made by their immediate supervisor. The supervisor is able to see all the effects of that decision; she is therefore at the lowest competent level for that decision. Suppose, though, that the decision involves whether or not to give a salary increase above the regular pay scale to one nurse who has threatened to resign if the raise is not granted. The immediate supervisor may wish to give the raise in order to retain the nurse, but she may not be in possession of the facts which would permit her to foresee all the consequences of that act upon the total organization. Such a salary increase for one nurse may throw a very tight budget out of line, and certainly it will lead to demands and the necessity for giving similar raises above scale elsewhere. Therefore the nurse's immediate supervisor should not be permitted to make the decision on whether or not to grant that raise. She is below the lowest competent level. This is a decision which must be made higher up in the organization, perhaps at the very top.

Saving time for busy top executives is the most obvious of the reasons why decision-making should always be pushed down to the lowest competent level. The phrase "pushed down" is used because often junior executives do not want to make the decisions. Since they are executives, though, they must. Among other reasons for having decisions made at the lowest competent level are these:

1. Generally the facts needed to make the decision are at that level, so communication problems in decision-making are reduced when the decisions are made on the same level where the facts relevant to the decision exist.

2. Decisions must be implemented on the lower organizational levels. If those individuals who are going to have to carry out the decisions make those decisions, or participate in the making of them, they then have a stake in the success of the decisions and will be more likely to see that they do work.

3. Permitting decisions to be made down on lower levels gives junior executives and supervisors the practice in decision-making they need to develop for promotion.

4. Pushing decision-making down in the organization will serve as a screening device for those junior executives and supervisors worthy of promotion. Some of the lower-echelon executives will try to avoid decision-making responsibilities while others will welcome them and make good decisions.

5. Permitting decisions to be made at lower organizational levels will make the job more interesting for good junior executives and supervisors, and these individuals will remain within the organization because of added job satisfaction.

6. The more democratic environment brought about by lower-level decision-making contributes to raising the morale throughout the organization.

IX. Decision-Making as an Art

The emphasis which has been placed on the science of decision-making should not obscure the fact that decision-making, no less than management of which it is a part, is both a science and an art. As Barnard[30] writes, "The fine art of executive decision consists in not deciding questions that are not now pertinent, in not deciding prematurely, in not making decisions that cannot be made effective, and in not making decisions that others should make." Surely there is no purely scientific approach which can determine the correctness of these points. Therein lies the art of decision-making.

This is not to say that the art cannot be learned. It must be learned in other than step-by-step methods, however. One can learn best through practice, trial and error, observation, and patterning oneself after a capable master. Learning the art can take place partly within a protected or semi-protected situation, as in an administrative residency where the preceptor not only serves as a model of administrative behavior but also protects the resident from making too many serious errors. The day must come, though, when every executive must stand on his own to practice the science of management and decision-making as he has learned it—and to acquire the art.

To say that the major emphasis in the study and teaching of management and decision-making (as well as most of the writing in those fields) has been on science does not mean that there has been none on the art. It should be noted, however, that there is a difference between the two approaches. The science is based on a methodology and on empiricism which permits its learning by a student in a logical, ordered fashion. The art, being based on the personal feelings and experience of the author and teacher, is necessarily presented in a less ordered manner. Books and articles emphasizing the art of management and of decision-making consist primarily of admonitions, exhortations, and tips. Compare, for example, books like Tead's *The Art of Administra-tion*[31] and Brown's *Judgment in Administration* with a volume like Terry's *Principles of Management* and the difference between the science and art of management becomes obvious. Even when Terry[32] deals with decision-making as an art, the twelve tips he gives are numbered and classified in sequence.

The essence of the art of decision-making is the judgment of the decision-maker—judgment in the face of risk. Brown has this to say about judgment: "The administrative area is the area in which choices must be made. It is an area that by definition is marked by gaps of uncertainty. They are gaps that can be narrowed by good information, but they are gaps that can never be eliminated. They can only be bridged by the administrator's judgment. In the midst of all his new found aids, the administrator's judgment still remains crucial."[33] In other words judgment is the cement which binds the science of decision-making together and which gives it implemented meaning.

X. Improving Decision-Making

Given the necessity of good decision-making to management and the information that studies have revealed about decisions, decision-making, and those who make decisions, it should not only be possible to teach decision-making but also to improve it within organizations. How can this be done?

First, by eliminating incorrect ideas about decision-making. A general acceptance of the fallacy that good executives are born, not made, would make it impossible for there to be any improvement in executive decision-making. Presentation of the facts proved about decision-making will be valuable in doing away with such incorrect assumptions. Teaching of scientific decision-making principles not only will help dispel mistaken ideas about decision-making, but since the science of decision-making can be learned, this will in itself improve decision-making. Continuing education of management personnel should have much emphasis on decision-making.

Since decision-making is based on communications, clarifying and improving organizational channels of communication will have the automatic effect of improving decision-making, as incorrect decisions based on erroneous or incomplete facts are eliminated. Providing feedback on the results of decisions is essential to improvement, especially as regards that part of decision-making which is an art. Just as teachers correct, grade, and return student papers so that students may learn and improve, so should the results of executive decisions be fed back to them so that improvement may occur. Just as those students who are vitally interested in the subject matter learn and improve most from feedback on their errors, so will such feedback result in improvement in decision-making only if the executive is vitally interested in his job and in improving his decision-making. Therefore it is impractical to think that executives who are not vitally interested in their jobs and in self-improvement will ever better their decision-making skills.

Finally in these days it is illogical to expect executives to make decisions without providing them with the data, methods, and tools available through computer technology, quantitative techniques, and the systems approach to management. Health administration has lagged in this regard, still expecting its administrators to produce capable decisions based on intuition, experience, rules-of-thumb, and outdated, inadequate facts. New concepts, new methods, and new tools exist now, and they must be made available to health administrators. The explanation of these modern concepts, methods, and tools occupies the remainder of this book.

XI. Conclusion

In this chapter decision-making was presented as one of the essential ingredients of management. Some characteristics of decisions themselves were given as well as some of the personal characteristics of executives which have a bearing on their decision-making function. The science of decision-making includes various classifications of decisions and theories of decision-making. This led logically into the section on steps in the decision-making process and problem-solving.

The importance of creative solutions to new and old problems in decision-making which takes place in such a rapidly changing environment such as the health field was the subject of the section on creativity. Decision-making by group creativity, the so-called brainstorming, was discussed there also.

A consideration of who should make decisions included a presentation of the important advantages of having decision-making pushed down to the lowest competent level in the organization. Decision-making, as an integral part of management, was discussed as being an art as well as a science. Finally some practical steps were given for improving organizational decision-making.

Section Two: Systems
THE SCIENTIFIC APPROACH TO MANAGEMENT

This section has only a single chapter—an indication of the importance of the subject. A system is defined as an organized, complex, functioning entity existing for a specific purpose or purposes and derived from the rational application of the scientific method to the organization and administration of this entity.

While the systems approach to management appeared after the other schools of management thought, it differs from its predecessors in not being just another school of management thought. Systems is total in its approach and concepts. It includes all of the other theories, for systems is the application of the total scientific method to all of management. Systems is a way of thinking.

Neither is systems just another of the quantitative and modern management methods and tools, as it has sometimes been presented. All of the other modern management methods and tools are merely parts of systems. Systems is the general theory which is then applied to management, using quantitative methods and tools.

Chapter Four

Systems

I. The History of Management Thought

In the attempt to explain the management of organizations and of people there have been many different approaches. In order to understand the most recent and most comprehensive of these —the systems approach to management—it will be helpful to review the other schools of management theory.

The first of these, which can be called the traditional theory of management, is based on a hierarchy of pure and relatively unquestioned authority. The boss gives the orders, and his subordinates carry them out. If the orders are not carried out well, the subordinate is disciplined or loses his job. If they are followed satisfactorily, that is merely what was expected.

Certainly this situation was never entirely true. Hence the traditional theory of management was never truly in existence in a pure form. In this respect it is like the "classical school of economic thought"—that of Adam Smith, Malthus, Ricardo, John Stuart Mill, and others. It is a construct by later students of the subject, intended to postulate and explain the earlier thinking. Yet such a construct does serve a useful purpose. Not only did this type of management exist in some form, but it was surely the most prevalent approach of managers prior to 1900 and is still practiced by some today. It also serves as a reference point on which to build the history of management theories.

Frederick W. Taylor (1856–1915) is widely known as the father of scientific management. Working as a shop foreman, he was impressed with the way that workers were able to control the primitive piece-rate plans used in those days. Since no one knew what was a fair rate, the standards were set arbitrarily and could be easily manipulated by management and workers. Taylor decided that job tasks could be analyzed and rates set which would be fair to both the company and the workers. This was done through time and motion studies. Based on the idea that there was a most efficient way to do each job task, data were collected by observation of workers on the job. Then analysis of these data led to the establishment of piece-rate incentive plans intended to secure maximum worker productivity. It was more important that this change led to a revolution in managerial thought—the replacement of traditional management by scientific methodology. As Taylor once said: "Exact scientific knowledge and methods are everywhere, sooner or later, sure to replace rule-of-thumb."[1]

Among those others most commonly associated with the school of scientific management is Henry L. Gantt, who among other contributions designed the Gantt Chart, still widely used today for measurement of job activities. Frank B. and Lillian Gilbreth, who were made familiar to the public by the book and movie "Cheaper by the Dozen," concentrated on improving the methodology of time and motion studies through the use of such modern devices as the motion picture camera and micro stopwatch. They measured job activities in very precise terms, using as the unit of measurement the "Therblig," which is Gilbreth spelled backwards.

It has become widely fashionable to criticize the leaders of the scientific management school on the basis that they treated workers as mere machines to be manipulated in the interest of higher productivity. Certainly this was not true of Taylor, Gantt, or the Gilbreths—all of whom were interested in making the workers' jobs easier and in returning the financial benefits of the increased productivity to both management and the worker. As is commonly the case, however, many others picked up scientific management solely for the improvement of worker productivity in order to increase company profits. Time and motion became a fighting term to workers and unions. Congress once even passed a law forbidding the use of time and motion studies by government agencies. The principles of scientific management were and are sound: only the partial application and misapplication of the theories by other than their originators have led to disfavor and partial disuse, as has been the case with all other schools of management thought.

From a chronological viewpoint (there is much overlapping in time of the various schools of management thought) the organizational theory of management should be considered next. This theory of management is based on an analysis of the characteristics of bureaucratic (in the sense of Max Weber) organizations within which the management takes place. In this approach the primary job of the manager is to establish the work organization by setting up functional units arranged in a vertical hierarchy. Delegation of responsibility and authority, staff and line positions and relationships, organization charts and job descriptions, and the concepts of span of control and chain of command are among the considerations of this school of management thought. Associated to a great extent with Fayol[2] and R.C. Davis,[3] this theoretical approach to management was prevalent in the late 1940s. (Fayol's work was first done and published immediately prior to World War I, but it was not rediscovered and appreciated until the 1940s.)

While being initially widely accepted, especially by members of business school faculties (because it lends itself so well to the teaching of management theory), the purely organizational theory of management has been subject to criticism on the basis that it is too broad to be of much practical application. It has also been criticized for being too rigid and formal since the job of the executive is managing people, not managing an organization. Empirical work has also proven that much of the theoretical presentations of the organizationalists is not supported by fact. The work of Suojanen in demonstrating the fallacies of the "span of control" theorists is a good example of this. The organization school of management has its contribution to make to management thought, but it is no longer accepted as a total theory.

The human relations school of management came into existence as a reaction against the scientific school of management. Instead of viewing the worker primarily as a cog to be inserted into the right place in the wheel, the human relations school viewed workers as human beings motivated not only by money but by a desire for understanding and approval. The weakness of the human relations school of management lay in its relatively simple and naive approach to workers' job needs and in the ease with which its methods could be practiced as a collection of obvious gimmicks. Although the human relations school, like the other schools of management thought, may not have provided a comprehensive theory, it did make some significant contributions to an understanding of management.

The behavioral science school of management grew out of the human relations school. This behavioral science school of management theory, based on research findings and the concept of man as an individual and as a member of formal and informal social groups, is still very much with us. It has made and will continue to make important contributions to management even though it is not a complete theory in itself, for management is more than merely meeting the personal and social needs of people or even of making these congruent with organizational needs.

Growing primarily out of the work of engineers, scientists, and mathematicians in World War II and implemented by computer technology, the quantitative approach to management has received much attention in recent years. It is based on the reduction of management to mathematical terms and processes and includes all of the many uses of mathematics and computers in management, especially in managerial decision-making, including the methods and techniques which will be described in the remaining chapters of this book. Its contributions have been significant.

However, like all of the other schools of management so far described, quantitative mangement is not a total theory. It has its limitations. Management is obviously more than the application of mathematical formulae and methods. Like all the other schools of management, the quantitative school has made its unique contributions by focusing special attention on certain aspects of management and primarily by providing managers with valuable decision-making tools. It has also led into the systems school of management, which is much broader than the mere quantitative approach and which embraces material from all the other schools of management thought.

II. Systems: The Scientific Method Applied to Management

Various authors have offered definitions of systems. Johnson[4] and others say that a system is "an organized or complex whole; an assemblage or combination of things or parts forming a complex or unitary whole." He also defines a system as "an array of components designed to accomplish a particular objective according to plan." Hall[5] gives this definition: "A system is a set of objects with relationships between the objects and between their attributes."

Kershner,[6] after pointing out that attempting to define a system is a very ambitious and perhaps foolhardy undertaking, offers this definition: "A system is a collection of entities and things (animate or inanimate) which receive certain inputs and is constrained to act concertedly upon them to produce certain outputs, with the objective of maximizing some function of the inputs and outputs."

Gibson[7] states that "a system is an integrated assembly of interacting elements, designed to carry out cooperatively a predetermined function." Kennedy[8] gives his definition of a system as an organization, whose components are men and machines working together to achieve a common goal and which are tied together by a communications network. Wilson[9] suggests that "a system is a set of components to perform some 'wanted' operation on an object."

Why is a system so difficult to define, with most of the definitions appearing so broad and vague? It is because systems is very broad in its conceptual framework—a true theoretical approach to management. Still, in spite of the difficulty of defining a system in simple terms, examples of systems are familiar to everyone. The solar system, the circulatory system, the legal system—all are well known. The key to each of them is its totality. Each is made up of individual functioning parts, but the focus is on the total system and its end products, not on the parts or on the functions.

For this discussion the following definition will be used: *A system is an organized, complex, functioning, total entity existing for a specific purpose or purposes and derived from the rational application of the scientific method to the organization and administration of this entity.*

III. General Systems Theory

On the broadest level systems is concerned with developing a general theoretical framework to describe all the relationships of the factual universe through utilizing the general methodology of science. While this may appear to be an impossible task, significant progress has been made in constructing systems models of some areas of knowledge and some interdisciplinary models have even been constructed.

Interest was focused on the general theory of systems by von Bertalanffy in 1951.[10] Much of the 1962 and all the 1963 systems symposium at the Case Institute of Technology was devoted to papers on general systems theory.[11] In one of the papers from the second symposium Mesarovic[12] says that a general theory of systems must satisfy these two requirements: it must be general enough to encompass all existing specific theories and it must be scientific, in that its concepts and terms cannot be vague, ill-defined, almost poetic analogies but must be uniquely defined within proper context so as to have practical meaning for real systems.

Boulding[13] has given a hierarchy of systems which Goode[14] has presented as shown in figure 4.1. Bertalanffy[15] presents another dimension of systems when he defines closed and open systems. A closed system is one complete within itself, neither receiving from nor contributing to any environment. An open system is one which receives input from the environment and sends back output, while at the same time maintaining an equilibrium so that it does not itself change. An open system is based on a flow concept, with whatever flows through the system having no change effect on the system itself. Therefore a business or health organization is an open system on the fourth level of Boulding's hierarchy.

This brief presentation of the fascinating subject of general systems theory shows that the systems approach to management is only one facet of a much broader theory. It is the application

Figure 4.1 A hierarchy of systems (after Boulding and Goode)

Key Word	Characteristic	Example of system at level
1. Framework	Static structure	Geography of earth, anatomy of cell
2. Clockwork	Predetermined motions	Steam engine, solar system
3. Thermostat	Transmission of information	Furnace, homeostasis
4. Cell	Open system throughput of material and energy, system maintained in the face of throughput	Flame, river, cell
5. Plant	Division of labor among parts but not at the sensory level	Any plant
6. Animal	Self-awareness, specialized receptors, increased intake of information to form image (different from the information)	Any animal
7. Human	Self-consciousness, knows that it knows, language and symbols	Human being
8. Social organizations	"Role" and communication, messages, music, art, history	Human societies
9. Transcendental systems	Unknowables	Unknowables

in the management field of attempts to obtain a total theory of the entire scientific universe.

IV. Definitions

In order to gain an introductory insight into the subject, here are some of the common terms used in systems (see figure 4.2).

Input. That which is fed into the system and upon which the system works. For example, a job applicant may be an input into

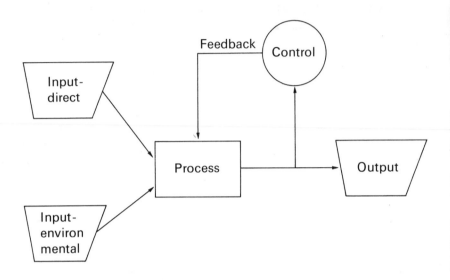

Figure 4.2   A typical system

a personnel system of a large health organization. Broadly speaking, there are two kinds of inputs, direct and environmental, as follows.

Direct input. That input whose specifications can be known, measured, and controlled. For example, the amount, type, and quality of a reagent put into a clinical autoanalysis system can and must be known, measured, and controlled exactly. It is therefore part of the direct input into that system.

Environmental input. The second type of input is that which feeds into the system but which is not controllable by either the systems designer or operator. An example of environmental input would be the kind and level of community educational programs in relation to a hospital's job training system. While the hospital cannot control the community educational programs, it is obvious that these programs will have a very important effect on the job training system. It provides a type of uncontrollable input into that specific system, and so it must be recognized by the job system designer and operator, who must know as much about it as possible.

Output. This is the product which is desired out of the system. Of all the system elements this is the most important because systems are output-oriented. In setting up a system, output is the first element which the designer must consider. Output must always be defined in very rigid terms, for the system can never produce the desired output unless this is done. Rigid definition of output is absolutely essential for effective control. An example of output would be the meals produced and delivered from a dietary system.

Process. The process is that which the system components do to the input to produce the output. Traditional management patterns tend to be function (i.e., process) oriented, but systems recognizes that process is only one of the four major components of a system and the one which is considered only after the system designer has defined output and input. An example of a process would be the interviewing of student applicants for admission to a medical school.

Black box. This term entered systems nomenclature from the experiments of MacArthur and Heigl[16] who tested how research teams attack problems by means of electrical resistance networks housed in small black boxes. Since exactly what happened within these black boxes was unknown to the subjects being tested, the term black box means a process not thoroughly understood or defined by the systems designer and systems operator. (This meaning is accepted here. By an odd twist many authors writing about systems use the term "black box" to mean "process"— not differentiating between processes which are understood and those which are not.)

An example of a black box would be the use by the personnel department of a certain test, which they do not fully understand, to select nurse aid job applicants. Ignorance is unscientific, and since systems is the application of the scientific method to management, black boxes are undesirable. How can the desired output be obtained and controlled if the process acting upon the input to produce the output is not understood? Black boxes are sometimes inevitable because in our present state of knowledge, much is unknown. For instance, it is not known what really goes on in the mind of an information clerk when her brain is fed input in the form of a question and the output appears as an answer. So her mental process is largely a black box at present.

However, even if there must be black box processes, at least their existence should be known, for one of the first requisites for knowledge is to pinpoint what is not known or understood.

Control. The fourth major element of a system (the others are input, output, and process) is control. A control is that mechanism which measures actual output against desired output and which automatically corrects the system if a deviation exists. An example of a control is the thermostat in a heating system.

Feedback. This is the information from the control back to the system (either to the process or, less commonly, to the input) triggering necessary adaptive system changes if there is a deviation from desired output. An example of feedback is budget performance figures supplied to department heads by an accounting system.

Adaptation. The automatic changing of a system in response to feedback from the control. In the example for feedback, expenditure reductions would be the appropriate adaptation to feedback from the accounting control center indicating deviations from desired budget output.

Component. The part of the system which carries on the process by working on input to produce desired output. Components are of two types: machine and human. An example of a human component would be a professor in the educational system of a graduate school of public health while his dictating equipment or his computer are examples of machine components.

Designer. The person, commonly a specially educated and experienced systems engineer, who plans, organizes, sets up and changes the system. A consulting engineer responsible for planning, designing, and setting up a materials handling system for a hospital is a designer.

Operator. The person responsible for the functioning of the system. The clean-cut separation of the designer and the operator is an important contribution of systems theory since it eliminates confusion over *who* is responsible for *what*. It also permits the designer to maintain a broader and more detached view of the total system than is possible when the designer and operator are the same person. If, as described above, a consulting engineer is the designer of a hospital materials handling system, the materiel manager of that institution would be the system operator.

Flow chart. A schematic or diagrammatic outline of the system. The flow chart is in skeleton form and is then filled in with written material, including instructions, forms, policies, procedures, methods and specifications to give body to the system. Figure 4.2 is a typical system and therefore is a flow chart reduced to its most basic form. Examples of flow charts abound in books on systems. Fold-out figures 3–8 and 3–12 in Young's book[17] are typical horizontal flow chart diagrams while examples of vertical flow charts are figures 5, 6, 7 and 8 in Bennett.[18]

Subsystem. Because a total system is complex and because the time and information needed to design one is great, it is more practical to work with subsystems. These are parts of the total system and are fitted together so that the output of one system becomes the input of another. Thus an output of the purchasing and stores subsystem (e.g., a sterile suture) becomes an input into the operating room subsystem. Both are parts of the hospital system.

V. Designing a System

Designing a system is simple and, at the same time, very complex. It is simple because fundamentally there are only four steps in designing the basic systems model; it is complex because this basic model must be then filled in with precise details. The steps in setting up the basic systems framework are these:

1. The first step is deciding what output is desired from the system. The system is strictly goal-oriented. It is keyed to results. Since the entire system is built around producing the desired output, the output must be determined and defined exactly or it can never be obtained. Failure to define exactly the desired output will also handicap setting up the process and make rigid control and adaptive adjustment of the system impossible.

2. Having determined the output desired and having defined that in rigid terms, the system designer next decides what direct inputs are available upon which the system can work to produce the output. The direct inputs are controllable, so these are specified in as strict terms as possible. Of course, there may be more than one type of direct input into the system (e.g., blood, reagents, distilled water, and electrical energy into an autoanalysis system). Then the systems designer attempts to discover and define as well as he can all the other factors which have a bearing on the system and its output. These factors are called environmental input. Although they are not controllable, or controllable only in part, by the systems designer, their existence, characteristics, and effect on the system must be known as much as possible so that the system can be constructed and adjusted according to these uncontrollable but very real inputs.

3. Now that the output is defined and the inputs known, the designer constructs a process or series of processes to act upon the inputs to produce the desired output.

4. Only one other step is now left: that of designing a control mechanism that will take samples (perhaps a small sample or possibly a continuous 100 percent sample, depending on the system) of the actual output and compare it to that output desired, making allowance for permissible defined tolerances. Then, if the deviation is above tolerance levels, the control adjusts the process automatically to make the necessary correction.

The steps described above comprise the designing of a system. Output (o) is decided upon; what there is to work upon, direct input (DI) is determined and other factors, environmental inputs (EI), affecting the system are taken into account; process (P) is designed to work on DI to produce o in the presence of EI; and control (C) is established to be certain the P is producing the desired o from DI.

As any systems engineer knows, this is deceptively simplified. Yet this simplification is valuable because it does give the essence of every system and it shows that systems is actually a total philosophical concept applicable to all management. As Boulding[19] has said, "General systems is a point of view." This simplification may also be all that the top health administrator needs to know about any given system. The details can be filled in by those working under him.

These details (including methods, machines, policies, tools, specifications and procedures) must be added in as precise terms as possible. There is no room in management by systems for hazy thinking. What is wanted *must be definitely known.* The acceptable and unacceptable levels of deviations from that *must be precisely defined;* how all this is to be accomplished *must be known exactly;* and it *must be certain* that all this *is being achieved* according to plan. To accomplish this, everything connected with the system must be defined precisely and completely. This is the job of the systems engineer.

VI. Systems Controls

Probably the major contribution of systems theory to management is its focus on output. The second most important contribution then is the emphasis on having a built-in control as an integral part of every system.

Figure 4.2 shows the place of the control in a system while figure 4.3 shows a typical control. A sample of the output (this may be a small or large sample or even a 100 percent sample of a continuous output, depending on the particular system) is taken. This is then compared with the standards set up for output desired; allowance is made by the control for defined permissible deviations from standards (this is called "tolerance"); and the results appear on some form of display panel, usually with a warning device of some kind for deviations beyond acceptable standards.

When the system is designed, adaptive changes to correct for deviations in output are built into the process. When deviations from standards are detected by the control, feedback to the process triggers the programmed adaptive changes, and these are automatically set into motion, correcting the problem and returning the output to that desired.

Occasionally, when appropriate in some systems the control feedback on deviations from standards may be fed to the input selector, if selection of different inputs is possible and will correct the problem.

While the anticipation of all possible deviations from normal desired output, with a programmed built-in adaptive response for correcting each type of deviation, may be theoretically possible, in reality this is never economically feasible. So, from a practical

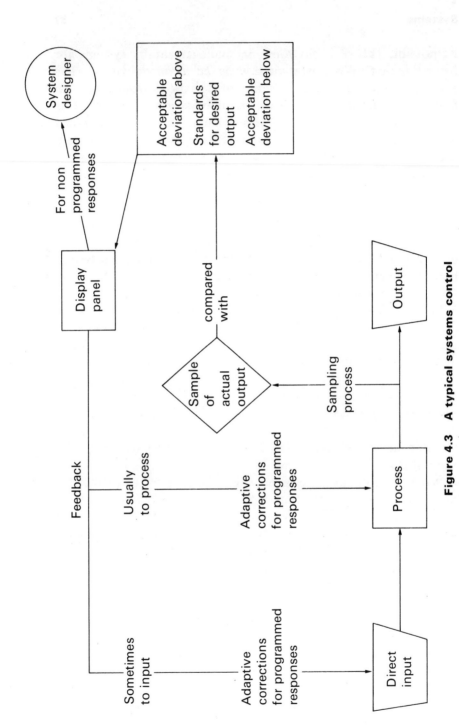

Figure 4.3 A typical systems control

standpoint, the system is designed with an adaptive response for most of the commonly anticipated deviations. Unusual situations or other deviations are then handled by having the feedback on these go to the systems designer who will decide at that time whether to change or redesign the system with an added programmed adaptive response, or whether to continue handling these non-programmed deviations on an individual basis.

While commonly systems controls are computerized, the fact that systems is a concept and not a collection of electronic devices is shown in that totally non-electronic controls may be the only ones existing in a very well-designed system. Take, for example, a total personnel system using as one control mechanism a report giving the top administration monthly personnel turnover figures by department (see figure 4.4). Acceptable personnel turnover

Figure 4.4   A non-electronic systems control panel

Memorial Hospital Monthly Personnel Turnover Report

Department	Number of personnel	Number of separations	Percentage of actual turnover	Percentage of acceptable turnover	Percentage of acceptable over-under
Laundry	20	1	5	5	—
Nursing	400	40	(10)	7	over 3
House-keeping	35	0	0	5	under 5
Main-tenance	25	1	4	5	under 1

rates would then be established for each department, acceptable deviations from these defined, and actual monthly figures recorded on the form. The monthly turnover report is thus the control display panel, and circling in red any unacceptable percentages serves as a warning flasher. Feedback on this may consist of a phone call from the administrator to the department head or to the personnel director. This may trigger adaptive changes within the department (e.g., group meetings to determine causes of separations and to receive complaints) or perhaps within the personnel department (which might be, for instance, better recruitment and selection of applicants for that department).

All the elements of a systems control are present in this example: standards for output, defined tolerance levels of permissible deviations from standard output, a display panel with a warning flasher, feedback, and a mechanism for adaptive corrections. Yet in this control example there are no computerized or electronic devices. Control *is* a concept.

VII. Components of a System

As previously defined, a component is that part of a system which carries on the process by working on the input to produce the output. The types of components are:

1. Human
2. Machine
   a. Computers
   b. All other machines.

Since in system design one goal is to produce the output with maximum efficiency, it is essential that each component chosen or designed for each task in the process be the one best fitted for that particular job. This has led, partly under the terminology of cybernetics, to the study and comparison of the advantages and disadvantages of human, machine, and computer components. For example, Sinaiko and Buckley[20] have studied these ten general characteristics of man as a systems component with the implications of each for systems design: (1) physical dimensions, (2) capability for data sensing, (3) capability for data processing, (4) capability for motor action, (5) capability for learning, (6) physical and psychological needs, (7) sensitivities to physical environment, (8) sensitivities to social environment, (9) coordinated action, and (10) differences among individuals.

The following is a summary of studies such as those in relation to choosing the right component for each job.

Machines have these following advantages over humans:

1. Machines are less subject to individual differences than are humans. In designing and setting up a system, it is important to have rigid specifications for each component so that the process may be uniform, predictable, and controllable. It is relatively easy to write out design specifications for a machine and to have as many of this same design obtained as are needed initially and for replacements. However, merely writing up standard job specifications will not ensure obtaining standard people to fill those jobs. In an admitting system as many typewriters as are needed can be purchased and with slight exceptions all will be similar. This is not so with the typists, however.

2. *Machines generally have a higher upper performance limit than humans.* While machines do sometimes "get tired"—that is, function at reduced efficiency if they are pushed to their upper performance limits, this is much less a problem than it is with people.

3. *Machines are less emotional and temperamental than are people.* Once a component is put into place, it is desirable that it continue to operate as planned. While some machines may act balky at times (e.g., the automobile which turns out to be a "lemon"), this is much less a problem than with humans whose emotional ups and downs affect their on-the-job functioning and interfere with the proper and smooth operation of any system.

4. *It is easier to check a machine's specification for the job.* To obtain the right human component, the personnel department must resort to testing, interviews, and checking past work history and references. These are all subject to inaccuracy and doubt. When a machine component is needed, however, the systems designer need only see what is available on the market and order it.

5. *Machines are easier and less time-consuming to modify.* Both the human and machine components of the system represent expensive initial and break-in costs. From time to time it may be necessary to change the functioning of a component to meet a change in the systems requirement. While people can learn new ways of doing things, some more easily than others, the amount of attention which has been given in management and behavioral science literature on the management of change shows that this is a major problem area demanding much of management time and effort. Not so with changing a machine. Replace a part here, speed it up a little there, adjust a screw, and the machine has been modified to perform its new operation.

6. Less turnover occurs with use of machines. Labor turnover is obviously a major problem, especially in the health field. No sooner is the medical technologist trained in her work than her husband is transferred out of town and she leaves. The auto-analyzer component of the lab system remains. Of course, there is some machine turnover due to obsolescence and deterioration, but this is slight compared to labor turnover.

7. It is easier and less costly to replace machines when necessary. Machines never complain or cause trouble when they can no longer do their jobs and it is necessary to discharge or retire them. They can then be sold as used machinery or scrap and represent income instead of a continued retirement expense.

8. Machines are in greater supply than human beings. This is generally true except for some very complex computers. The systems engineer can usually order all of the cardiac monitors he needs, but finding the nurses to operate these may often be impossible.

Man seems to have one major advantage over machines in general. Man is more versatile and more flexible than machines. This is a highly important advantage when, for some reason, a system component cannot be defined as rigidly as might be desired. Without exact specifications it may be impossible to construct a machine to do that job, but a man can be plugged into that spot, and with his flexibility and versatility he will shape himself to the job, or the job to himself, and thus carry it on adequately. Then, too, if the system demands changes, the human components can adjust to that change automatically without requiring system and component redesign. In spite of this, though, the preponderance of machine advantages indicates clearly why industry has sought to replace human workers with automated machinery.

While the computer is a type of machine, its special qualities require that it be compared to man in a different manner. In some regards comparing humans with computers is actually comparing two types of computers against each other. Some engineers have used the term "wet computer" to apply to the brain, as compared with "dry computers," which are electronic. The human brain actually is a type of computer. Electronic computers, since they are designed by humans, are necessarily models of the human brain to some extent.

These are some of the advantages of the computer over the human brain:

1. Computers make far less errors. While malfunctioning may cause computers to make some mistakes, these are rare. On the other hand "To err is human."

2. Fatigue is less a problem in computers. While excessive use at upper capacity limits may cause a computer to show some symptoms which can be called fatigue, this is not a common thing. The human brain tires easily.

3. Computers will work any and all hours. There is no difficulty when the computer is asked to work weekends, nights, or holidays, or to work for twenty-four hours straight. No bonus pay is required. As is well known to health administrators, even liberal premium differentials often will not motivate humans to work at undesirable times. Of course, humans cannot be criticized for this because their brains, being more easily fatigued, do require recreation and sleep to be restored to a desired functioning level. Computers need no recreation or sleep.

4. The computer is better on search functions. Searching is simply a process in which all possible combinations of answers are produced and tried. Producing all the possibilities for the opening of a combination lock is simple for a computer but a tremendous task for the human brain.

5. The computer far excels the brain in long-term storage and retrieval of information. The human memory is an imperfect thing and little understood. While it is possible, even likely, that every single bit of information which a man's senses have fed into his brain over his lifetime is still stored there somewhere, it is not easily obtainable. On the other hand the computer never has something "just on the tip of its tongue." The information it has been fed is stored within its memory unit, and it is easily retrievable.

6. Computers have no personality problems. They do not worry about the fact that they are merely servants or slaves. The computer does not balk on doing the work fed into it by a remote control input unit merely because it does not like the color of cabinet the input unit is wearing or the tone with which it gave its message.

The reasons for the fantastic rate at which computers are being utilized can thus be easily seen. Does this mean that humans will eventually be entirely replaced by computers? Not likely, for there remain certain advantages of the human brain over computers, described by Edwards:[21]

1. The human brain is better on pattern recognition, especially visual. As Chapanis[22] points out, a computer cannot read printed material because of the difficulty of building perception into a machine. No wonder that efforts to develop a computerized typewriter which can type material from spoken dictation without having a secretary to do this seems almost insurmountable at the present time without restricting the executive to a small, patterned vocabulary. What can the machine do when the boss says "er— er—ah, let's see, where were we? Oh, yes, ah—hmmm." How will the machine handle "and so on, you know what I'm trying to say. Type it up and I'll sign it." The secretary can do this because her brain is able to recognize the pattern which seems to be developing. Not so the computer.

2. The human brain is better at translating uncertainty into probability. Computers are made to deal with certainties. They can handle probabilities, but uncertainties are beyond them.

3. The brain has a higher tolerance for ambiguity and vagueness. As a matter of fact, the common computer term of "GIGO" (garbage in, garbage out) shows that computers can only deal with precise facts. That is not the material of which life is made, though. All human life is filled with ambiguity. It has been said that "growing up" for the human child is learning to deal with ambiguity—that little is absolute and eternally true. Since this is true and since human beings can deal with this ambiguity while computers cannot, it is easy to see that man is not going to be replaced by computers.

4. While the human brain may make more errors, it is much more likely than a computer to recognize an error and correct it on its own. When something is wrong, like an obvious mistake in a program, the computer may often go on throughout a very lengthy operation, turning out the material with the same error over and over.

5. Human brains, at present, are in greater supply than computers and hence are less expensive. A story is told which illustrates this. A news story appeared which said that it was possible at our present stage of computer technology to fly planes safely from takeoff in New York to landing in Los Angeles by means of a control computer on the ground and an operational computer on the planes. Someone asked a pilot if he wasn't worried about losing his job to such a computer system. "No," he replied, "not when the cost of paying for just the computer in the plane alone would be $50,000 a month while I get paid $50,000 a year."

The reason why systems theorists have determined the above comparisons between men and machines, between the human brain and computers, is to aid systems engineers in making the most efficient choice for each component in the system they are designing. If the process calls for the preparation of the organization payroll every two weeks (which is a routine programmed function involving simple factual comparison of hours worked for each employee with stored information on his pay rate and deductions), the components chosen to do that work should be machine and computer. For a process calling for recognition of vague and unexpressed fears and uncertainties, so that a patient may be treated psychologically and as a total being, the human brain is indispensable, and the component of that system must be human.

VIII. Systems and Human Relations

From the preceding section one could get the idea that systems is inhuman and that the systems engineer views workers merely as cogs in a wheel. This accusation has been frequently made but actually this is far from true. The systems engineer is not interested in disregarding the worker nor in driving him beyond his human capacity. This would be as stupid as designing a system that overloaded and overworked the machine components so that expensive machinery was broken down most of the time. If a machine component can produce an optimum production figure of 350 units an hour, with an absolute top capacity of 500 units, an engineer will build his system around the 350 figure and he will know that he cannot exceed the top figure. An engineer who did not do this would be illogical, inefficient, and unscientific. He would not be using the systems approach.

If the systems engineer knows that the machine component should function at optimum level and cannot exceed its top capacity figure, he certainly will be equally as aware of this in regard to the human components. The systems engineer is interested in determining human capabilities in comparison with machines and computers so as to put the workers into the system where they can function better than machines. Put into such positions, workers will have less routine drudgery and less frustration and hence a more satisfying job. The workers can then command a better wage rate since they can do that work better than a machine and therefore are not in cost competition with a machine. Such a worker is not likely to be replaced as soon as the company can afford a machine to do his work, for the worker was put into that position because it was a job that a person could do better than any machine.

As a matter of fact the traditional approaches to management tend more often to disregard the worker through unawareness of the worker's limits and of the worker's peculiar advantages over machines. For example, it is obvious that any type of operation—personal and organizational—will have unusually heavy demands put upon it at some times. In setting up and staffing his organization, the traditional manager seems to be unaware of this, or at least he commonly fails to make any provision for such increased demands. When these extra demands arise, they are met by overworking or exploiting the human components, for no provision was made to handle them, and although the machine components do have a higher upper performance level than the workers have, the top capacity of the machines is still an absolute limit. The overworked personnel then may respond by sloppy work and personal strife created from their tension and frustration as they try to keep up with the extra work load.

The systems engineer is well aware of potential fluctuations in system load and the fact at times there will be extra demands on all components of the system. The systems engineer also knows that there are only three ways to deal with extra demands on a system: (1) by opening extra facilities, (2) by speeding up the process, and (3) by queuing. So the systems designer utilizes one or more of the above to build provisions into the system for dealing with emergency or excess demands. He does not permit these extra demands to be met by overworking and exploiting the human components.

In other ways also the systems approach to management is good human relations because the system is designed around the capabilities of the components. The system must always be designed and operated within the capacities and characteristics of the workers. The workers should never be bent to fit the system.

IX. Conclusion

The strengths of the systems approach to management are many. Systems is a total approach. It forces the manager to look at the "big picture"—his total organization and its environment. Too much of organizational and personnel behavior is oriented towards a function, a department, or a person. Usually when we ask what a registered nurse does, we get the answer that "she nurses," or possibly, that "she is a professional nurse." The systems analyst would ask, "Why?" Continued questioning and investigation would disclose that what the RN really does is help get the patients well, among other things. Once this point was established, the focus could turn away from a functional approach to nursing to an output-oriented approach. When this occurred, new patterns of thinking would emerge and the nurse could stop merely "nursing" or being a "professional nurse"—she could concentrate on the output of well or improved patients.

So systems is output-oriented. It is the goal-oriented management about which Schaffer,[23] Schley,[24] and many others have written. Management by the systems approach forces planning, which is the most basic function of management and probably the most neglected. Systems cannot exist without planning, because for the system to exist and function it must be set up. Setting up the system *is planning*. Function-oriented traditional management can limp along without planning but the system cannot even come into existence without planning.

Systems has control as one of its four basic elements. Here again systems forces good management by making the establishment of adequate control an essential part of the system. Systems demands the establishment of adequate output-oriented controls—a system is not a system without them. At the same time the systems approach permits the rational establishment of such controls.

Finally systems does not permit the manager to act as his organization existed in a vacuum—a fault too common in health organizations and institutions. Systems calls attention to the existence of the uncontrollable outside world in which the system must live and adjust. By defining these as environmental inputs, the system is then constructed with these environmental inputs given importance at least equal to the controllable direct inputs.

The above demands and advantages of the systems approach show why it is revolutionizing management theory and practice. Is it, however, just another management theory? Will it make its contribution and then be supplanted by a more current and fashionable theory, as has its predecessors? Probably not, for, unlike the other theories of management, systems is total in its concepts and approaches. It is completely tied to our world of today and will be to the world of tomorrow, for systems is no less than the application to management of that which has created the world of today and will even more create that of tomorrow—the scientific method.

Section Three:
Modern Management in
Production

The application of the scientific method to management (called systems in this book) can improve both production processes and managerial decision-making. Its application to production is the subject of this section, which includes chapters on automation (in its production sense), work simplification, and value analysis.

Chapter Five

Automation

The first of the modern management methods to be considered will be automation. Like so many other terms used in modern management this word has a variety of meanings as is shown by its many definitions. Its first use was to refer to mechanized materials handling equipment. Hence the word "*automation*," from *auto*matic *mat*erials handling. Blumberg[1] says that automation is "any labor saving device going back to the invention of the wheel." The Webster dictionary[2] definition of automation is an "automatically controlled operation of an apparatus, process, or system by mechanical or electronic devices that take the place of human organs of observation, effort, and decision." Ferguson[3] gives these three definitions which he states are offered by others: the use of new and complicated equipment to perform in one operation processes that had previously required several; the use of automatic feedback devices (servomechanisms) that observe and adjust operations to fit pre-set specifications; and the use of electronic devices in administration to record, store, process, summarize, and interpret information. His own definition is that automation is "the automatic control of automatic machinery."

So the word automation has a gamut of meanings from a production operation using any kind of tool, to the use of machinery in production, to the use of *self-adjusting* production machinery. Then, as computers came to be used as control mechanisms in automation, some authorities began to use the word automation for any and all computer applications, thus broadening the term until it became synonymous with what is also called automatic data processing (ADP), electronic data processing (EDP), computer technology, computer science, information systems, or even the entire field of quantitative management and the use of the scientific method in management —defined as systems in this book. For example, an article titled "How to Automate a Hospital"[4] actually refers to the hospital installation of a computer based information system. Another article "Automating Nurses' Notes"[5] sounds like a good trick if automation has the definition used in this book. Hospital accountants especially use the word automation for ADP, EDP, computer technology, computer science, and computer based information systems [see as an example "Automation of Building Fund Campaign" by Conrad[6]], even though the word did not appear as a subject heading in the index to their professional journal until 1964.[7]

With such a wide range of meaning for the word automation, the reader must determine what is meant by context each time he hears the word. Which of the meanings are right? In one sense all of them, for as Humpty Dumpty says in Lewis Carroll's *Through the Looking Glass*, words mean exactly what the user wants them to mean. Therefore any given definition of the word automation is correct in a sense as long as the writer has a specific definition in mind (which is sometimes doubtful in the case of some who use the term in health field applications), so long as it is understood that more than one common usage of the word exists and that both writer and reader have the same definition in mind.

However, it does seem as if a word like automation should be reserved for something beyond the use of tools or even of complex machinery, for which the perfectly good word "mechanization" already exists. Buckingham[8] gives four essentials for a process to be considered as automated. These are: mechanization, continuous process, self-contained feedback, and rationalization (the application of reason to solve a problem). Thus it is apparent that automation, when used in this sense, is the true application of the systems concept to production. It is the application of the scientific method to one phase of management—that of production. All of the elements of the typical system are to be found in automated processes: input, process, output, control.

Strictly speaking, automation is not new. Watt's original steam engine of 1788 was an early example of automation with a simple centrifugal weight as a governor. This acted as a control and feedback device.

Automation has as its essential ingredient a programmed continuous production operation with a control mechanism which automatically corrects product deviations which are beyond defined acceptable tolerances by means of feedback mechanisms. If the deviations are beyond correctable programmed response levels, the control sounds a warning alarm and shuts off the machine. Bowen and Mangum[9] give a definition of automation which fits in with the concepts of this book. They write that automation is *"the application of electronic (or other) controls, including self-adjusting feedback mechanisms, to mechanical production processes."*

A familiar example of automation is a thermostatically controlled heating or cooling system. Samples, usually continuous, are taken of the temperature and the heating or cooling machinery adjusts its output to meet the desired temperature previously chosen. Hospital heating and air conditioning systems, as well as dietary and blood bank refrigerators, are thus true applications of automation as the term is defined in this book.

Good examples of the use of true automation in the health field are difficult to find. First, because most of the articles purporting to present automation are concerned actually with computers, information systems, or electronic equipment of some sort. Even Ferguson[10] after giving three common definitions of automation, plus one of his own previously cited, proceeds later in his article to discuss ultrasonic cleaning of surgical instruments as an example of automation, apparently overlooking the fact that ultrasonic cleaners are merely electronic and sonic machines with no elements of control feedback.

Another reason why it is difficult to find good examples is simply that true automation has not been used much in the health field. The main reason for this is, of course, that individual, personalized patient service does not lend itself well to total automation. Health agencies are in the production business but their product is a service. Little of this product can be manufactured in continuous mechanized processes with self-adjusting controls. Where such conditions do exist is where automation has made its appearance in the health field—in the processing of records and information, in laundries, central service departments, clinical laboratories, accounting, and business offices.

Even here, however, progress towards automation has been slow. In repeating the traditional caution that health services are personal and can never be given by machines, health administrators often overlook that *all* health services are not personal. Many of them, especially those of an ancillary supportive nature, are simple production processes in which industry has made valuable use of automation. Even where the product is personal services performed by health personnel, the use of automated machines, computers, and systems related to them can serve as invaluable aids to those rendering the personal service and to the ancillary personnel.

A sophisticated application of the automation concept in the health field is the programming of banks of hospital elevators. The input is people and objects, the process is vertical movement, and correctly delivered people and objects are the output. This is only mechanization, even with "automatic" elevators, until a control mechanism is added to automate the process. Through feedback mechanisms, the movement of each of the component cars is coordinated with the movement and location of all other cars in the bank. A pre-programmed schedule design provides optimum elevator use and avoids unnecessary delay occasioned by all the cars being at the same end of the run at the same time.[11]

Many pieces of complex hospital equipment have been truly automated in recent years. One type of steam sterilizer automatically programs the entire cycle, whether for fabrics, hard goods, or liquids. In case of a temperature drop or any other interruption, the control automatically corrects the cycle and the process.[12] Automatic wash machines in the laundry perform over fifty operations automatically, feeding supplies in the correct amounts at the right times and adjusting temperature through the use of their own timing and sensing control units.[13]

Memorial Hospital in Worcester, Massachusetts, has applied automation to their soiled laundry delivery system. When dirty linen is inserted into the laundry chutes through a double door lock, a moving stream of air carries the linen to a collector. This automatic collector then deposits the linen into a hand truck for movement to the wash machines. Control is present in this mechanized system since if one load is in transport, additional deposited loads will be stored by the system, which then moves these stored loads when the system is clear and ready for them. Movement of soiled linen from nursing units to the hand trucks takes an average of three seconds.[14]

Other examples of true automation in the health field will be given in later sections of this book covering computer applications, for often it is the addition of computer control that changes mechanized processes into automation. That is the manner in which North Memorial Hospital in Robbinsdale, Minnesota,[15] converted their entire complex of mechanical equipment into a type of automated system. An electronic surveillance system was installed to monitor all of the important mechanical equipment in the institution. If something goes wrong with any of the equipment an alarm sounds in the system's control center pinpointing the problem, and the central control unit operator turns off the malfunctioning equipment, turns on a standby spare unit, and dispatches a repair crew to correct the problem. While perhaps not complete automation in the sense that the machine does not adjust or fix itself when the trouble is detected by the control, it is a step in that direction and certainly elevates the machinery above the mechanization level into that of a controlled system.

An example of a similar type of control system is, of course, the patient monitor unit. The continuous monitoring and automatic recording of some of the patient's vital signs (for example, pulse rate, blood pressure, and temperature) is compared against previously programmed danger levels. When a danger point is passed, an alarm sounds to alert the nurse and she takes necessary corrective action. Again, this is not true automation because there is no feedback to correct the detected danger condition (as, for instance, the automatic administration of appropriate medication or electrical stimuli) but instead there is a mechanical control device which alerts the nurse. A human nurse component must be included for effective functioning of the system, but in true automation, human components are not needed nor included. Still, this and the electronic surveillance of mechanical equipment are excellent examples of what can be accomplished by applying the systems concept and modern computer technology.

Within recent years, there has been a growing interest by hospitals in automatic materials handling systems. Strictly speaking, these systems do not fit this book's definition of automation because they are not actually production processes, but they do provide excellent examples of many of the principles of true automation.

Health administrators have an obligation to keep up-to-date on modern applications of the automation concept in order to investigate similar applications in their own institutions.

Chapter Six

Work Simplification

The second area of application of systems to production processes to be considered is that of work simplification. Nadler[1] points out that work simplification is both old and new. It is new because of the emphasis placed on it for increasing production and reducing costs; old because in the broad sense man has always applied work simplification to tasks. That, however, depended primarily upon individual ingenuity. Now work simplification is a well-recognized field of management with its own skilled practitioners who have their own special tools and methods.

Significant scientific work simplification undoubtedly began with the work of Frederick W. Taylor, who developed time study of jobs to properly determine what constituted a fair day's work. The subject has been much expanded since that time as indicated by some of the definitions given for work simplification. Reynolds[2] says that "it is a method used to coordinate work habits by simplifying the drudgery jobs and putting the challenge back into work that must be done and at the same time makes the work more interesting." Zinck[3] states that the whole essence of work simplification is embodied in two statements: it is a way of getting something done, step by step, by breaking the problem into simple statements, and it is an organized, common sense attack upon the way in which the work is done now, with a view to doing it better. Lehrer[4] describes work simplification as a systematic analysis of all factors affecting work being done, or all factors that will affect work being done in order to save effort, time, and money.

For the purpose of this book, *work simplification is defined as the application of the scientific method to production functions through the use of systems analysis.* This definition is not at variance with that of Lehrer[5] who has expressed his definition in the form of a formula SWS = (PWS + TWS) HF where SWS is successful work simplification, PWS is the philosophy and attitude of work simplification, TWS is the tools and techniques of work simplification, and HF is the consideration of the human factor. The systems approach is an attitude and a philosophy; it has its tools and techniques; and the consideration of the human factor is an integral part of systems.

Work simplification includes five major subdivisions: (1) time and motion study, (2) tool and machine design, (3) physical plant design, (4) work standardization, and (5) production control.

I. Time and Motion Study

The basic methodology of work simplification is time and motion study. According to Barnes,[6] time and motion study is the systematic study of work activities for the purposes of developing the preferred system and method of doing the work—usually the one which is most economical, standardizing this chosen system and method, determining the time required by a qualified and properly trained person working at a normal pace to do a specific task or operation, and training the worker in the preferred method.

Mundel[7] says that the fundamental philosophy of time and motion study involves three assumptions: (1) that there are numerous ways to perform any task but, with the knowledge available at any one time, one method is usually superior to others; (2) that the scientific problem solving method is more productive of better work methods than is undisciplined ingenuity; and (3) that a standard of performance or time value for work may be determined so as to permit dividing the basic labor inputs into an organization, thus permitting the creation of true managerial design. Time and motion studies are applicable only to routine, continuous, short cycle work tasks, therefore not to many health jobs.

II. Tool and Machine Design

The second element of work simplification is tool and machine design. R. C. Davis[8] writes, "A tool may be defined as any implement or instrument used directly by a man or machine in performing work. Machine tools is a term used for machines which apply the tools to materials in performing work. An example of this would be a cast cutter in a hospital emergency room. Hand tools are those used for manual performance of work, for example a surgeon's knife. Much time, effort and planning goes into the design of most tools and machines in the health field. Consequently, with the exception of a certain amount of gadgetry and the high costs, tools and machines for use by health personnel are well thought out. The Health Industries Association has made important contributions in that regard over the years.

III. Physical Plant Design

According to R. C. Davis,[9] physical plant design is "the function of determining the physical relationships between the operations that must be performed on parts and assemblies, and such physical performance factors as plant, equipment, storage areas, materials handling equipment and other facilities." He further says that "Good plant layout increases turnover of work in process, reduces manufacturing lead time, lowers materials handling costs, and contributes other values. Materials handling is concerned with the internal movement of materials and work in progress."

Abramowitz[10] states that "an effective plant layout properly integrates site location, building design, materials handling, human engineering, and product and process requirements. . . . A good plant layout influences output and costs by: (1) permitting a faster flow of work in process. This reduces the need for high in-process inventories, thus reducing the inventory costs; (2) reducing the waiting time for materials. This keeps the amount of idle machinery and manpower at a minimum; (3) eliminating bottlenecks by adjusting the flow operations; and (4) providing adequate space for inventories, production facilities, and service areas."

The effect of plant layout and design on the other factors of work simplification is obvious. Without a correctly designed physical work area, tool and machine design and work standards arrived at by time and motion studies and regulated by production controls cannot work together to achieve the best possible work simplification. The great number of poorly designed hospitals and other health facilities in this country (planned by others than those who were to use them and had the knowledge needed for planning a good plant layout had they been asked) testifies to the truth of that statement.

IV. Work Standardization

A term commonly confused with and used synonymously for work simplification is work standardization. However, standardization is only one element of work simplication.

The American Management Association[11] groups standards into three types: historical, market, and engineered. Historical standards are based on past performance results. Market standards are based on comparisons with what competitors are doing. Only the third type represents true standards in the sense of work simplification. Work standards were originally derived only from specific individual time and motion studies. Now, however, they can be based upon previously developed data systems such as "methods-time measurement"[12] in which work tasks are analyzed by the basic motions needed to perform them and these assigned a predetermined time standard or the "master standard data system"[13] which is a set of predetermined standards based on a simplification of "methods-time measurement." For a hospital use of methods-time measurement, see Hansen.[14] Both of these, and other such systems, merely give predetermined standards for basic human job motions and thus do away with the necessity of measuring each job individually. In any case, when the standards are determined each job is then set up so that all workers can be trained to perform it in the most simple manner.

V. Production Control

The fifth major element in work simplification is production control. The presence of the control function shows clearly that work simplification is systems oriented, for as was stated previously when systems was discussed control was defined as an essential element of any system.

R. C. Davis[15] says that "Control is the function of constraining and regulating action in accordance with plans for achievement of specified objectives. Functions of control are: (1) assurance of correct performance as specified by plan; (2) well-coordinated action to accomplish the mission with a minimum of time, effort and expense; and (3) a minimum of losses due to interferences with the proper execution of the plan."

According to Eilon,[16] production control "begins as soon as production operations begin, in fact it begins slightly earlier in the actual issue of the production orders to the shop floor. The four stages of control are: (1) triggering off the operations—observing progress and recording it; (2) analyzing the data by comparing progress with the plans and with achievements of competitors; (3) taking immediate action to modify plans and redirect activities in order to attain targets; (4) postoperative evaluation feeding back information and conclusions to the planning section in order to improve future planning."

So production control is more than merely measuring the product. It is continuous, beginning with the planning stage. According to Eilon[17] it also includes quality control (of which so much is heard these days in the health field), inventory control and cost control (another subject not unknown to health and hospital administrators). Even more important though is the overall co-ordinating activities of production control: pulling together all of the elements of work simplification. As R. C. Davis[18] has written, production control is the coordination of manufacturing activities in the execution of product and production plans and programs.

Because two excellent volumes exist on the subject[19] the methodology of work simplification in the health field will not be presented in this volume.

Work simplification applies to all activities of any health organization from the simplest to the most complex, for a basic premise of work simplification is that improvement is always possible. Another way of expressing this is what Zinck[20] calls reducible waste. He says that waste is everywhere—as transportation, storage, inspection, and failure to use faster devices. Zinck points out that transportation adds nothing to a product or service except cost. In transportation waste he also includes time and effort wasted for personnel to move from one place to another to perform their work. Storage wastes time, space, and work moving things about, as well as adding to inventory cost. Inspection is a waste, he says, because it is a constant reminder that it is not known how to do the job adequately without wasting resources checking up on it every now and then. (This is the essence of Halpin's "Zero Defects" program[21]: to do things right the first time.) Failure to use faster machines is an obvious waste. So the objective of work simplification is to reduce the waste.

Management attitude is probably the key ingredient in the successful expansion of the concept of work simplification. People tend to act the way they are expected to act. So if top management shows interest in and support of good work simplification programs, they will work. Otherwise, never!

Employee suggestion systems are an excellent method of encouraging "amateur" work simplification. Poorly planned and poorly operated employee suggestion systems have caused an aversion to them in some managers, but if well planned and properly run, they can turn up many good ideas for work improvement plus building up organizational morale through employee participation. However, it is not only the management which has the feeling that the suggestion system will not work. The employees, having gone through it all before and having seen their ideas ignored or rejected; having received the impression that employee suggestions are taken as criticisms by the foreman; and having seen numerous suggestion systems come and go, are very dubious. Here is where top administration must believe in the system as a part of the organization's total work simplification program, and must express this strongly to management on all levels and to the workers. Then and only then will a suggestion system work. Of course, even then the suggestion system must be well planned and well operated, with special emphasis on feedback regarding suggestions received.

Work simplification has had many other names: methods improvement, operation analysis, job study, methods research, work measurement, methods study, and industrial engineering, to name a few. What it is called is not too important as long as it is recognized as a total process with the objectives of measurement, analysis, evaluation, standardization and improvement of production tasks. Since obviously job tasks do exist in hospitals and other health institutions, it is equally obvious that such institutions are good subjects for work simplification. Yet, the concepts and accomplishments of that area of systems, although much discussed, have made few inroads into health management. Smalley and Freeman[22] in discussing industrial engineering in hospitals give some of the reasons why. They ascribe it to traditions, to general resistance to change, to the existence of educational and research functions alongside of patient care, to the employment of submarginal labor, and to the personal medical and spiritual needs of patients. Smalley and Freeman also say that the uniqueness and supposed uniqueness of the hospital has led to the nonuse of work simplification in hospitals and even to the belief that there is no place for industrial improvement methods there. Included among this real and assumed uniqueness would be the division of authority between management oriented trustee-administration and the physicians with their clinical orientation; the traditional motivation and compensation of health personnel being primarily non-financial; the extremely conservative trust generated attitude of the governing boards' attitudes towards expenditures, even for the reduction of operating expenses; the non-profit motive and attitudes that patient life and well-being comes before costs; and that hospitals are already being operated as efficiently as possible, if one only understands their special problems and unique mission.

In spite of all this, there has been a growing interest in the application of work simplification to hospitals. Smalley and Freeman[23] cite Gilbreth's work on time and motion study in surgery, undertaken in 1913, as the first example of this method being applied to hospitals. Isolated studies were carried out and some were published up through the late 1950s; these are described by Smalley[24] in 1957 and by the American Hospital Association in 1958.[25] Since then with encouragement from many sources, especially the American Hospital Association, work simplification in hospitals has expanded, usually under the name of methods improvement. Still, the surface has been barely scratched. For instance, in 1968 there were still only two schools in the United States (the Georgia Institute of Technology and the University of Michigan) offering special university education for hospital systems engineering, and together these pioneer programs have only a handful of students.

The hospital literature is full of articles citing the results of work simplification. For example, Hansen[26] reports the results of work simplification studies in the dietary department of "a 300-bed hospital in Indiana." The first step in that program was a determination of the existing dietary practices. These were divided into three categories: food preparation, food service, and cafeteria–coffee shop food preparation. Each of these was then further subdivided into five or six functions. Once the functions were defined, work sampling determined how much time was devoted to each function. Observations were made at randomly selected times for seven days. Each observation was recorded and summarized at the end of each day to determine the amount of time spent on each function.

One of the important things disclosed in this study was that 30 percent of the dietary activity was non-productive, as compared with the acceptable standard of 20 percent non-productive time for personnel rest periods and inevitable delay. This non-productive time was then pinpointed and it was found that much of this was lost during patient tray assembly.

This then led to the second phase of the project: a search for possible improvements. One of these was the combination of the regular and special diet kitchens into a single operation. Floor serving kitchens were discontinued and centralized food service substituted. The coffee shop and cafeteria were combined. Smaller improvements included such as measuring food in graduated containers instead of weighing the servings, and changing certain personnel work times to coincide with peak work loads.

At the start of the work simplification study, the dietary staff had sixty employees. This was reported as reduced to forty-five with a payroll saving of $40,000 a year, while at the same time, the nursing service reported an improvement of patient meal service.

After several years of administrative study and planning, a methods engineer was employed at Toledo (Ohio) Hospital. Some of the initial results of the work improvement activities he conducted were reported in 1961.[27] Time study of the radiology department jobs showed that various tasks could be combined and so several jobs were eliminated. Patient X-ray requisitions were traced, by means of a flow process chart, from arrival at the radiology department until final results were filed. This showed that there were thirty steps in the process. A study of each step to show its purpose resulted in the reduction of these to nineteen.

In an attempt to determine how the operating rooms could handle more cases, studies were undertaken to determine time and man hour requirements for the various types of surgical cases. This showed that 13.21 employees per day were needed to handle a full surgical schedule and that the department had 13.5 employees per day working. This disposed of the contention of the chief of surgery that more personnel were needed to handle the existing load of surgical cases. Improvements included some changes in operating room policies and better scheduling of cases. These enabled the handling of an added ten cases a week with no added personnel.

Community Hospital, a 114-bed institution in Winona, Minnesota, undertook a work simplification study of their housekeeping, laundry, and dietary departments.[28] Studies of a time and motion nature were used to establish work standards. With the use of these new standards in training and supervising the employees, more than $15,000 was reported as saved annually.

Work simplification, as the systems approach to production functions, is more or less closely related to the subject of the next chapter, value analysis, which is the improvement of physical product value by the systems approach. Both are systematic, scientific, organized, planned searches for efficiency and economy —work simplification in the area of work functions and value analysis in materials.

Chapter Seven

Value Analysis

In 1931, the General Electric Corporation employed a young engineer named Lawrence D. Miles. After serving with General Electric in a number of responsible positions, he turned his attention shortly after World War II to an activity which he felt would bring better value to the use of materials. This later became known as value analysis, which Miles himself defines as the identification of unnecessary costs and decision-making which eliminates the identified unnecessary costs.[1]

There are other definitions of value analysis, of course. One article[2] says that value analysis is "the detailed study of every aspect of every purchased part, material, or service to see where and how unnecessary parts can be eliminated." Fallon[3] gives as his definition: "Value analysis/value engineering is a functionally oriented scientific method for improving product value by relating the elements of product worth to their corresponding elements of product cost in order to accomplish the required function at the least cost in resources." Miles himself expanded his brief definition by writing that: "Value analysis is a philosophy implemented by the use of a specific set of techniques, a body of knowledge, and a group of learned skills. It is an organized creative approach which has for its purpose the efficient identification of unnecessary cost, i.e., cost which provides neither quality nor use nor life nor appearance nor customer features. . . . It focuses engineering, manufacturing, and purchasing attention on one objective—equivalent performance for lower cost."[4]

The definition used in this book will be that *value analysis is a systematic, planned program of increasing product value by the application of the scientific method.*

One of the examples Miles gave was value analysis directed towards a tiny pin used in clock motors. The pin cost one-third of a cent. As a result of his efforts the cost of this pin was reduced to one-fifth of a cent. While this may seem insignificant, this pin was used in such large quantities that the result was an annual savings of $112,000 to General Electric.[5]

How did value analysis accomplish this? Essentially, by a step-by-step approach. Miles[6] gives three basic steps in value analysis: (1) identify the function, (2) evaluate the function by comparison, and (3) develop value alternatives. To do this Miles says that five questions must be asked: (1) What is the item? (2) What does it cost? (3) What does it do? (4) What else would do the job? and (5) What would that alternative cost?

Miles[7] gives another interesting example of how value analysis saved $45,000 for one company. The company was building a new lab which, because it included a powerful X-ray machine, would require a horseshoe shaped concrete wall, seven feet thick and fourteen feet high, erected outside the building at a cost of $50,000. Paying this much for a mass of concrete that had no supporting function bothered the general manager but he approved the contract. However, he told the lab manager that if he ever decided to move the lab, he would have to take his concrete wall with him. This caused the lab manager to think further, so he began a value analysis asking:

1. What is this item? A concrete shielding wall.
2. What does it cost? $50,000.
3. What is its purpose? To stop X-rays.
4. What else would do the job? Lead plates or a dirt wall fourteen feet thick and fourteen feet high.
5. What would the alternatives cost? (*a*) Lead would cost much more than the concrete, which is why lead is used for radiation shielding only where space is at a premium, as inside buildings. (*b*) The dirt wall would cost only $5,000 and would have the added advantage that when sown with grass it is more attractive than a mass of concrete. Also, if the lab moved, the dirt could be easily removed also.

After this analysis of comparative values, the decision was easy. The dirt wall was chosen.

The American Society of Tool and Manufacturing Engineers[8] states that the results of value analysis can be applied in fourteen different general ways: these fourteen, with suggested applications to the health field by the author of this book, follow:

1. Improve function. An example of this would be analyzing the scheduling and handling of patients in a neighborhood community health center in order to avoid waste of time by both patients and health center personnel.

2. Improve worth by lower cost or more utility. Use of multiphasic clinical laboratory tests, which can be done cheaper on a quantity basis and have been shown to save money for most patients over waiting for the attending physician to order only some of these tests on an individual basis. An example of the improvement or worth by increased utility is the combining of outpatient and emergency room facilities in smaller hospitals, thus using some of the same facilities for two purposes.

3. Improve esteem through better aesthetic value. Value analysis of a dietary food service to hospital inpatients may not save any money but may result in the serving of hot food hot and cold foods cold, as they should be served.

4. Decrease direct labor. Usually by replacing health personnel with machinery: for example, replacing lab personnel with equipment such as Coulter blood counters can decrease labor.

5. Decrease indirect labor cost. Replacing supportive health personnel by machinery: for example, replacing hand folding of hospital linen by adding an automatic folder to the flatwork ironer can decrease indirect labor cost.

6. Decrease required labor skill. The use of licensed practical nurses and nurse aids to perform nursing duties formerly handled only by professional registered nurses can decrease required labor skill.

7. Decrease direct materials cost. By supply conservation of items used for direct patient care, materials cost may be decreased.

8. Decrease indirect materials cost. Cost savings through eliminating unnecessary forms as a result of an organized form review program is an example of indirect materials cost which can be decreased.

9. Maximize use of standard items or practices. Requiring the use of standardized drugs, ordered by generic instead of brand names, as in a hospital formulary system can maximize use of standard items.

10. Optimize the manufacturing process. Better coordination of health personnel working schedules with patient work loads will optimize the use of the personnel and patient time.

11. Improve the production program. Decreasing the paper work required of professional personnel, for example, is an improvement of the production program.

12. Decrease capital cost. Included in this are all of the analytic studies which go into building programs for health facilities, with the intent of getting the most building and equipment for the money.

13. Improve quality assurance. Quality control programs in clinical laboratories are of this nature.

14. Improve vendor reliability and liaison. A good example of this is the relationships entered into by some hospitals and vendors in which the vendor sets aside in its warehouse the standard amount of certain items used by the hospital in a certain period, say three months. This then permits the hospital to reduce its inventory which saves both warehouse space and the money tied up in inventory.

Viewing the foregoing, it may appear that value analysis is merely cost reduction. If this is the case, then the health literature —especially in the hospital field—abounds with it. Take for example the 2 March 1968 issue of *Hospitals*, chosen at random from the hospital journals in the library of the graduate school of public health at the University of Pittsburgh, which had three different articles on cost reduction.[9] Are these value analysis articles?

Even Miles[10] has written that value analysis is a common sense approach. However, it must be more than that or any bright worker or supervisor could do it. Instead, there are people who devote a lifetime to value analysis. An entire vocation of value analysis engineering exists. There is a whole field of literature on the subject and the magazine *Purchasing* devotes an entire issue each year to value analysis.[11] So how does value analysis differ from cost reduction by the application of "good old common sense"?

First of all, value analysis is more than just cost reduction. Many of the fourteen areas for the application of value analysis just listed result in no reduction of cost. Instead, more value is added for the same cost. Value analysis is the *analysis of value* to increase value. Cost reduction is the *reduction of costs* to cut costs. This is no mere tautology because it demonstrates that there is only one way to cut costs but there are two ways to increase value: either by obtaining the same product for less cost or a better product for the same cost. Actually, value analysis may even result in a quality reduction if study shows that the lower quality, produced at a much lower price, will meet the customers' needs as well.

Another characteristic of value analysis is that even though there may be professional guidance, improvements are thought up by everyone. Time and motion studies done by "outside experts" are not value analysis, because in true value analysis the worker and supervisor are encouraged to figure out their own ways to improve the work process and materials.

Value analysis is a formal organized program of cost reduction. It is a constant search for better and more economical ways to do things. It does not depend on the worker or foreman to get a bright idea. As Dale and Michelon[12] say in comparing value analysis with employee suggestion systems: "Ordinary suggestion systems generally depend on sudden inspiration, which may or may not occur. With the value analysis technique, the search for improvement is a systematic one—and if the technique is constantly employed, some improvements are practically bound to come to mind."

Besides being formal and organized, value analysis is scientific in nature. The relation of value analysis to scientific problem-solving is easily seen from the basic steps and questions it asks. Value analysis is the application of systems to product improvement, with the desired output of better ways to make the product. Since value analysis is scientific, it can therefore be taught and learned—taught by value engineers and learned by everyone in the organization.

Because value analysis programs are formal and organized, they must be initiated by someone in the organization who has authority and responsibility. All of the writings on organizing a value analysis program agree with Martin[13] who writes: "Without the backing of top management, a value engineering program will never get off the ground."

Value analysis programs are organized in one of two ways. Either they are headed by a value engineer or by a value analysis committee. The employment of a full time value engineer with his own staff has proven to be worthwhile by industry. The savings far outweigh the costs of employing the engineer and staff. If there is a committee under such an arrangement, it is advisory only and primarily intended to involve key people in the program.

Formal value analysis programs in hospitals are rarely headed by a full time engineer: instead, a committee of key people are responsible for the program. Still, the concepts of value analysis are so sound and the scope for improvements in hospitals so great, that even this committee approach is widely reported as achieving highly successful results.

The use of value analysis in other health institutions and agencies besides hospitals seems virtually non-existent, probably because of their generally small size. The concept and opportunity for savings exist there also. In these situations and in hospitals which are too small to employ a full time value engineer there are the following possibilities of obtaining some professional assistance and utilizing the advantages of value analysis.

1. To share a full time value engineer between two or more health institutions and agencies.

2. To use an engineer on a consulting basis.

3. To employ a full or part time systems technician, backed up with the services of a consultant. Georgia Tech, for example, prepares such technicians by giving special training to selected personnel sent to them and by supervising their work when the technician returns to his own health institution.

4. Obtaining an engineer or committee of engineers from local industry on a volunteer basis. The Society for the Advancement of Management has been particularly helpful in this regard. The

author of this book received invaluable volunteer assistance (and invaluable personal education) from a committee of SAM. members in Canton, Ohio, who assisted Aultman Hospital in establishing a point factor job evaluation system in 1956 through 1959.

However, as Smalley and Freeman[14] have written on this subject, any approach except that of employing a full time engineer is "deficient in one respect or another. It is important to remember that a *permanent* professional program requires an industrial engineer who is a full time hospital employee. . . ."

As stated in the previous chapter, both work simplification and value analysis are systematic, scientific, organized, planned searches for efficiency and economy. Work simplification focuses on human work processes and functions while value analysis is primarily concerned with materials. Each arose from different backgrounds and with different parentage: Frederick W. Taylor for work simplification and Lawrence D. Miles for value analysis.

In reality these two approaches are not so totally different. Work simplification studies may sometimes concern themselves with changes in a material product if studies show that this is needed for improvement of the work function. Value analysis has expanded into finding better ways of doing any and all things in work organizations. Thus, any sharp lines between the two have blurred and they can both be considered as contained in the field of industrial engineering.

Industry has clearly shown that a formal organized value analysis program, headed by a full time value engineer, can result in substantial savings. It is a proven fact. Hospitals which have entered this area, even on a committee or part-time basis, have also reported significant results. Unfortunately all of this has made little impression on many health administrators and governing boards who continue to pinch pennies and lose the opportunity to save thousands of dollars.

Section Four:
Modern Decision Methods;
Operations Research

The term "operations research" is one that has been applied to all of the scientific approaches to management, thus taking on a meaning far beyond its original one. Because the application of the scientific method to management has already been defined as systems in this book, operations research is considered in its original meaning: the application of mathematics to managerial decision-making by the use of models.

After a brief presentation of the entire subject of operations research, this section then includes five other chapters—one each on the specific operations research methods of linear programming, non-linear programming, queuing theory, simulation, and gaming.

Chapter Eight

Operations Research and Models

I. Operations Research

In World War II, Great Britain, having suffered a catastrophic defeat at Dunkirk, was faced with the knowledge that the Battle of Britain would soon begin. Although the German air force was far superior numerically, the British had the best plane—the Spitfire—and excellent pilots but far too few. To help determine how to best meet this threat, the familiar economic problem of the allocation of scarce resources, half a dozen scientists were assigned to the Royal Air Force. The techniques they used were mathematics and the scientific problem-solving method. Their success is shown by Goodeve's comment:[1] "It is estimated that radar itself increased the probability of interception by a factor of about 10, but that, in addition, this small operational research team increased the probability by a further factor of 2, which together meant that our air force was made twenty times more powerful." Goodeve also gives several other examples of the use of these successful accomplishments of scientists in World War II, including fighting German submarines by computing the most likely areas in which they would have to surface to recharge their batteries.

Since this technique was research applied to military operations, it was named, appropriately enough, operations research. In its original meaning, the essential characteristics of operations research were the application by mixed research teams of the scientific method to problem-solving, using mathematical techniques. Different possible solutions to the problem are constructed as mathematical "models" (that is, sets of equations) and then the results of the various solutions are tried out by solving the equations.

Since that time, operations research (commonly called "OR"— not referring in this case to the more familiar health field abbreviation for operating room) has expanded into many fields, especially into business and managerial decision making. No management textbook is complete without its chapter on operations research. The journals are full of OR articles and journals in the health fields are no exception. Libraries have shelves of books on the subject. The Operations Research Society of America issues its own journal, *Operations Research*.

As the use of operations research has expanded, so has its definition been stretched until it is now commonly used to apply to all uses of the scientific method in management. This would be a logical extension of terminology, for one of the three major characteristics of OR from the very first was its total approach to a problem (the other two characteristics being a mixed-research team and the use of mathematical models). However, this extension of meaning has led to three difficulties.

1. It makes it appear that there is nothing really new about operations research. Simon[2] expresses this when he writes, "No meaningful line can be drawn any more to demarcate operations research from scientific management. . . . It is not clear that operations research embodies any philosophy different from that of scientific management." However, there is much new about operations research. To broaden the use of the term until it is synonymous with all of scientific management is to obscure these important new and different contributions.

2. It gives the impression that operations research is synonymous with systems. Dale and Michelon[3] seem to believe that these are the same when they write: "The most sophisticated aids to management decision-making are those used in management science, which is also known as *operations research*, or OR for short, and as *systems analysis*." This obscures the differences which do exist between operations research and systems, and this confusion may weaken the impact which the systems approach can have and is having on management.

3. It adds to the confusion in the field of modern management. Duplication and overlap of terminology, of which the use of

the term operations research is a good example, makes the ordinary executive, who already feels inadequate and unsure in the face of all of the new approaches to administration, feel more so when even the experts cannot agree on such basic things as terminology.

One of the objectives of this book is to aid the understanding of health administrators by arranging all of the modern management methods into a logical order, without overlap and duplication in terminology. Therefore the term "operations research" will be "rolled back" to its original meaning of *the application of mathematics to managerial decision making by the use of models.* The term "systems" will be reserved for the scientific approach to all of management, as has already been defined in a previous chapter. Because it has emerged as a discipline in its own right, I do not feel that mixed research teams are a necessary part of operations research any longer.

Of course, it is realized that the definitions in this book will have no effect on changing definitions used by others, regardless of the confusion created by the existing duplicating definitions. However, the definitions in this book do serve the purpose of producing internal consistency throughout the volume as well as calling to the reader's attention confusion of terminology, duplication, and overlap of meaning when they do exist.

With this definition of operations research, all managerial decision-making by use of mathematical models becomes subheadings of this general term. These include linear and non-linear programming, queuing theory, simulation, and gaming. Each of these will be covered in a separate chapter.

II. Mathematics in Management

Since operations research has been defined as the application of mathematics to managerial decision-making by the use of models, it is appropriate to consider briefly the role of mathematics in management. Commonly referred to as quantitative management, a better terminology is quantitative methods or techniques, for obviously management is more than mathematical. However, as aids to management, quantitative methods and techniques obtained through the use of mathematics can be invaluable.

The use of mathematics has several very important contributions to make in managerial decision-making. Probably the most important is that the rigid methodology required in setting up the equations may aid the manager to understand the nature of the problem and of the system with which it is involved. Rogers[4] expresses this when he says: "There is no escaping the iceberg analogy for quantitative analysis—the bare structure of equations through which values are to be found to get answers is the one-tenth that shows above the surface; the reasoning from which the equations derive, the qualifications attached to them, the preliminary steps to be completed before they can be used and the interpretation of the answers when they are secured compose the hidden remainder."

For many problems, mathematics may actually provide specific best answers which would not be obtained in other more usual decision-making methods, especially when the variables and their relationships are numerous.

Mathematical methods in management have their disadvantages also. Hicks[5] points out one of the most significant of these when he writes: "The first and most basic limitation of quantitative techniques has to do with the nature of mathematical models or equations, and quantitative techniques almost always involve the use of such mathematical expressions. Assumptions, either explicit or implicit, are incorporated in the derivation of an equation or a model." Failure to understand this and to grasp the effects of the assumptions will lead to incorrect decisions at worst or to irrelevant solutions. It is this which has led operations research to be defined as "a solution in search of a problem."

The cost of using mathematics in management is often far from inconsequential. While the cost of computer time is high it does not seem nearly so expensive when compared to the salaries of the engineers, mathematicians, and all of technical personnel needed. Also this cost disadvantage may be overcome by using mathematical methods and techniques only for decisions involving a potentially high payoff.

Management, of course, is much more than the mere use of quantitative methods and techniques. If this is understood, then there is no danger in aiding the manager by giving him assistance derived from mathematics. It is only when a manager actually believes in the apparent exactness of the data and the correctness of the answers fed him from the computer, that the use of mathematics in decision-making constitutes a danger. "Exact" and "correct" do not mean the same thing.

III. Models

Because the word "model" will appear often from now on in this book, it seems an appropriate time for definition and comments on that subject. First of all, what is a model? Many lengthy and complicated definitions exist, but as good a one as any is that of Allen[6] who says: "*Models are condensed statements of relationships.*" Another approach would be to say that a model is a logical construction of a system with pertinent "real world" elements abstracted and simplified.

Models may be purely descriptive in nature or geometric or mathematical. If geometric, they consist either of plane or three dimensional figures. If mathematical, they are made up of either algebraic or calculus formulas. The manner in which models are used is to vary the model by changing one factor at a time and observing the results of this on the other factors and on the total system represented by the model.

There are certain generally accepted rules in the use of models. Morgenstern[7] gives the following rules for the construction of mathematical models. They must be similar to reality. That is, they must bear some relationship to the real world situation being considered. Secondly, the model must be mathematically manageable. It cannot be too complex or impossible of solution. Finally, the model should lead to results that may be computed numerically.

Nagel[8] points out one pitfall in the use of models in that some unessential feature of the model may be mistaken for an essential part of the real system. Allen,[9] in commenting on the use of models says: "However, a mathematical statement can be used to prescribe a correct course of action only when it is supplemented by knowledge of how the process occurs in the real world."

With these comments, some of the uses of operations research (that is, mathematical models in managerial decision-making) will be presented in the next five chapters.

Chapter Nine

Linear Programming

I. Definition

Linear programming is an operations research method for use
with a common management problem—the allocation of resources
in an optimum manner. As defined by Ferguson and Sargent,[1]
linear programming is: "a technique for specifying how to use
limited resources or capacities of a business to obtain a particular
objective, such as least cost, highest margin, or least time, when
these resources have alternate uses. It is a technique that system-
atizes for certain conditions the process of selecting the most
desirable course of action from a number of available courses
of action, thereby giving management information for making
a more effective decision about the resources under its control."
In other words, as expressed by Hicks,[2] whose definition will be
the one accepted here, *"Linear programming is a mathematical
or graphical technique that can be used to determine the best use
of scarce resources to accomplish a defined objective."*

II. History

Linear programming is a direct descendant of "input-output
analysis," developed by the economist Wassily W. Leontief,[3]
in the 1920s. This was an attempt to create a general model of
industrial production by the solution of a set of simultaneous
equations. The application of this same methodology to specific
industrial problems was called by its innovator, George B. Dantzig,
the "simplex method."[4] This was in the early 1950s and led directly
to linear programming.

III. What Is Linear Programming?

Linear programming is basically a search technique. Through mathematical means, it sets up a problem and tries all possible solution until the optimum one is disclosed. Linear programming is used when problems have these characteristics: (1) The problem is one of "mix," that is of combining together two or more variables. (2) The problem needs an optimum solution—not just a feasible solution but the best one, taking into account all of the variables. (3) There are constraints upon the solution—there are certain solutions which are outside the range of usable answers. (4) A linear relationship exists between the variables: when one varies, the others do also in direct proportion.

It is important to understand number 4 above. This has given the name of "linear" to linear programming. The term linear means that "straight line relationships" are involved. In the equation $x = 2y$, x and y vary in direct proportion. Therefore, when this equation is plotted on a graph, it appears as a straight line. This is a linear relationship.

With the equation $x = 2y^2$, x and y do not vary in direct linear relationship with each other. Plotting this equation on a graph gives a curved line. This is a non-linear relationship. No relationship can be linear if the equation contains a term raised to a power higher than one—that is, squared or cubed or so on. Since the equation $x = 2y^2$ contains y squared, it cannot be linear. Only linear relationships are used in linear programming. Otherwise the relationships become too complex to produce meaningful solutions to practical problems. (See the next chapter for a discussion of non-linear programming.)

So linear programming is a search for an optimum solution to a mix problem, in the presence of constraints and when the relationships are linear.

IV. Examples of Linear Programming

Linear programming is probably the quantitative management technique most commonly used in the health field, except for statistics and accounting. Almost every health administrator uses a simple type of linear programming called break-even analysis, which determines the point of institutional or agency activity where income equals expenses. The variables are fixed costs, semi-fixed costs, variable costs, fixed income, and variable income. Plotting these on a break-even chart gives the break-even point as well as the amount of surplus or deficit at all other levels. All of this leads to decisions regarding the planning of levels of expense and service load as well as setting service charge rates, personnel salaries, and staffing patterns.

Young[5] presents an approach to linear programming based on the relationship between a patient's degree of illness, his ability to care for himself, and the amount of nursing care he will require. If this is accepted as linear, which it probably is or at least very close to linear, then it is possible to predict the number of nursing personnel of each type needed for each nursing unit based on information concerning the number and degree of illness of each patient. This can be done immediately before each shift reports for duty by a computerized program matched against current patient illness characteristics, and the assignments of nursing personnel can thus be made on a predicted patient care *need* for the next shift rather than just on the number of patients on each unit, or even worse, merely based on the number of beds in each unit, as it is done in most hospitals.

A much simplified example of linear programming is this hypothetical problem of determining the average staffing of a medical-surgical nursing unit in the most economical manner. Assume that RN's, LPN's, and nurse aids are to be used. An LPN is paid 75 percent of an RN salary and a NA is paid 55 percent of an RN salary. Also, the average amount of nursing care required on that unit is 4.2 hours per patient per day and the average number of patients is 27. It is assumed further that an RN is the equivalent of 2 LPN's and of 3 NA's in the production of nursing care.

This, then, is a search for an optimum solution to a mix problem: what mix of RN's, LPN's and NA's will provide the most economical staffing of the unit. A linear relationship exists as all factors have simple straight line relationships to each other. Putting all of the relations into the form of separate algebraic formulas gives:

$$S = \text{solution to problem}$$
$$XRN = \text{number of } RN's$$

$YLPN$ = number of LPN's
ZNA = number of nurse aids
$ = RN salary per month = \$500

$$S = XRN + YLPN + ZNA$$

$RN = 2LPN$
$RN = 3NA$
$LPN = .667NA$
$RN\$ = \$$
$LPN\$ = .75\$$
$NA\$ = .55\$$

Solving all of these equations simultaneously gives a continuum of solutions from which the most economical one may be chosen. Not quite though. If this were the case, then it would be obvious that the unit should be staffed entirely with RN's as it costs only \$500 a month to get one unit of work from an RN but \$750 a month to get this equivalent amount of work from LPN's (\$375 × 2) and \$825 to obtain this from nurse aids (\$275 × 3).

Here is where the fourth element of linear programming comes in, for it is obvious that the shortage of RN's will make it impossible to obtain all that would be needed for total RN staffing. This then imposes a constraint on the range of possible solutions. Staffing the unit with 20 RN's and no LPN's or NA's is not a feasible solution if only 7 RN's can be obtained.

Also, it is a fact that RN's and LPN's and nurse aids are completely interchangeable only up to certain points. This then imposes additional constraints on the range of solutions. Suppose too that the state hospital licensure law requires there be an RN on duty on each unit each shift. This is another constraint. So, as in any linear programming problem, constraints are present and the optimum solution must take them into account.

V. Advantages of Linear Programming

The major advantage of linear programming is in the decision-making function itself. Linear programming permits the determination of an optimum solution with mathematical certainty, even when the number of variables and constraints may be very large and the relationships complex. Sometimes the number of variables and constraints may be beyond those which can be grasped by the unaided mind of any manager, even when these variables have been simplified, but linear programming can handle these mathematically and provide the manager with one or more optimum solutions which he not only can grasp easily but in which he can place confidence.

Along with many other applications of systems to management, another advantage of linear programming lies not only in the solution it provides but in forcing management to think through all aspects of the problem and thus to become aware of all variables and constraints concerned. In constructing the linear program, it is necessary to establish objectives and then to discover, isolate, define, and quantify pertinent variables and constraints as well as the relationships between these. Even when it is necessary to simplify these so that they may be handled in the program, their existence and relations often lead management to obtain new insight into the situation with which they are dealing. In other words, linear programming forces broad management thinking in rigid terms, focused on the particular problem under consideration.

The preceding example of linear programming in staffing a nursing unit points out another advantage of linear programming —the presentation of not one but a range of solutions from which not only the optimum one may be chosen but from which other solutions may be obtained at a later date if conditions change or added constraints are applied. For example, if the chosen solution to the nursing staffing problem requires eight RN's because it is thought that this number can be obtained, a worsening of the nursing shortage to where only six RN's can be employed would permit an easy determination of the mix of LPN's and nurse aids to go along with six RN's to provide the new most efficient and economical solution. In fact, linear programs may produce a range of solutions in some situations which can be provided as a guide program to permit the varying of the mix, as certain factors may vary, without further managerial decision-making intervention.

The objectivity achieved in decision-making is another important advantage of linear programming. The subjectivity of human judgment, based on non-rational and irrational factors, is well known. A certain type of human subjectivity is the ignoring of some of the variables or not taking them fully into account. Linear programming considers all variables objectively and when solutions are presented, "the chips fall where they may."

VI. Disadvantages of Linear Programming

Like everything else in life, linear programming has its disadvantages as well as its advantages. While these may not be fatal, since the advantages far outweigh the disadvantages, it is important for the administrator to know both.

Linear programming requires that all information must be available in exact terms. Obviously, all information needed in many problems is not available in such exact form. This then limits the application of linear programming in such problems. This is not serious for there are plenty of problems in which all of the data is exact and for which linear programming would be the decision method of choice. For the other problems, other decision methods can be used. What is really serious is the application of linear programming to problems where the quantification of the data in exact terms may lead to incorrect results. This should never be done. However, in some cases, to permit the use of linear programming, inexact data may be treated as exact known facts. Even this is not serious if the fact that this was done is remembered when the solutions are worked out. If it is realized that the solutions are only as good as the assumptions which went into them, then quantifying inexact data for linear programming is not wrong. It may be very right, for the basically inexact and guarded solutions presented may be the best obtainable and may give indications which are extremely important to the decision-maker. It is only wrong when the inexact nature of the solutions, based on forcing rigidity upon inexact facts, is not known or is overlooked by the decision-maker.

The necessity of treating all relationships as linear is another disadvantage of linear programming. In reality, few administrative relationships are that simple. To treat them as such is to again make assumptions which will affect the solution. Again however, this is not detrimental if the assumption of linear relationships is known and considered in choosing the solution. As will be seen in the next chapter non-linear programming does not have this disadvantage since it permits the variables to assume the complex relationships they may have in real life. This, however, has the disadvantage of often making the variables and their relations impossible to manipulate and solve, so that no solutions can be reached.

Often, the number of variables in a linear program are so great that their simultaneous solution becomes lengthy or impractical. This is less a problem as computers become faster but it still adds to the cost, which is another consideration in linear programming. With the necessity of collecting exact data to be analyzed and programmed by a mathematical engineer for solution using expensive computer time, the cost is often too much for the results which can be obtained. The temptation then is to reduce the number of variables but this again has the effect of reducing the correctness and value of the solution.

Chapter Ten

Non-Linear and Dynamic Programming

In the previous chapter, it was stated that one of the necessary conditions for the application of linear programming is that the relationships between the variables being considered must be linear—that is, of a simple straight line nature. When one variable changes, the other variables change only in direct proportion.

However, this necessary condition imposes a limitation on the realistic use of linear programming to solve practical problems. While there are some management problems which do involve simple linear relationships, many others consist of variables which have complicated relationships to each other and in which more than one of the variables may be changing at the same time.

Take for example, the nursing staffing problem in the last chapter. It was assumed that the relationships between the number of RN's, LPN's, and nurse aids was linear. That is, when the number of RN's was reduced by 1, it was necessary to increase LPN's by 2 or nurse aids by 3, or some combination of this. Actually, of course, the relation between the numbers of these three types of nursing personnel is not that simple. It is very complex since it depends on so many factors. Changing needs of individual patients, individual qualifications of each RN, LPN, and nurse aid, legal constraints on the functions each may perform, are but a few of the numerous—perhaps innumerable—variables involved. Then for some functions of an RN, no number of LPN's or aids can replace her.

Whatever relationships are involved in this simple problem, perhaps it is impossible to determine or even be aware of all of them, it is very obvious that they are not related in a linear manner. They are non-linear, as are most real life relationships with which administrators must deal. This then means that the equations which represent the variables and their relationships are difficult to set up and probably impossible to solve. The problem then has no feasible mathematical solution.

This does not mean that operations research has nothing to offer in the solution of non-linear problems. As a matter of fact, many of the most exciting and important contributions have been in this area. Non-linear programming covers the same problem areas as does linear programming with the exception of linear relationships. That is, non-linear programming deals with resource allocation (mix) problems seeking an optimal solution in the presence of constraints when the relationships are non-linear. A good example would be RN's working on a certain nursing unit. Suppose that 1 RN can produce x amount of patient care, then perhaps 2 RN's will produce $2x$ and 3 RN's will produce $3x$. However, a point is reached where the "law of diminishing returns" begins to operate for the nurses will begin to get into each other's way, communications problems will arise, or perhaps the large size of the group may encourage more chit-chat. For example, 5 RN's may produce $5x$ but adding a RN will result in a total patient care output of $5.75x$, and 7 RN's may only produce $6.5x$, and so on.

Most of the examples given in the literature as non-linear programs are actually examples of a single non-linear function, because non-linear programs are complicated to even explain to readers. Also, most work on non-linear programming is to be found in economics and not in management writings. This is an indication that this modern management method is still primarily theoretical, not practical. Probably the most practical use of non-linear programming is in what its inventor, Richard E. Bellman,[1] calls "dynamic programming." This is an attempt to provide optimum mathematical solutions to complex, non-linear problems by successive approximations. In other words, it is a search for the optimum solution by a type of trial and error methodology which gradually narrows the area of correct solutions by discarding at each step of the computations those solutions which appear furthest away from the desired solution.

It is "zeroing in on the problem."

This is actually a realistic way to deal with administrative problems because most executive decisions are not really "one shot, all-or-none" actions; instead they are usually multistage. That is, the executive makes a certain decision on the basis of the facts he has on hand at that time. Later, when the results of that initial decision are apparent, he makes a second decision and so on. Such multistage decision making is the methodology of dynamic programming.

Bellman[2] gives as a common example of multistage decision-making the bidding in a bridge game. Each player makes an opening bid and then, as more facts appear based on the successive bids of the other players, each player makes another decision each bidding round as long as he remains in the bidding.

The mathematical techniques used in dynamic programs are of a complex nature involving quadratic equations, calculus, and the Lagrange multiplier. No details of the actual mechanics of dynamic programming will be given here. Interested readers can find them in Bellman,[3] Bellman and Dreyfus,[4] and Zangwill.[5]

Bellman makes an interesting and important point when he writes that the objective of dynamic programming is not necessarily to arrive at an optimum mathematical solution, for most of the multidimensional allocation processes with which dynamic programming deals are too complex for that. Instead, Bellman says that the objective of dynamic programming is to disclose the optimal policy involved and that the solution is not reached by the successive approximations until the optimal policy involved is understood. In this respect non-linear or dynamic programming is similar to the systems concept of which it is a part, for one of the major contributions of systems and its various applications to management is not so much the solving of problems but the understanding of the factors involved in the problems.

Non-linear programming and its contributions, while fascinating, remains highly theoretical. As Lindsey[6] writes: "Since dynamic programming is clearly in the development stage, its applications should be limited to situations of high potential payoff and situations where management is prepared to regard the necessary expenses as it would research-and-development expenses. Because of the complexity of most management problems of a dynamic nature, it may be that simulation will provide a more practical approach to most problems than will formal dynamic programming."

The reasons why non-linear or dynamic programming is so little used in the health field are obvious. Health institutions have little money to spend for research and development expenses in administrative decision-making. Also, simulation is better known, more widely accepted, more practical, usually more effective, and covers many of the same areas as does non-linear programming.

Since non-linear programs are usually converted to linear programs when the principles of that particular problem are revealed by non-linear programming, this is another reason why non-linear programming is not well known in the health field.

Chapter Eleven

Queuing Theory

I. Introduction

Every hospital administrator is aware of the public relations aspects of the hospital emergency room. Many times he has had the experience of having someone come to him with a complaint about having to wait too long on a recent emergency room visit. The tale is usually embellished with gruesome details about the suffering of the patients and their families, dying like flies in the waiting room while the cruel and calloused doctors and nurses ignore them. Then, to top it all off, today the patient received a bill for thirty dollars and all they had done was to examine him and give him some pills. The administrator, having heard all of this many times before, listens with interest, asks a few questions which may disclose that most of the waiting patients were minor medical cases, that a nurse or a doctor had seen them briefly on arrival and told them to wait and that they would be taken care of as soon as reasonably possible, that the emergency room was especially busy at the time as a half-dozen seriously injured automobile accident victims had just been brought in, that most of the patients were actually awaiting the arrival of their own family physician without whose presence and orders the hospital personnel were unable to proceed beyond rendering first aid emergency care, that no one really died nor worsened medically during the wait, and finally that the entire length of the wait complained about was only forty-five minutes. When the administrator has brought out all of this by experienced questioning and explained the problems of staffing the emergency room at the correct level to meet emergency needs without having to pay for too much idle time, the individual ends his complaint with a typical comment such as, "Well, everyone knows hospitals aren't being run very efficiently. When people come to the emergency room, they shouldn't have to wait around. Something ought to be done about it!"

Now the administrator knows that people are under great strain when they come to the emergency room. He knows the bad public relations which can build up when patients are made to wait. He probably is an efficient, well-educated, experienced administrator. Still, people do have to wait in the emergency room. Why *doesn't* he do something about it? It is because he is up against a problem of allocating resources in the most efficient manner. Emergency room usage is subject to erratic unpredictable fluctuations of use —high peaks of demand followed by hours of no patients at all. Staffing the emergency room takes personnel and these employees must be paid. It is not only dollars involved, for nurses, interns, and others are in short supply and if they are just sitting around in the emergency room waiting for a patient to come in there are other patients in the hospital at the same time who need their services. If the administrator staffs the emergency room too lightly, true emergency services may not be available when needed; if he staffs the emergency room with too many people, professional services and money are wasted. This is a common problem in modern life, not only in hospitals. It is known as a queuing problem. Industry faces it and so do banks, theaters, and supermarkets. Planes trying to land at a busy airport are a queuing problem. Man has always had to wait, but this is an increasing problem in a crowded urban society.

It is not only people who must line up to wait for service. Physical items may be visualized as customers waiting to receive service. For example, disposable intravenous sets on the shelf of the central service department wait to be used. Automobiles in a service station wait to be worked upon. Requisitions and work orders get queued. Items placed in stock wait to be used. Production assembly lines may be viewed as a queue and intermediate products along the line as customers waiting to be served. Inventory control is a queuing process since the effect of inventory levels, order processing time and shipment time have their effect on customers. Too small an inventory will result in delays in filling orders and customers will take their business elsewhere. However, too large an inventory ties up capital unnecessarily and also increases losses due to deterioration and obsolescence.

II. General Queuing Theory

Faced with these waiting line problems, industry and the military have turned to a type of operations research called queuing theory. This is a mathematical analysis of queuing problems in order to arrive at optimum decisions. Simulation, the next chapter in this book, is also used to solve similar problems and is therefore related to queuing theory. However, simulation is a trial and error method, while queuing theory is more formal in its approach.

The origin of queuing theory is credited to A. K. Erlang for his work in 1908 having to do with the elements of demand on the Copenhagen telephone system. A key aspect of Erlang's work was the assumption that demands arose independently of each other and outside the control of the system—still very basic assumptions in most queuing models. During and after World War II, interest in queuing theory grew, especially in its applications to communications, transportation, and production, until as Flagle writes,[1] there were times when queuing theory all but preempted the pages of operations research journals.

The object of queuing theory is to determine the optimum service level in correlation with customer demand and customer willingness to wait, so as to provide a balance between too little service, which leads to undesirable results such as loss of customers or bad public relations, and too much service which results in costly waste of service on an unused standby basis. Defined more briefly, *queuing theory is a mathematical method of balancing waiting time of both customer and customer-serving personnel in an optimal manner.*

III. General Queuing Characteristics

Looking at general queuing problems, it can be seen that they all have certain characteristics. A customer (1) arrives at the service facility, (2) enters the queue and waits for his turn, (3) is served, and (4) leaves. In our specific case, the patient (1) arrives at the emergency room, (2) is seen briefly and asked to have a seat in the waiting room, (3) is taken care of, and (4) leaves the emergency room, to return home or to be admitted as a hospital inpatient.

Therefore, the length of time between the arrival of the customer and his departure depends on these factors:

1. *Customer arrivals.* How frequently do they arrive? Do they arrive singly or in batches? Is their arrival at a uniform rate or is it erratic?

2. *Customer waiting time.* Although this is usually all the customer is concerned with in a queuing situation, it is affected by the number of serving stations open and how they are staffed. Also, by the order in which the customers are served. Is it first come, first served, or are there some favored special or priority customers? This order of serving customers is called the "queue discipline."

3. *Customer service time.* How long does it take to wait on a customer?

4. *Customer departure.* How rapidly does the customer clear out when served?

Again, back to the emergency room. The efficiency and speed with which the patients are handled depends upon those above factors:

1. *Patient arrivals.* The unpredictable and erratic nature of patient arrivals makes it very difficult to handle all patients smoothly as they arrive. If the patient arrives at a slack time, he will be taken care of immediately. If he arrives when the emergency room is full, he will have to wait his turn.

2. *Queue discipline.* The order in which patients are served is a key factor in the hospital emergency room. Patients are not taken in order of arrival but instead, they are seen and graded into medical priority categories (when this is done in a formal manner, such as during disasters, it is known as *triage* and the patients are divided by the screening physician into critical, serious and slight injuries). Then the most serious are handled first, which adds to the anxiety and aggravation of the less serious patients and their families who do not understand why they are being kept waiting while other later arrivals are receiving medical care already.

Besides, the first arrivals probably think they are more serious cases anyway. Of course, the number of emergency room personnel of specific types, the number of emergency rooms available, and usually to a lesser extent the amount of equipment available has its influence on the actual waiting time.

3. *Length of service.* How long it takes to serve each patient is highly variable in the emergency room. Fortunately, the most serious patients over whom personnel may work for hours, are usually transferred out of the emergency area into surgery or intensive care. Still, some orthopedic outpatients may require hours of work while others are impatiently awaiting their turn.

4. *Customer departure delays.* Usually patients depart from the emergency room rather promptly when finished, but occasionally some linger around, perhaps waiting for transportation, thus taking up personnel time and adding to the waiting time of others still unserved.

Other factors affect the queuing situation. The nature of the service being provided must be considered. It is one thing to choose to wait in line all night to purchase tickets to the world series and still another thing to make patients wait so long in an emergency room that some may die before being seen by a physician. The importance of a reputation for providing quick service has a bearing. So does how long a customer will wait without leaving. Industry is well aware of the latter, known technically in queuing theory as "customer patience," for loss of waiting customers will result in loss of sales. However, this seems to be considered less in the health field where the long lines and day long waits for service in outpatient departments are often not the result of inefficiency in scheduling but instead, are actually planned so as to conserve physician and nursing time at a maximum level. If the patient has to do all the waiting, the physician or nurse never has to wait at all, for the next patient is ready immediately whenever they are ready for him. Queuing theory applies both to the waiting *of the customer and to that of the personnel who will serve him.*

Lengthy patient waits in the offices of physicians and dentists are primarily the result of breakdowns in excessively optimistic scheduling but they may also result from intent to save the utmost in professional time. Although the patient cannot very easily get up and leave the office (the indigent outpatient especially cannot get tired of waiting and leave the hospital to go elsewhere), customer patience is tried, with resulting poor public relations and political pressure for governmental medicine.

IV. The Poisson Function

As previously noted, in his pioneer work on queuing theory Erlang assumed that demands on the telephone system were independent of each other and also outside of the control of the system itself. These assumptions are still essential to most applications of queuing theory. Such assumptions of random independence leads to the input into the system being considered as a Poisson distribution, a theory of great importance in mathematical decision making. Named after the French mathematician Simeon Denis Poisson (1781–1840), its major characteristic is that there is a constant probability of any event occurring at any time, no matter what has happened to other events during the time intervals. In other words, if a situation exists where the chance of any event occurring at any time is completely independent of the occurrence of any other event, then the Poisson distribution applies and the likelihood of the occurrence of the events can be predicted as a statistical probability.

Whether heads or tails comes up on a single flip of the coin has nothing to do with how often heads or tails has come up in all previous flips of the coin, so a Poisson distribution applies and from this, the likelihood of series of heads or of tails can be predicted with statistical accuracy. Hence, if the time of arrival of patients to a hospital maternity department is by pure random chance, then the staffing of the delivery and labor rooms can be computed by queuing theory based on this assumption of randomness and on application of the Poisson function.

This does show however one of the limitations of the Poisson process and the queuing theory models based on it, for how often in the health field are events truly random and completely independent? While perhaps the phases of the moon may not be the factor affecting the pattern of newborn deliveries as so many obstetrical nurses claim, neither can it be said that these deliveries are totally random in occurrence. Factors like June weddings, power failures in cities, and holiday military leaves, for example, have a causative effect on the date of births. Therefore, staffing which is based only on Poisson assumptions will be in error.

Also, it is interesting to note that one of the characteristics of the Poisson function is that it is ultra-conservative. Staffing patterns based on Poisson assumptions will very rarely provide too few personnel, but neither will they permit the administrator to take calculated risks and to perhaps plan his staffing a little on the light side in order to use the scarce human resources elsewhere.

V. Health Applications of Queuing Theory

Although health agencies and institutions have the same types of queuing problems as does industry, the application of this type of mathematics to the health field has been slight and of recent origin. Smalley and Freeman[2] give three examples of the use of queuing theory in health facilities. The first, by Bailey,[3] is an application of queuing theory to waiting times in outpatient clinics, the second by Whitson[4] concerns staffing of the operating room, while Hudson[5] applies his use to the pharmacy. Thompson et al.,[6] give an example of queuing theory applied to delivery room usage. Williams et al.,[7] improved the outpatient waiting system at the University of Missouri Clinic using queuing theory.

A specially interesting application of queuing theory is reported by Stricker.[8] Complaints about excessively long lines at the University of Chicago Medical Center hospital cafeteria led the administration to undertake a review of the situation. It was found that the hospital and medical center personnel were given thirty minute lunch periods. As much as ten minutes could be spent in the cafeteria waiting line with another three to four minutes being consumed in going through the serving line. Add to this the travel time to get to and from the cafeteria and the time required to wash up and it was obvious that personnel were being forced to overstay their thirty minute lunch period.

A specially trained operations research engineer was assigned to this project. He noted these facts:

1. There were two cafeteria lines planned for straight line flow only. That is, the customer had to enter at one end of the line,

proceed in order through the line, and come out the other side. No jumping from one serving area to another, a la super market, was possible.

2. The cafeteria lines were located some distance apart so that changing from one line to another was difficult since it involved walking through eating areas.

3. Both lines opened at eleven A.M. The load was light until noon when it became heavy. Peak serving times (and consequently, longest waiting lines) were at 12:10 P.M. and 12:40 P.M.—a reflection that most of the employees were taking their lunch periods at noon and 12:30 P.M.

4. The lines did not always move evenly or at the same speeds as there were shortages of supplies, like silverware, and variations in cashier checkout speed.

5. The visitors slowed up lines as their unfamiliarity with the cafeteria line led to their moving more slowly than the personnel.

After these observations and data had been collected, they were analyzed by a member of the administrative staff who was an operations research specialist. He formulated a plan for improvement based on an objective stated as follows: "Logic is based on reallocation of the variability in waiting times between the two lines. To state this in simpler terms, this meant that the shorter waiting times would be given to employees." The following changes were then made:

1. One line was restricted for medical center employee use only. This was controlled by signs and the use of lunch control cards issued to the medical center departments.

2. Medical center departments were asked to let their personnel off evenly throughout the lunch periods (11:00 A.M. to 1:30 P.M.) instead of all at noon or 12:30 P.M. This was controlled by issuing each department only enough lunch control cards to permit about one-fourth of their personnel to be gone at any one time. Then, these had to return and surrender their cards to other departmental employees, a further control on the thirty minute lunch period.

3. Department heads and supervisors were asked to provide better supervision of the scheduling and duration of the lunch periods of their employees.

4. Better dietary supervision ensured that the lines did not run

out of silverware and other supplies.

5. A turnstile gate was installed for use with the employees' lunch control cards. Inserting the card into the turnstile permitted passage of the card holder. This was only for the one serving line restricted to employees.

6. A bypass route was established between the two serving lines, although the initial poor construction planning still made this difficult.

Three years after all of these changes were made, the following results were reported: employee waiting time was nil and even the waiting time for the public was less than before. Peaks of usage had been leveled out. The bypass route between the two lines had been eliminated as unnecessary and a priority system which was under consideration for such employees as operating room nurses never became necessary.

So queuing theory worked in this case and solved the problem. It is particularly interesting that when analysis showed that the customers were not arriving in an independent and random fashion, planning was able to eliminate the "batching" and to ensure a smoother timing of arrivals. While this is not always possible in all of hospital waiting line situations, it does show that a random independent Poisson distribution is not always absolutely necessary for the use of queuing theory because planning and scheduling can often approximate it. Even if that cannot be done, if the non-random, non-independent nature of the customer load is known, then such known patterns can be used in the formula and a successful solution obtained.

In *Modern Hospital*,[9] the following suggestions were made for application of queuing theory to hospitals: accounting—posting sequence; admitting office—waiting lines; cashier—functions and procedures; central supply—inventories; credit and collections —waiting lines; delivery room—staffing schedules; dietary— inventory control; housekeeping—night cleaning schedules; laboratory—batch processing; laundry—production and staffing schedules; medical records—filing and processing; operating room—schedules; pharmacy—work scheduling; radiology—examination scheduling; storeroom—requisitioning procedures; and X-ray—film filing.

VI. Queuing Theory and the Emergency Room

Queuing theory can provide a method for determining the proper staffing of the emergency room in order to have an adequate number of personnel on duty at all times to keep patient waiting to a low level acceptable to them and still to avoid having personnel sitting around when no patients are there. To use queuing theory in solving this problem, one must first assume that the arrival of patients at the emergency room is random and as likely to occur at one time as another.

Now the pattern of case load must be determined to see what type and number of personnel are needed and how much service time the patients of different types will require. Then it must be decided what length of waiting time is acceptable for different types of patients, taking into account both patients' thoughts on this and medical reality. The order in which different types of patient will be taken must be established. The availability of major items of equipment and the number of emergency rooms and their use limitations are other factors to be determined. How the emergency room is staffed by physicians is an important variable, as is also the way in which physicians are assigned: by patient choice or by whoever is on duty or on call. Finally, some determination must be made of what other activities emergency room personnel could be doing during slack periods as well as sources of other available resources (space, equipment and personnel) in case of excessive disaster or near disaster demands.

Having obtained all the data, defined all of the variables, decided on desired levels of service, the administrator and his operations research mathematician can now set up the equations and solve for the optimum staffing, equipment, and physical space requirements. When this is all completed, it still must be remembered that underlying all of this is an oversimplified assumption that patient usage is on a random independent basis. Of course, the administrator knows this is not true, for emergency room visits are tied to certain hours of the day (for example, traffic rush hours), to certain times of the year (for there are more accidents in the summer), to the office hours and days off of physicians, to weather conditions, and, of course, automobile and other accident victims tend to arrive in clusters.

This gives some idea of the factors involved in figuring out proper emergency room staffing. Add to that such other things as whether or not the patients are truly emergencies and also the availability of physicians, both in the emergency room and in the community and it is easy to see that the "something which ought to be done about it" isn't that simple to determine, even with modern mathematical methods like queuing theory.

VII. Conclusion

It has happened too often that health administrators have been taken to task for failing to solve the problems of their institutions by "doing it the way it is done in industry." When the majority of the governing boards of voluntary health institutions are business men, such statements are to be anticipated, but they show a lack of understanding of the complexities of health care institutions. Queuing theory is a good example of a relatively simple application of mathematics which has solved many industrial problems. Since health institutions have the same types of problems, why not use queuing theory to solve them?

This chapter has already given the answer. Queuing theory assumes customer arrival in random independent fashion, or else that the customer arrivals can be controlled and scheduled to approximate random independent arrival. If such random independence of customer arrival does not exist, incorrect solutions will be obtained through queuing theory. If the administrator does not understand this basic assumption and implements the incorrect solutions, this will aggravate the problem—not solve it. Since very few simple queuing problems involving random independence of customer arrival exist in health institutions, queuing theory has limited application.

To say this is not to overlook that there are some important solutions which can be obtained for vexing problems through the application of queuing theory. When customer arrival can be scheduled, random independence is approximated and queuing theory is valid. Examples of this were given in this chapter and others suggested. Knowledge that health institutions are different and the methods which work well in industry are often not applicable to the health field should not obscure the situations in which successful industrial methods can be applied with equal success to health institutions.

Then also, as is true with all systems applications, the application of queuing theory and the discipline of setting up the equations lead to an understanding of all factors involved, to an appreciation of the total system of which the queuing problem at hand is only one small part.

Chapter Twelve

Simulation

I. Introduction

Among the most commonly used quantitative management techniques in the health field is that of simulation or alternate model building. Simulation means to have the appearance or form of something without its reality. In management, *simulation is a decision technique in which alternate models of real life situations are constructed and tested to see which brings the most desirable result.*

Because the essence of simulation is models, attention is called to the presentation of the characteristics of models in the earlier chapter of this book on operations research.

In theory, the above definition embraces the construction and testing of all types of models. The designing, constructing and testing of different shapes of automobile bodies in a wind tunnel, to determine the one most streamlined, would then be simulation. In reality, however, simulation only refers to quantitative model building.

II. What Is Simulation?

The concept of simulation is very simple. It is a "dry run" of possible solutions to a problem. The essential elements of the problem are determined and these are then defined in mathematical terms, as are also the relationships between them. Then these elements and their relationships are set up in an equation or series of equations. This constitutes the basic simulation model and this is then programmed for a computer. The pertinent actual present and anticipated future data relating to the problem is also programmed and then run through the computer to determine how the model functions in the presence of that data. By this method, time is compressed and the results of many years of future operations can be obtained in a few minutes.

Simulation is basically a rather primitive method of managerial decision-making. It is based on a systematic trial and error search for the best solution which is then accepted and all other answers discarded. This could be extremely time consuming and wasteful if it were not for computers. In one sense, simulation is not a mathematical decision-making method. It is based on empirical data, not theory. The result of simulation is a series of different answers, not a single optimum answer as in the other operations research methods such as linear programming and queuing theory. However, as Schull and Levin[1] write: "Simulation methods admittedly lack the appeal of explicit mathematical statements, but if one is pragmatic, these methods hold great promise for an early insight into a variety of interesting and important problems. In fact, at this juncture, it may well be that numeric analysis is more rewarding than an analytical, mathematical approach." Khoury and Nelson,[2] commenting upon the same point, say: "Simulation is particularly useful in this area because it can be applied to problems that are too complex and have too many variables to be reduced to optimization formulas."

Simulation models are of two basic types. The first is the static model described in this chapter, in which the basic model is constructed; applicable past, current, and future data is fed into the computer; and alternate answers are obtained of what will happen over a period of time, by varying the model or the data.

The second type of simulation model is similar to the first except that decisions are continuously being made, based on the results of the computer data manipulation and printouts. Then these decisions are fed into the computer, becoming themselves part of the model and of the data, to affect subsequent manipulation and printout results, which then affect future decisions which are fed back into the computer and so on. This dynamic use of models is called competitive simulation or gaming, and it will be the subject of the next chapter.

Dickie and Throndsen[3] say that to use simulation, four things are necessary:

1. A plan
2. A computer
3. Plenty of actual facts
4. Three specialists:
   A. The substantive expert, who is the person thoroughly familiar with the operation being studied
   B. A systems analyst who constructs the model
   C. A computer programmer who converts the data and the model into terms the computer can use.

The six steps of simulation, according to Dickie and Throndsen, are: (1) defining the project, (2) gathering the operating data, (3) formulating the model, (4) programming the computer, (5) the test run which is then corrected and debugged, and (6) the actual run and analysis of the results.

III. How Can Simulation Be Used?

Perhaps a few simple examples may make this all clear. Suppose a hospital wishes to know how many operating rooms to construct so as to take care of demand in a reasonable manner without having idle facilities. Anticipated demand for operating rooms is determined, based on population growth, current usage, age and number of surgeons, and all other factors deemed essential. These figures are fed into a computer along with alternate models built about different numbers and types of operating rooms (for example, model A could have two major rooms and one minor; model B with two major and two minor) and the results of these alternate possibilities can be easily seen as predicted usage, idle time, backlog of elective surgery, and waiting time for elective surgery.

The value of this is obvious. It permits trying out different alternate decisions without risking investment loss. In the example above, it would obviously be impossible to construct alternate surgical suites with different numbers and combinations of operating rooms. What is done instead is to estimate (using experience, past usage, and projections) the "correct" number and combination of operating rooms and then build them. If this turns out wrong, little can be done about it—but when the *model* of a combination of operating rooms discloses undesirable results, the model is merely changed or discarded.

If the laundry is chronically behind in their work, the question of whether to expand the physical facilities, purchase new automatic equipment, or to put on a night shift, or all combinations of these can be tested by simulation to see which will be best without actually putting the various alternate solutions to test.

These simple examples may be misleading in that it appears obvious that the answers to specific problems could be figured out with reasonable accuracy without having to actually build too many operating rooms or hire and train an entire crew of laundry workers and then lay them off shortly thereafter. However, the mistakes which have actually been made in similar decisions testifies that it is not so easy to come up with the correct answers, even in simple situations such as these. Then given some of the complex situations in the health field, with the multitude of essential elements and variables affecting the decisions, the value of being able to try out the effects of alternate decisions without making costly and serious errors becomes obvious.

IV. Advantages of Simulation

Alberts[4] gives these reasons for the use of simulation:

1. For purpose of experimentation or evaluation; in other words, to try and predict the consequences of changes in policy, conditions, methods, etc., without having to spend the money or take the risk to actually make the change in real life.

2. To learn more about the system in order to redesign or refine it. The very complexity of most of our business and industrial systems makes necessary a means to provide understanding of both the system as a whole and of its parts.

3. To familiarize personnel with a system or situation, which may not exist yet in real life.

4. To verify or demonstrate a new idea, a new system or approach; in other words, quantify the risks and benefits and demonstrate the chances of success.

Number one, experimentation without risk, is the most important advantage of simulation. Simulation has been called a "management wind tunnel" and also "hindsight in advance." Either the model or the projected data can be changed with equal ease and no actual effect on operations results. If a model with two major and two minor operating rooms does not seem to predict optimum usage, the model can be changed to have three major and one minor and the results of this obtained from the computer. If it is not certain what projected usage will develop (for instance, will an important local industry expand or cut back on its facilities and number of employees, or remain the same), then the different projections can be easily fed into the computer and the results of these on the alternate solutions easily seen.

Often, a system is in operation and any experimental substitution of alternate ideas for change would be impossible. For example, Giffin,[5] in his presentation of a simulation analysis of alternatives for operation of a central blood bank, writes: "a radical plan for altering shipping schedules of blood to outlying hospitals might never be tried in the real system for fear of possible shortages and attendant risk of human lives. The same plan can be tested by the simulator for just the cost of machine time. If it appears better than existing techniques, it can then be used in the real system with a certain degree of confidence."

Number two shows that simulation, being a part of the systems approach to management, has the same advantage of all other systems methods in leading to a better understanding of the situation and system under consideration.

Number three may be used in the design of system components and in training. Number four has a very important function in the health field where so many new things must be sold to others—governing boards, medical staff, professional societies, planning bodies, governmental agencies—before they can be approved and implemented. A good example comes to mind. In 1958, with the drop in birth rate, a 500 bed general hospital found its two maternity postpartum units, totalling about sixty beds, running at a 40 percent occupancy. State law at that time forbade any but OB patients on maternity units. At the same time, medical and surgical units were extremely crowded. The obvious answer seemed to the administrator to be the conversion of one of the maternity units into a medical-surgical unit.

However, when he discussed this with the physicians on the obstetrical staff, he was reminded that OB had occasional high usage peaks. A study of census figures indicated that such was the case but that there were only about ten times in the past year when the OB census exceeded the number of beds on one unit, and then only by two or three patients at a time. The administrator called attention to the declining birth rate and suggested that these few times of peak demand could be met by earlier discharge of a few patients at that time. He then attempted to take into account such factors as the declining birth rate, the population growth, the example of the other hospital in the city which also had a low occupancy OB unit, and other factors in constructing two models—one with sixty maternity beds in two units and one with thirty beds on one unit. Without a computer it was difficult to manipulate all of the factors and turn out projected usage figures showing average census, peak load times, and the census for each day for a five year period. Therefore the governing board and even the administrator lacked confidence in the results and predictions based on the experiment, and the obstetricians quickly found fault with the recommendations.

Even so, this early and unsatisfactory use of simulation for a health problem did lead the governing board to approve the closing down of one OB unit on a trial basis, but not to go as far during the trial of converting it to a medical surgical unit. However, when a peak census did overcrowd the other maternity unit one day, the obstetricians complained and the governing board ordered the second unit reopened. Had good simulation data been available to prove how rarely and at what a low level for only a short period of time this overcrowding would be, then the board would have undoubtedly "stuck to their guns." Just the impressive appearance of the mountains of computer printout and the unfamiliarity of the physicians with all this would have probably carried the day, even without the obvious increased value and accuracy of the computerized simulation.

The accuracy of prediction of even this simple non-computerized simulation was shown by the continued low census, with peak days very rarely reaching even 90 percent, for one unit during the next five years until finally the problem was solved when a long overdue change in state law permitted the admission of clean gynecology cases to the maternity unit.

V. Disadvantages of Simulation

Of course, simulation has its disadvantages also. These are the same as many other quantitative methods—the necessity of making simplifying assumptions which may destroy the real life value of the results. Still, such simplification is less necessary and less dangerous in a method such as simulation, which uses computers and which is built around a consideration of all factors concerned rather than based upon purely intuitive management decision-making where the limitations of the human brain can lead to even more simplifying assumptions which may not be recognized.

VI. Some Examples of Simulation Use in the Health Field

With simulation dependent on computers for practical application and with the increasing availability of computers to health administrators, it is not surprising to find a very large and increasing number of reports in the health literature on the successful use of simulation. Because there are so many, only a few can be mentioned here, chosen to show the variety of applications.

Giffin's simulation model of the Columbus, Ohio, regional blood bank included details on the operation of a fifty hospital regional blood bank using 60,000 units of blood a year, in order to increase efficiency and to insure the availability of adequate blood of the right types at all the individual member blood banks.[6]

Thompson et al.[7] describe simulation for predicting maternity unit requirements. Assuming admissions to be random and independent of each other allowed the use of the Poisson function. The model includes scheduled and unscheduled patients broken down into normal deliveries, Caesarean sections, and undelivered cases. Physical facilities in the model were labor, delivery, and postpartum rooms. Predicted future usage levels were printed out on a once-an-hour basis for the period being forecast. This simulation usage permitted the prediction of physical needs for that maternity unit, by sub-units (delivery, labor, and postpartum) to permit the handling of peak loads with minimum facilities.

Kavet and Thompson[8] also constructed a simulation model for the surgical system at Beth Israel Hospital in Boston. The model was simple because no intensive care unit existed at the hospital and it was further simplified by deciding that an operation would be considered the starting point of each patient's stay in the hospital, which thus excluded surgical patients not having an operation.

The sample from which the data was collected consisted of all pre- and/or postoperative patients in October 1966. Each patient's stay was determined in regard to where and how long they were during their stay. Also, whether they were elective or emergency surgery patients was considered. Of course, the physical facilities available were already known. Other simplifications were that operations and patients were not broken down by surgical sub-specialities.

After the simulation model was designed, predictions of the model were run for forty-two days and compared with the actual situation in the hospital for those same days. This showed that the model was actually representing the real system. Then an alternate model was constructed to measure the effect on the system of providing separate beds for pre- and postoperative patients. This would permit all preoperative patients to be in one area for necessary preoperative work. It would group patients undergoing the same physical and psychological experiences and it would eliminate what the authors call "pathological and psychological contamination between preoperative and post-operative patients." These goals were considered desirable—the question was one of feasibility. Running the same data on patient load through both models showed that the system being currently used, that of mixing pre- and postoperative patients, would require a maximum of 174 surgical beds and a minimum of 111. While, of course, the 111 beds would be occupied at all times, the maximum of 174 would be needed only 4 percent of the time. Overall, the average occupancy was 89.1 percent with an average census of 155 patients.

This compared with a requirement for a maximum of 214

beds for the revised system in which pre- and postoperative patients were separated—40 more beds to give the same amount of care. The occupancy rate would have been 72.4 percent with the number of patients obviously being the same at 155.

Because of the need for an additional 23 percent more beds to implement the more desirable system, it could not be adopted. If the decision had been made to adopt the revised plan, the simulation method would have showed the added number of beds needed, as well as their capital and operating cost.

Brooks and Beenhakker[9] were responsible for a very comprehensive application of a type of simulation to the prediction of future bed needs of a community. For this work, Beenhakker was very appropriately awarded the first prize for student papers at the May 1963, meeting of the Operations Research Society of America. The problem was that of providing a more rigorous method of predicting future needs of Community Hospital, Indianapolis, Indiana, than merely depending on the long range estimates made by the administrative and medical staffs. The fantastic total of 117 factors were included in the model. These are listed in the reference article. The simulation model was constructed by means of a mathematical technique known as multiple regression, in which variables are correlated with each other and their significance to the problem is determined. An interesting aspect is that Beenhakker's prediction was confirmed by a study performed one year later by a national consulting firm.

Knickrehm[10] presents a simulation study of a problem to which queuing theory has often been applied—how to increase efficiency and reduce customer waiting time in a cafeteria line. Instead of focusing on the customer as in queuing theory, this study attacked the problem by observing the effect which changes in cafeteria layout and serving methods would have on length of waiting time. To do this, two models were set up and programmed into a computer. One was based on theoretical data, the other on empirical. When it was shown that the theoretical model approximated reality, then changes in operating procedures and layout of facilities were simulated to study the effect of these changes on customer waiting time, rate of customer flow, and utilization of facilities. Knickrehm concludes that, "simulation appears to be a technique which can be used by food service administrators to plan or revise operating procedures and facilities." She further writes that simulation has advantages and disadvantages. It is too time consuming unless computers are available. Accuracy and adequacy of input data imposes limitations, as the results of the program are only as good as the data used to create them and the intelligence exercised in interpreting them. The discipline needed to define the problem precisely and to determine the exact questions to be answered are among the main advantages of simulation. It is easy to use and does not require a high level of mathematical ability. It is also versatile and the results are easily communicated to the users.

Greenwald[11] reports the use of a simulation model exercise as a training device in a hospital. The problem was that of professional RN staffing. Considered were RN recruitment expense, RN wastage, and RN allocation. Multidisciplinary teams of key hospital personnel participated. The primary intent of the exercise was to demonstrate the factors involved and to see the problem as an integrated whole.

The National Center for Health Statistics reports a computer simulation of hospital discharges.[12] After the model was constructed including 10,000 discharges broken into various age groups covering a period of 108 weeks, it was checked against the actual figures gathered from patient interviews held on thirteen interview dates, each 28 days apart. Deficiencies between the data predicted by model and actual information were noted, for one of the objectives of the study was to acquire a better understanding of the impact of measurement deficiencies in health interview surveys. The second objective was to work out methodology.

VII. Conclusion

The foregoing examples and the hundreds of others in the literature should provide evidence of the broad application that simulation has to the health field. This and the increasing availability of faster and faster computers will certainly lead to the use of this tool by health administrators more and more, especially in the area of regional health planning.

Chapter Thirteen

Gaming

Under the general heading of operations research, four mathematical decision methods have been presented in the previous chapters: linear programming, non-linear programming, queuing theory, and simulation. All use mathematical models and, with the exception of dynamic non-linear programming, all are static in their methodology. That is, the problem situation being considered is "frozen" in the model, free of all changing conditions.

Of course, management is not really like this. Organizational situations are fluid, changing. They are altered every time a single decision is made. They are affected by forces from outside and especially by the actions of competitors in the same and related businesses. Therefore any approach to managerial decision-making which uses static models has a certain unreality. To overcome this, the decision method of gaming has been devised.

In gaming the initial steps are the same as in simulation. The pertinent data is collected by empirical observations and assumptions and is put into a computer. The model of the situation is then programmed. A decision is then made and its results determined by running the model, as altered by that decision, through the computer so that the effect of the data on this may be determined. The computer then prints out the result of that decision. In simulation, if this is not what was desired, the decision-maker starts over again. A different decision is tried, and so on, until the best answer is obtained. This is, then, a series of trial and error approaches with everything, including the time element, considered as frozen at the moment the model was constructed.

Gaming differs from this in that the results of the first decision, once made and determined by the computer, are irreversible and the decision-maker must proceed from there with his next and all subsequent decisions. In other words the model assumes a dynamic form, for once altered it can never be returned to exactly its original form. The decision-maker, once having altered his model with a decision, must live with the results of this, for even when he draws back and reverses the original decision, the situation never will return exactly back to where it was. This is the way life really is in management. It is as Heraclitus said so long ago, a man can never jump into the same river twice.

Now add to this more than one person "playing the game" and making separate independent decisions at the same time, with their effect on the data influencing the model. This provides a very close approximation to actual management, where everything one manager does is affected by what his competitors do and by external changes not caused by any of the competing managers. It is a game situation but one close to reality.

Games of this type are usually called business games—sometimes management games and also business simulation. Kibbee[1] says that the use of the term game is an unfortunate one because it brings to mind play and fun. He suggests that better terms would be "simulation exercise" or "dynamic decision-making sessions." Gaming of this general type is age old. Chess was once an actual simulated war game. The military have a variety of simulated war games that they play now. Simple telephone "c.p. exercises" (command post exercises) are an example, but complex computer games of many types are used. The famous "Link trainer," in which pilots are trained to fly without leaving the ground, is a simulation "game."

As might be concluded from this, the primary use of gaming is in training. Two organizations developed the first non-military business games at about the same time in 1956. The American Management Association used their game, called "top management decision simulation," for the first time at a management training seminar at Saranac Lake, New York, using a computer specially installed for the purpose. McKinsey and Company developed their game about the same time. It was a game using a consumers' goods simulation while the American Management

Association was a capital goods game.[2] Hundreds of similar games have been developed since then. As early as 1962, sixty-four schools of business in the United States reported using business games for education of their students.[3]

Greenlaw[4] offers this definition which will be the one accepted in this book: "*A business simulation or game may be defined as a sequential decision-making exercise structured around a model of business operation, in which the participants assume the role of managing the simulated operation.*"

In defining gaming, great emphasis must be put on drawing the distinction between this and a similar term in quantitative management—game theory. Game theory has an entirely different meaning since it is concerned with competitive decision-making under uncertainty. As such, it will be covered in that later chapter of this book. The terms have often been confused. Even Terry[5] in his fine book on the principles of management writes: "To give reality to a situation, gaming can be utilized. Actually this is a type of simulation. The theory of games was developed by the scientists Von Neumann and Morgenstern." Unfortunately, while gaming is as Terry describes it, a type of simulation, the contributions of Von Neumann and Morgenstern are to game theory, not gaming.

Business games are related to other methods of teaching management, including the case-study method, critical incidents, role-playing, and in-basket exercises. Obviously, all of these are types of simulation in that they are "one-shot" in nature, lacking the dynamic continuing aspects of gaming.

Business games are of two types: general company or industry wide games involving all important phases of the operations (production, marketing, finance), and functional games in which only one element (e.g., production or inventory) is considered.

Business games have now become highly developed, many of them introducing external reality into the game with such unpredictable events as strikes, acts of God, shortage of transportation, channels of communication suddenly closed, executive resignations, even the switch of executives to other companies (teams), forced evaluation of other executives (players), needed information not available or late, and special reports suddenly demanded with very brief deadlines. The University of Chicago has developed an international business game in which revolutions and consequent complete reversal of governmental policies in foreign countries are one aspect.

In the health field, the graduate program in hospital administration at Baylor University U.S. Army Medical Service Field School has developed a hospital administration game which they use for both education of graduate students and continuing education of hospital administrators.[6]

The IBM Corporation has also developed a fairly simple hospital management game with up to ten hospitals in one city. This game was recently updated, expanded, and converted for more modern computers by the health administration faculty of Georgia State University. In its revised version, this game is played by teams of graduate students in health administration at Georgia State in competition with each other. The students are evaluated against how well they are able to achieve the hospital objectives they set for their own hospital at the beginning of the game. One realistic aspect of the game was the unannounced entry into the game, halfway through the quarter, of a new team consisting of an instructor whose hospital was proprietary, for profit.

Greenlaw[7] gives these steps in playing a management game: (1) briefing and orienting the players; (2) organization of the teams and distribution of the initial data; (3) the first decisions are made and turned in; (4) the results of these decisions are then computed and fed back to the teams, along with additional environmental and competitive data now available; (5) the cycle is repeated as many times as desired; (6) the game results are analyzed and criticized in group sessions.

According to Kibbee,[8] the use of gaming in the education of both executives and business students teaches: (1) the importance of planned, critically timed decisions; (2) the need for flexible organized effort; (3) the need for decision assisting tools; (4) the significance of reaching a dynamic balance between interacting managerial functions; (5) it shows the power of mathematical models and the scientific approach to management; (6) as a byproduct, it teaches human relations.

Of course, all of the preceding concerns the use of gaming as an educational method. This is not a book on education, it is one on the use of modern management methods in health administration. So what does playing a management game have to do with this?

While the main use of gaming has been in teaching, two other uses do exist. The most important of these is the use of gaming as a dynamic decision-making technique—as an extension of simulation. Used in this way, gaming tests out the results of an entire series of managerial decisions. The operational and environmental data are collected, the model is constructed, and proposed decisions are made. These results are then followed up by further decisions and so on as long as the manager desires to see the simulated results of his decisions.

As in simulation, no risk occurs because these are all paper decisions. However, gaming used in this operational fashion is more related to real life situations because the results of one decision affect the next, and an entire series of decisions going through a definite time period can be tried out. Also, the possible results of alternate competitor decisions can be seen, as well as the effect of environmental factors—expected and unexpected. Add to this the education of top executives during this entire game and it is easy to see why Stewart[9] says that most game designers think this use in actual management operations is likely to be the most significant long run application of gaming.

Stewart further admits that there is little in the management literature reporting the use of gaming for operational purposes —there is more talk than apparent action. However, she does say that this does not mean that there has been little use made of this, for if the results of usage have been unsuccessful this is likely to have been reported while if the results were successful the company would mark them top secret and not for publication.

In using gaming for operational purposes, most companies construct their own model. However, there is one game which does claim to be realistic enough for testing of actual business strategies. This is AMSTAN, a marketing game with three hundred simulated accounts, designed by the American Radiator and Standard Sanitary Corporation, written up in *Business Week*,[10] and described in detail by Greenlaw.[11]

AMSTAN has also been used for another operational purpose —executive testing for employment, placement, and spotting weak areas for added training. Again, this seems to have great promise but little has been written on it.

Like all other modern management methods, gaming has its strengths and weaknesses. As a purely educational tool, Kibbee[12] says that the advantages of gaming are: (1) providing of objective feedback on decisions; (2) a realistic use of time, including both the continuing nature of the game and time deadlines; (3) establishing a balance between objectives and resources; and (4) a high degree of student involvement.

The disadvantages he gives are: (1) the comparatively high cost of both computer time and personnel time needed in planning and conducting the game; (2) the building up of intense rivalries between students and the often heavy emotional drain on individual students; and (3) the validity of this teaching method has actually not been proven by research.

Probably the above apply also to gaming as a management decision method and executive testing device, and there is the added disadvantage that so little has been published on these uses.

Section Five: Other Modern Decision Methods

This section presents the modern quantitative decision-making methods which do not require the use of mathematical models. Chapter 14 includes the two well-known planning methods of PERT and CPM. The relatively simple managerial decision-making techniques of payoff tables and decision trees constitute chapter 15.

In chapter 16, decision-making is classified as occurring under conditions of certainty, of risk, and of uncertainty. Special attention in this chapter is paid to the latter two categories.

Chapter Fourteen

Program Evaluation and Review Technique (PERT)

I. Introduction

In the preceding section of this book, the applications of mathematical models to managerial decision-making were presented. At least, strictly speaking, that is the main element of linear and non-linear programming and queuing theory. With the use of equations, an optimum solution is obtained for management problems. However, simulation was different from that, since it was a trial and error search for a solution. Some authorities quoted even state that simulation is not a mathematical method. Gaming is even less mathematical, for it includes a series of human decisions in its methodology. However, the relationship of gaming and simulation to the other operations research is shown by their use of mathematical models.

There are other modern quantitative decision-making methods less mathematical than operations research since they either do not use mathematical models, formulas and equations or their use of them is incidental and mixed with other tools and techniques. The first of these to be considered is program evaluation and review technique—called PERT.

II. What is PERT?

An early Navy definition described PERT as "a fast, flexible, management control tool for coordinating complex research and development programs."[1] Another definition states that PERT is a method for planning, controlling, and monitoring the progress of complex projects. The emphasis is on time scheduling.[2] Both of these contain the key points for a definition of PERT—planning and control. As a planning method, it forces orderly sequential thinking of all factors involved in the project being scheduled. As a control, it permits measurement of actual accomplishment related to projected progress.

The basic foundation of PERT is the network, which is a two dimensional graphic presentation of the plan for carrying out a project. This network consists of an orderly progression of steps which must be taken and completed to reach a desired objective. (See figure 14.1 for a simple PERT network.) The PERT network consists of events and activities arranged in a logical order intended to reach the objective most efficiently. In PERT notation, a network proceeds from left to right.

An event in PERT is a task or objective which must be reached and accomplished at a particular point in time. Events are indicated by circles in PERT notation. Each event, when selected and placed in its proper place in the network, is then fully identified by title and number.

An activity in the PERT network is a link between events. It represents the time required to complete a particular task and move on to the next one. Activities are represented as arrows. They begin at one event and proceed to the next event. An activity cannot begin until the event at which it originates is fully completed.

In planning a PERT network consisting of events and activities, Stires and Murphy[3] say that three methods may be used: backward, forward, and middle. In the backward approach, the final objective is first entered and then the activity from this to the next-to-final event is drawn in, and so on proceeding backward to the beginning event. The forward method is just the opposite as it begins with the first event and proceeds to the final objective. The middle method employs both the forward and backward techniques.

While it may be true that there are these three methods, the correct way to lay out the PERT network is to begin with the final objective and work backwards. Since PERT is a systems application the output must be first determined. The time of reaching the final event must be set and then a program laid out to achieve that goal. Of course, once the final event is set and the backward construction of the net begins, the planners move backward and forward constantly in order to achieve the most efficient arrangement, eliminating non-essential events and activities as well as doing away with slack. Slack is wasted waiting time which occurs when one of several activities leads to a specific event and one takes longer to complete than the others.

The third component of a PERT network is time. Each activity is assigned a definite time for completion. Time estimates between events are set by the use of a formula. Three times are estimated for the completion of each activity. The optimistic estimate is the minimum time thought to be required for the completion of an activity if everything goes perfectly. The most likely time is that average which the estimator thinks, based on his experience, the activity will take if it were performed one hundred times. The pessimistic estimate is the very maximum time required if everything goes wrong. Then, an average of these three times is obtained, with the most likely estimate being weighted four times as likely to happen as either the pessimistic or optimistic guess. The time computation formula is:

$$T_e = \frac{T_o + 4T_m + T_p}{6}$$

T_e = expected time
T_o = optimistic time
T_p = pessimistic time
T_m = most likely time

When the events, activities and times have been decided (this is first done on individual cards), the network is laid out so as to waste as little time as possible in reaching the final objective. Then one of the most important parts of constructing a PERT network occurs. The "critical path" is determined. This is the path, from the beginning event to the final objective, which has the longest elapsed time from start to finish. Therefore, any delay in the activities on the critical path will delay the entire project. Other activities, not on the critical path, involve slack time which can be used to compensate for delays.

So in planning the project, the critical path shows where more and better planning might be able to save total time. In control,

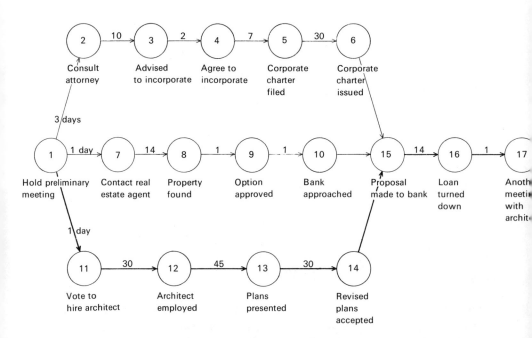

Figure 14.1   A simple PERT network for construction

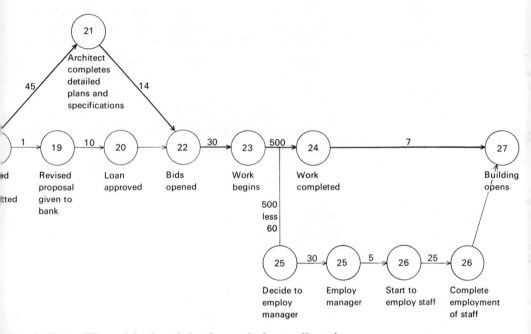

...cians' clinic. (The critical path is shown in heavy lines.)

the critical path is a type of "management by exception" for it is on activities and events along the critical path that management should concentrate. Any gains along the critical path will be gains in total completion time while any time loss on the critical path will delay attaining the final objective. This means that detailed progress reports, tied to specific assigned intermediate target dates, must be given to management regularly. Prompt management action is then imperative to correct deviations from schedule, especially when these are along the critical path.

While this concept may be applied to the simplest project, in reality it is primarily used when the project is so complex that no one can work out the schedule in his head. Then a computer is utilized. Events, activities, and time estimates are fed in and the computer manipulates these to achieve the optimum solution and to plot the critical path. Progress data fed into the computer regularly will be compared with programmed targets, in order to provide management with control reports.

In summary, PERT is defined as *a managerial planning and control method, intended to save time by coordinating a series of job events in a logical schedule by using the systems approach.* Its methodology is to: (1) set a desired target date for completion of the project; (2) identify all of the jobs that make up the project; (3) relate them in a logical network; (4) estimate how long it will take to complete each job and move on to the next one; (5) feed this into a computer to obtain a realistic program with each step arranged in optimum order and the longest total completion time determined; and (6) obtain regular reports from the computer for control and possible revision.

III. History of PERT

In any of the social sciences, completely new discoveries are rare. What passes for new is usually a slight addition to an old theory, the application of known theories to a new field, or the rearrangement of previous knowledge in a novel way. This observation should also apply to management science since it is one of the social sciences. Yet, when it first appeared in 1958, and continuously since then, PERT has been hailed as a revolution in management thought.

PERT is another contribution of the military to management. By the middle 1950s, the "cold war" was in full flower. The key to winning this war was to continually develop new offensive and defensive weapon systems through basic research and then to make them operational as soon as possible. This was becoming increasingly difficult as the weapons (like intercontinental ballistic missiles with nuclear warheads or atomic powered submarines with nuclear weapon) were not only becoming more complicated but the new supporting and delivery systems were so complex and huge that they were difficult to conceive and construct. Besides, building up these systems was very time consuming as each step meant experimentation and new methods to be invented and tried. The time lag was becoming more and more a problem and increasingly dangerous to our national security.

At that time, the Navy turned to a national consulting firm (Booz, Allen and Hamilton) for assistance with their program to arm nuclear submarines with ballistic missiles (the Polaris Fleet Ballistic Missile Program for the Special Projects Office of the U.S. Navy Bureau of Ordnance). Together with personnel from the special projects office and the contracting corporation, PERT was designed as a new type of planning and control system. Its success was proven when the coordination and control of the work of over 3,000 contractors and agencies on this project was advanced at a time saving of two years.

Whether PERT is completely new is open to question. Certainly, elements of the idea are to be found as far back as the scientific management of Taylor. The Gantt chart, a planning and scheduling bar chart device, was an obvious predecessor of PERT in a way. The critical path method (CPM) is so close to PERT, especially at present, that they are defined as the same in this book. Yet CPM first appeared in 1957 and PERT in 1958. However, whether or not PERT is something completely new or merely a logical development in management thought is unimportant. PERT does represent the ultimate practical approach to managerial planning and control using the total systems approach, and as such it has had a terrific impact on management. In spite of the managerial resistance pointed out by Schoderbek,[4] the use of PERT has spread into almost all fields of management. Even Communist nations use PERT, for according to an article in *Business Week*, PERT was to be used in planning the USSR economy for 1963.[5] The field of health administration, always traditionally slow to use new management ideas for a variety of reasons, has also begun to use PERT, as our examples will demonstrate.

IV. Critical Path Method (CPM)

In giving the brief history of PERT, the critical path method (CPM) was noted as having been developed one year before PERT. The objective of CPM was to reduce time and cost of routine plant overhauls at the DuPont Company. Its success was demonstrated in its saving of one million dollars in the first year of its use.

CPM is very similar to PERT in that it is a planning and control method using a scientifically constructed network with a critical path. The definition given previously in this chapter applies equally well to CPM as to PERT. Yet many authors claim that there is a difference.

It is true that there is a difference between CPM and PERT. Two differences in fact. One is a difference in concept—CPM includes both cost and time in their planning and control network. This would be expected in a method developed in industry where cost might be more important than in a major national defense program, which could be expected to concentrate on time. Yet, the old saying that time is money has much truth in it. How did CPM save the DuPont Company a million dollars the first year? Mostly by saving time in factory shutdowns for overhaul. Certainly, the two year saving in time which PERT produced for the Polaris program resulted in the savings of millions of dollars—perhaps billions. So both are concerned with both time and costs, even though CPM approaches both elements directly while cost savings are only a byproduct of time saving in PERT.

The other difference between PERT and CPM is one of procedure. In computing time estimates, PERT uses the formula given previously in this chapter. CPM does not use a formula but instead relies entirely upon the best judgment of those who are operationally skilled in that particular area. Two estimates are obtained for both time and costs. One is an estimate of the time if everything goes along smoothly, or the "all normal" estimate. The other is the estimate if top priority in time and money is assigned to that activity and is called "all crash." Then a considered average is determined between the two.

Again, is this really a true difference? CPM uses an estimating method based frankly upon the experience of those best qualified by experience to judge. PERT has a scientific formula. Yet how scientific is the PERT method? The results of any mathematical computation are only as good as the basic data used in the computation. Therefore, although the PERT formula is rigid and scientific enough, the data which goes into it are still only three estimates. Then what is so magical about weighting the "most likely time" by four? Why not three or five? So, in reality, this is not a true difference between PERT and CPM, because in both cases the times are based on estimates and computed by what is considered to be the best method.

Since the supposed differences between PERT and CPM do not actually exist and since they are both obviously similar in the use of the systems approach, in using a planning and control network, and in critical path analysis, they are considered as the same method and the names PERT and CPM are synonyms.

V. PERT–COST

With the realization that PERT produces cost savings only as a byproduct of time savings, that the concentration of PERT on time may even result in increasing project costs, and probably stung by criticism of the CPM advocates, PERT engineers have designed an application of PERT to cost. This is called PERT–COST and was developed in 1962.[6]

As described by Schoderbek,[7] "PERT–COST is an extension of PERT for planning, monitoring, and controlling cost progress as well as the time progress of a program." This then permits the planning and control of costs as well as time in a PERT network, and shows clearly the costs (in time and money) for trade-offs of time and costs.

PERT–COST may be viewed as an extension of ordinary budgetary cost control, because it is a running comparison of actual and estimated cost. Newman[8] does point out that PERT–COST is more than that when he writes: "The distinctive aspect of PERT–COST is its direct association with each separate step in the total operation. PERT provides a unique way to measure how much progress has been made, and if we have a standard for costs at each step, we can also tell whether costs are running ahead of accomplishment. Normal accounting does not keep track of costs in this way, so we do have a new potential cost control."

PERT–COST, then, does seem to have a future, but so far it has not proved too practical in its application. Evarts[9] says that it is unlikely that PERT could have a cost budget built into it because there are too many problems involved. Newman[10] states that the unique features of PERT–COST are also its drawbacks. Costs for each step in a network are difficult to estimate, budget, and record. The frequent new applications of PERT make cost estimating difficult and since PERT deals with large projects involving many departments, the allocation of overhead and indirect costs is difficult. Newman concludes by writing: "Consequently, we still have much to learn about making a PERT–COST system work smoothly."

VI. An Example of PERT

Perhaps running through a highly simplified problem might lead to a better understanding of PERT. Let us suppose four physicians decide that it would be wise to build a doctors' office building and clinic near a hospital. They then go through these steps:

1. Hold a preliminary meeting.
2. Three days later, they consult their attorney.
3. Ten days later, their attorney advises them to incorporate.
4. Two days later they hold another meeting and agree to incorporate. They phone this information to their attorney.
5. Seven days later the attorney has the papers prepared and files them at the state house.
6. After the required thirty-day waiting and publication period, the corporate charter is issued.
7. The physicians now contact a real estate agent about purchasing some property near the hospital.
8. Fourteen days later, the real estate agent tells them there is a piece of property for sale for $75,000.
9. Next day the physicians hold a corporate meeting and

direct the agent to secure an option. They also vote to approach a bank to see about a loan.

10. The next day, the physicians go to a bank and explain their plans and need for a mortgage loan. The banker asks how much they will need and what do they intend to build. He states that he will present the matter to his board as soon as the sum needed and what is to be built is firmed up.

11. Next day, the physicians hold another corporate meeting and vote to hire an architect.

12. Thirty days later, after several other meetings, an architect is employed and he begins to draw plans.

13. Forty-five days later, the architect presents the plans to the physicians, who suggest several major changes.

14. Thirty days later, the architect submits the plans again and these are accepted along with a cost estimate by the architect of $750,000 total cost.

15. Next day, all this is presented in writing to the bank. The physicians will put up $100,000 with a bank loan of $650,000.

16. Fourteen days later, at the next regular meeting of the bank's board of directors, the loan is turned down as being excessive. A suggestion is made that a loan of $350,000 might be considered.

17. The next day, a meeting is held with the architect and he is asked to scale the job down to $450,000.

18. Thirty days later, the architect returns with a revised plan he thinks can be built for $450,000.

19. The next day, this is taken to the bank.

20. Ten days later, the bank board meets and approves the loan.

21. Forty-five days later, the architect has the detailed plans and specifications ready and they are put out for bids.

22. Fourteen days later, the bids are opened and the low bid of $438,500 is accepted.

23. Actual work on the building begins thirty days later.

24. Completion time was promised by the contractor within 365 days but two brief labor disputes and the late delivery of most of the materials resulted in the building being completed in 500 days.

25. After starting to interview staff for the new clinic, it was decided to employ a clinic manager. This took thirty days.

26. Employment of the needed staff began five days after the employment of the clinic manager and was completed in twenty-five days.

27. Seven days later, the clinic building opened.

All this took 887 days, during which building costs rose and the physicians had to continue to pay high rents for their offices in other people's properties.

So far, this all represents a traditional approach to a building project. If this were shown as a diagram of events and activities, it would be a long single track stretching in one straight line from the preliminary meeting to the opening of the clinic building. The critical path would thus necessarily be the total track because that is the only path which exists with this approach.

Even the most cursory glance shows that this project could be speeded up by doing several things at one time. However, to get the maximum efficiency the PERT approach would require each event to be entered upon a separate card with the times estimated for the movement from one event to another. Laying out these time and event cards would permit them to be rearranged as in figure 14.1. The critical path charted leads to a completion time of 747 days—a saving of 140 days.

VII. Health Examples of PERT–CPM

Although CPM and PERT were developed in 1957 and 1958, receiving immediate and continued publicity since then in professional journals, popular magazines, books and speeches as a new management tool, they have made little effect on health administration. The first article on the subject was not published in a health journal until November 1963.[11] In this, CPM is explained as related to a hospital building program. Schematic CPM diagrams and a sample computer CPM printout add to the value of the article. The author, Sando, asks the interesting question of how CPM is able to do things which engineers and architects have been striving to accomplish in all previous years with only partial success. Sando says this is because CPM identifies the cohesive and divisive forces in any construction project. These are, he says: (1) *Cohesive forces:* (*a*) clear and complete plans and specifications, (*b*) effective supervision, (*c*) contractual obligations, (*d*) a common goal, which is the successful completion of the project, (*e*) good fast decisions from the owner as needed, (*f*) a good full-time liaison team to work with the architect, (*g*) good project reporting procedures, (*h*) capable contractors and subcontractors with construction management ability. (2) *Divisive forces:* (*a*) labor, material, and equipment shortages, (*b*) inclement weather, (*c*) profit motives of contractor, (*d*) job changes, (*e*) lack of coordination, (*f*) lack of communication between engineers and contractors as well as between owners and engineers, (*g*) contractors with limited constructing planning skill.

Then, Sando states, CPM strengthens the cohesive forces and weakens the divisive forces. Add to this that CPM becomes the common language that keeps the building team working together, exchanging ideas, and helping each other get the job done as fast as possible without sacrificing quality.

Nalon and Ballinger[12] explained CPM with the aid of a hypothetical example of the scheduling of construction and financing of a 100-bed hospital. A PERT network and a critical path are presented as figures in the article. The presentation of a budget schedule of meeting the construction costs as they become due, tied in with the PERT construction network is a valuable part of the article, for it is important to have money available to pay the bills when they are presented.

This brings to mind the administrator and board of trustee time which could have been saved had such PERT finance scheduling been a part of the $4,500,000 construction program of Aultman Hospital Canton, Ohio, when the author was administrator there in 1954. Interim financing seemed necessary because pledges were payable over a three year period while the building was to be completed in two years, so it was decided to obtain a million dollar mortgage loan. Since the local banks were unable to handle that large a loan, this was obtained from a Cleveland bank. This necessitated numerous trips to Cleveland plus a special board meeting and mortgage papers and appraisals. However, not one cent of the loan was drawn upon, since the flow of cash, plus drawing on general fund and operating surplus, met all of the needs. Certainly, a PERT financial schedule of the type described by Nalon and Ballinger would have disclosed this. However, PERT had not been developed then.

O'Brien,[13] also writing on CPM as a construction planning, control, and expediting method, makes the following points: (1) CPM offers the only truly methodized and disciplined method of scheduling hospital construction, both before and during the actual construction. (2) CPM offers potential savings of at least one to four percent of the project cost for an investment of about one-quarter of the savings. This is actually incidental to the real goal of earliest practical completion. (3) CPM is not a cure-all and does not guarantee success. It does offer competent management the means to success. (4) CPM does not replace the need for competent contractors; however, it does identify an incompetent rapidly. CPM will make a good man better and point the finger at a poor one.

Noroian[14] gave the details of how CPM saved Pittsburgh's Presbyterian University Hospital two and one-half months of time in a $7,500,000 construction program. The article includes an illustration of the critical path of the project from 1 May 1963 through 9 March 1964.

From all of the foregoing examples, it would be easy to get the idea that PERT–CPM is only used in construction projects. Such, of course, is not true. As a systems approach, PERT–CPM may be used for any management project requiring planning and control, therefore anything in management. For example, Carlisle[15] describes how Bethesda Hospital in Cincinnati used PERT in eighty-four projects carried out in 1964, and expected to use it in the 147 projects planned for 1965. Among these projects using PERT and critical path analysis were linen distribution (described in detail with illustrations of the network schedule and critical path), central service operation, irrigation of grounds, community relations, revising the purchasing system, electric power distribution, dietary department reorganization, and credit and collections. This variety shows that PERT is not merely for use in construction projects. It is a systems approach to planning and control.

Smalley and Freeman's book on hospital industrial engineering[16] includes two critical path applications. One was a critical path study of the emergency tracheotomy in an attempt to identify those activities to concentrate on in order to shorten the time needed to perform this life-saving operation and also to provide a basis for writing a standard procedure for all personnel involved in this emergency procedure. The article describes the collecting of the data, arranging the network, plotting the critical path through the network, and improving this from the time the nurse first detects the patient's inability to breathe normally until the operation is performed and the patient taken to the recovery room. The surgeon involved did find the critical path method to be a useful, logical, and readily understood approach to the analysis of surgical procedures which have critical time restrictions.[17]

The second PERT application in Smalley and Freeman is the conversion of a hospital to a computerized patient accounting system. The author believes that the use of critical path analysis for this project was valuable, especially in making necessary last-minute revisions on two occasions when delivery of key equipment was delayed.[18]

VIII. Conclusion

In this chapter, the new planning and control technique called PERT was presented. Two related or identical techniques, CPM and PERT–COST were also described. All three are similar in being a systems approach, using a network schedule with critical path analysis.

The strengths of PERT as a management method are impressive. Moder and Phillips[19] give these as being the key advantages of using PERT: (1) It encourages logical discipline in planning, scheduling and control of projects. (2) It encourages more long-range and detailed project planning. (3) It provides a standard method of documenting and communicating project plans, schedules, and time and cost performance. (4) It identifies the most critical elements in the plan, thus focusing management attention on the 10 to 20 percent of the project that is most constraining on the schedule. (5) It illustrates the effects of technical and procedural changes on overall schedules.

Perhaps all of the advantages of PERT may be summed up in saying that, like all systems approaches, it forces good planning. Also, like all systems, it forces a consideration of all factors relating to the problem.

The merit of PERT lies as much in control as it does in planning, since these are always inextricably tied together with regular intermediate target goals tied to the final objective. PERT offers management a constant check on progress as well as conservation of management time by focusing on the critical points, thus being true management by exception.

Thomas E. Terrill, assistant professor of hospital and health administration at the University of Pittsburgh pointed out another advantage of PERT for lower level management. With an accepted PERT schedule, the assistants can force top management decisions when these are needed by pointing out the effect that delay in making the decision at that time will have on time of completing the project. Otherwise, top management will get the idea that they have plenty of time to make the little decisions along the way, but with the PERT schedule to spread before his boss, the assistant can show clearly that the decision must be made right now. Also, it is not the assistant who is bothering his boss: he is merely carrying out top management's schedule as he was instructed to do.

Of course, PERT has its weaknesses too. Schoderbek[20] wrote an entire article on these, which he gives as: (1) "padding" of estimates to play it safe; (2) inevitable changes in estimates as the project proceeds makes control difficult as it is to compare the actual "new" program with the anticipated "old" one; (3) it is difficult to obtain reliable data on which to base a PERT program because PERT usually deals with complex, one-shot programs in which there is much innovation and little experience; and (4) cost allocations by departments are often arbitrary and meaningless.

On close examination though, the criticisms given above seem to apply to most management programs involving controls and budgeting. Padding, revisions, obtaining reliable data, and allocating costs correctly are not only problems of PERT. It is up to management to solve these and PERT seems to give a better way to do this than traditional scheduling, budgeting, and cost accounting.

Sando[21] warns that PERT–CPM can be misused. He tells of a contractor constructing a large utility company office building, who attempted to use CPM as a planning tool only. Without control, without special training in CPM, and lacking the managerial ability to implement CPM properly, the contractor's efforts were valueless and the building was finished seven months behind schedule.

Perhaps the only valid criticism that can be made of PERT is that of cost. Like any major planning project, PERT is expensive. Miller[22] says that the use of PERT doubles planning time and cost but that it easily is worth it due to resultant savings.

It is difficult to envision any other management tool which has so many real advantages and so few drawbacks. PERT is proof of what may be obtained through the application of systems to management.

Chapter Fifteen

Payoff Tables and Decision Trees

I. Introduction

Most of the modern management techniques described in this book are highly mathematically oriented and deal with very complex situations involving a multitude of factors. Therefore, these techniques could not have been used on a practical basis until computers became easily available, for the manipulation of a mass of data within complex mathematical models is far too time-consuming and prone to errors when performed without computers.

However, it has been stressed that each of these techniques is the application of systems (i.e., the application of the scientific method to management). Therefore, while the use of computers in all of these may be essential from a practical standpoint, from a theoretical point of view computers should not be absolutely necessary. If the problem to be solved or the decision to be made is relatively simple, then the systems approach should be helpful without utilizing a computer. The truth of this is proven by payoff tables and decision trees which are modern management decision-making techniques that are usually relatively simple, are not highly mathematically oriented, and therefore do not necessarily require computers for their use.

II. Payoff Tables

Decision-making involves all three time dimensions: past, present and future. The decisions are made in the present and are usually based on past data. However, the consequences of the decisions lie in the future. Traditional decision-making has often relied too heavily on information from the past. With the rapid changes of the twentieth century, where tomorrow's conditions may bear little resemblance to that of the past, this can be fatal to good management.

One of the major contributions of modern quantitative methodology has been its concern with the future—with the dimension in which the results of the decision will be implemented. This is the essence of payoff tables which are an attempt to project into the future the estimated results of alternative decisions. *A payoff table is a well-defined tabular presentation of the probable result of alternate decision choices.*

In his article on this subject, Magee[1] gives a simplified example of a payoff table. The situation he postulates is that a cocktail party is to be given for seventy-five guests. The alternate locations for this party are a house that is not too large or a very large and pleasant garden which immediately adjoins the house. It is time to make the final decision of whether to set up for the party in the house or in the garden. The sky is overcast. Moving from one location to another after the decision is made is too difficult for such a large party.

Therefore, the decision-maker is faced with two alternate decisions and two possible outcomes of each decision. Arranged as a payoff table, they appear as in figure 15.1. The alternatives are clearly shown and the decision-maker must now make his choice and live with the results of his decision.

The problem could have been made more realistic and more complex by supposing that a partial commitment to one course

Figure 15.1 Payoff table for location of cocktail party in face of overcast skies (after Magee)

Choices	Events and Results	
	Rain	No rain
Outdoors	Disaster	Real comfort
Indoors	Mild discomfort but happiness	Mild discomfort but regrets

or the other could have been made initially, with opportunities for alternate adjustments to the initial decision as the day progressed and thus with consequent intermediate results. This would then be an example of decision trees, which will be covered later in this chapter.

Also, the problem could have been made more realistic and given a stochastic element (i.e., a statistical approach based on a known probability with random chance of occurrence), if the weather bureau had been called and had given a certain probability of rain other than 50 percent. For example, if the chance of rain had been predicted by the weather bureau as 75 percent, then the payoff table would appear as in figure 15.2.

Figure 15.2   Payoff table for location of cocktail party in face of overcast skies and 75% chance of rain

Choices	Events and Results	
	Rain (75% chance)	No rain (25% chance)
Outdoors	Disaster (37.5% chance of a right decision)	Real comfort (12.5% chance of a right decision)
Indoors	Mild discomfort but happiness (37.5% chance of a right decision)	Mild discomfort but regrets (12.5% chance of a right decision)

Then too, the element of the importance of a successful party could have been taken into consideration. If the guests were merely neighbors and the ultimate results of a wrong decision would merely be good-natured joking for the next several months about what a fiasco the party had been, that certainly would have affected the decision one way. Compare this to what the decision might have been if the guests included the president of the company in which the host was employed, especially if the host was being considered for a promotion into a position of considerable responsibility among the qualifications for which, as expressed by the president, was the ability to take a conservative outlook and "hedge" against all possible disastrous risks.

Figure 15.3 gives a payoff table of a different type. It does not give alternate events and results but compares alternate choices with one predicted outcome for each choice. It still is a payoff table since it clearly presents the results of each alternative decision.

Figure 15.3   Payoff table on expenditure of different amounts on student nurse recruitment (capacity of each class is 75).

Total recruitment expenditure	Predicted number of SN's recruited for fall class	Predicted number of SN's recruited for future	Recruitment cost per SN
$ 1,000	10	10	$ 50
5,000	40	100	36
10,000	60	200	38
20,000	75	225	67
100,000	75	250	308

In this hypothetical example, the decision to be made is how much total money to spend on the recruitment of student nurses. The limit on the size of the entering class is seventy-five students. As can be seen from the figure, the lowest recruitment cost per student recruited is at the expenditure level of $5,000. At that level, forty students will be recruited for the incoming class and 100 for future classes, at a recruitment cost of $36 per student. Still, that may not be the alternate chosen. The importance of enrolling a full class of seventy-five students and the cost of unused nursing school capacity might lead to a decision to spend $20,000. However, a decision to spend $100,000 certainly would not be a wise one.

It can be seen from this that a payoff table is a logical presentation of the anticipated results of alternative decisions. Payoff tables do not give management the answer to any particular problem. They merely present the alternatives in a clear manner so that the decision is facilitated.

As in all other applications of systems to managerial decision-making, the actual end product—in this case, the payoff table and the decision—may not actually be the most important result. The clarification of what issues and factors are involved in the problem, plus the necessity of presenting alternatives in a rigid format, may often be of more benefit in solving the problem than the actual final decision itself.

Because payoff tables do not require complicated mathematical presentations and manipulations, they should be utilized more than at present as a simple method of clarifying management thinking on problems and for clearly presenting decision alternatives. Just a simple payoff table scribbled out by the decision-maker on a scratch pad can be an improvement over pure "seat-of-the-pants" management, by making the manager aware of the alternatives, and the results which may occur through the interaction of the alternatives and the events affecting them. Certainly this is an important contribution to decision-making from such a simple technique for practically no cost.

III. Decision Trees

While the use of payoff tables does give management a simple technique for improving decision-making, it suffers from one major defect. Decisions are not one-shot affairs, for the result of one decision is the necessity of making others. Each decision alternative is merely a fork in a road leading to other alternative decisions.

Figure 15.4 gives a sample of a modern management technique which is based on the payoff table but which recognizes the decision-making as a continuous process. This is a decision tree. In the example, the initial decision to be made is whether or not to remodel the clinical laboratory of a group practice clinic at a cost of $100,000. Then, when that decision is made, the next question which arises is whether or not to purchase $100,000 worth of new lab equipment regardless of whether or not the decision was to remodel the lab or not.

It is assumed that this is a profit-making lab so that the only criterion is financial return on investment. When various probabilities are predicted, it can be seen that two alternatives will

	Payoff first year (odds × increase in income)	Percentage return on investment first year
No chance income will be $200,000 year	—	—
1/4 chance income will be $250,000 year	0 for $200,000	0
3/4 chance income will be $300,000 year	$37,500 for $200,000	18.5
1/4 chance income will be $200,000 year	—$12,500 for $100,000	—12.5
1/4 chance income will be $250,000 year	0 for $100,000	0
2/4 chance income will be $300,000 year	$25,000 for $100,000	25
1/4 chance income will be $200,000 year	—$12,500 for $100,000	—12.5
1/4 chance income will be $250,000 year	0 for $100,000	0
2/4 chance income will be $300,000	$25,000 for $100,000	25
2/4 chance income will be $200,000 year	—$25,000 for 0	No investment
2/4 chance income will be $250,000 year	0 for 0	0
No chance income will be $300,000 year	—	—

Buy new equipment cost $100,000

Do not buy new equipment cost 0

Remodel lab cost $100,000

Buy new equipment cost $100,000

Do not buy new equipment cost 0

Do not remodel cost 0

Present lab income $250,000 year

Figure 15.4 A decision tree (The question is whether or not to remodel clinical laboratory and/or to buy new laboratory equipment, with the only decision criterion being financial return on investment.)

both bring 25 percent on investment: remodeling the lab and not buying new equipment—as well as not remodeling but buying new equipment.

This is, of course, a highly simplified hypothetical example of a decision tree. It oversimplifies or ignores much pertinent material, e.g., changes in expenses of operating incident to remodeling and/or purchasing new equipment. Also, experts on this subject will recognize that this decision tree is presented in a manner which deviates somewhat from conventional usage and presentation. This is done with the intent of making it easier for the non-expert reader to grasp the general principles of the use of the decision trees in managerial decision-making.

The example given does show some of the important characteristics of this decision-making technique. First, it emphasizes that the first decision merely opens the way to other alternative decisions which must be made. It should not be thought that this decision tree really ends where it does in the figure. In reality, every decision tree can be visualized as continuing indefinitely with more and more branching.

The example shows that the results of one decision cannot be accurately predicted until the results of the decision possibilities which the first decision opens up are themselves predicted. A payoff table on the alternatives of whether or not to remodel the lab would show (see figure 15.5) only that the lab should be re-modeled at the cost of $100,000 in order to obtain the maximum payoff of a 50 percent chance of obtaining an income increase of $50,000 in the first year.

Not evident at all in this simple payoff table (figure 15.5) but clearly obvious in the decision tree (figure 15.4) is that the same results could be obtained without remodeling the lab if new equipment were bought instead at the same cost of $100,000. Other considerations, (for example, that of less inconvenience, less dust, less noise than comes from lab remodeling) might then have made that the decision of choice—but this alternative does not show in the payoff table. This is a weakness of mere payoff tables as compared to decision trees.

Figures 15.4 and 15.5 also show the relation between payoff tables and decision trees. Decision trees are a series of payoff tables presented in a branching continuum projected further

Figure 15.5   Payoff table giving results of first decision alternate choices from figure 15.4

Choices	Probable results (and payoff)
Remodel lab Cost $100,000	1/4 chance income will be $200,000 per year (−$12,500 payoff) 1/4 chance income will be $250,000 per year (0 payoff) 2/4 chance income will be $300,000 per year ($25,000 payoff)
Do not remodel lab	2/4 chance income will be $200,000 per year (−$25,000 payoff) 2/4 chance income will be $250,000 per year (0 payoff) No chance income will be $300,000 per year

and further into the future. This is realistic since the results of today's decisions lie in the future. A decision tree permits the manager to look into the future and to choose the results he hopes to obtain, then to retrace the decision pathway leading to the projected future results in order to make the first decision today which will lead to the right decision tomorrow and then on until the hoped-for result is obtained. Using a decision tree provides the manager with a decision-making road map which he can use to be certain that he takes the right direction leading to where he wants to go every time the road forks or divides— that is, every time he must make a decision.

The definition of a decision tree is: *a series of payoff tables projected into the future giving the branching results of alternative decisions.*

While payoff tables and decision trees are a technique of systematic managerial decision-making and do not necessarily require the use of computers or quantitative methods, some of the problems for the solution of which management is required to make decisions are so complex that the use of payoff tables and decision trees in the solution of these may be impossible without a computer.

For example, a desired result may extend so far into the future, require so many thousands of small decisions along the way, have so many alternatives at each step with each alternative having its own complex outcome probabilities, that the decision tree and its intermediate payoff tables can only be constructed by the use of computers and mathematical models.

However, such complicated use of payoff tables and decision trees have not yet emerged to any extent in industry, and not at all in the health field. Therefore, these techniques should still be viewed as simple, non-computer, non-mathematical applications of the systems concept to decision-making which can be of great value to the health administrator.

IV. Conclusion

It is surprising that such potentially valuable managerial decision-making techniques as payoff tables and decision trees are not more widely known or described in the literature, especially since the ordinary manager can use them even without access to a computer or the necessity or using complicated mathematics.

The classic article on the subject is that of Magee[1] already cited. Dale and Michelon[2] present these subjects in a very simple manner in one paragraph of their book. Brabb[3] does the same thing in a much more complicated presentation in his book.

If any articles presenting the subjects of payoff tables and decision trees as decision-making techniques in the health field exist (with the exception of an article by the author of this book)[4] they have not been found by this author. This is unfortunate because any decision-making techniques with the simplicity and advantages of payoff tables and decision trees should certainly be known and used by health administrators and decision-makers in the health field.

Chapter Sixteen

Decision-Making under Risk or Uncertainty

I. Introduction

Because management is at least partly a science, it is to be expected that it would be subject to classification because this is one of the tools of science. As a basic element of management, decision-making has been classified in a number of different ways. One of the more important of these classifications is that which divides decisions into controllable and non-controllable factors. Factors which are totally under the decision-maker's control are called strategies or alternatives. An example of this would be a choice by a clinic manager of whether to purchase four-drawer or five-drawer files for the office. This is a choice between alternatives. A decision by a planning executive whether to put a certain item on the agenda of the next board meeting or whether to "sit on it awhile" and await the outcome of certain possible developments is an example of strategy. In each case, the decision-maker has the decision completely under his control.

Non-controllable factors are called "states of nature" in recognition that they represent the influence of the decision-making environment. An example might be trying to predict the demand for cobalt therapy when considering whether to install such a unit in a hospital. Some idea of the demand can be obtained and predicted but the actual usage depends on many factors outside the control of the decision-maker.

So based on the level of control of the decision factors, that is, the level of uncertainty, decisions have been divided into three types: (1) Decisions made under certainty (the result is known) the decision-maker has control of all of the decision factors. (2) Decisions made under risk (the result cannot be known for certain) some of the factors are outside the control of the decision-maker. (3) Decisions made under uncertainty (the result cannot be known at all) all of the factors are outside the control of the decision-maker.

Perhaps this can be understood better by assuming a player is rolling dice ("shooting craps") with dice, one of which has all faces with sixes and the other all ones. Each roll will always result in the player throwing a seven and thus winning. This is "decision-making" under certainty. If the dice are regular ones, probability odds of winning can be calculated and this is decision-making under risk. However, if one die has nine faces and the other ten, while both are irregular in shape and size, having weird combinations of spots from zero through twelve and very few sixes and ones, and if they are each "loaded" with shifting pieces of mercury, then betting on such a game is decision-making under uncertainty.

II. Decision-Making under Certainty

Certainty is, of course, the ideal for which all decision-makers hope and strive — to be absolutely sure of the results of the decision. That is why executives collect facts, consider all possibilities and weigh everything, in an attempt to narrow the decision down to one single certain choice. Of course, this does bring up the question whether decision-making under certainty is actually decision-making at all. In a previous chapter decision-making was described as a choice between two or more alternatives. So how can decision-making under conditions of absolute certainty be decision-making?

Actually, the certainty does not mean that there is only a single possibility. It merely means that the results of each possibility can be known with certainty. The executive still has to consider the results and choose the alternative or strategy he wishes to bring about the result he considers most desirable. The decision is still there; it is just that the results of each possibility are known with certainty.

Many modern quantitative management methods are attempts

to bring decisions into this state of certainty. Linear programming is an example of this. After the facts are collected, the simplifying assumptions made, the model constructed, then the answer given to the manager is a certain one—it is the correct solution for that problem.

III. Decision-Making under Risk

While management science often seems to be proceeding with the basic assumption of absolute certainty existing and being attainable, fortunately this is not often the case (fortunately because absolute certainty can rob life of that unpredictable quality which gives it flavor and meaning). Risk is an inevitable part of management. If there were no risks, then there would be no managers—only computers, programmers and mathematicians. As a matter of fact, one of the results of computer use is said to have been the elimination of much middle management decision-making.

However, there is risk. Newman and Logan[1] say that risks can be handled in four ways: (1) reduction of hazards—for example, employee safety programs; (2) insurance—spreading the risk, as with workmen's compensation insurance; (3) hedging—sort of an intuitive calculation of probability; for example, computing the amount of blood of each type to carry in the blood bank by using Monte Carlo theory and then adding several extra pints of O-, "just in case"; and (4) calculation of profit—another way of saying the use of tight budget controls.

All of the above are traditional, conservative, intuitive ways in which the art of management handles risk. However, modern quantitative management has given a fifth way: the use of probability theory in decision-making. This way is used in decision-making when each alternative or strategy can lead to a set of known possible outcomes—each outcome occurring with a known probability. This too has a certain unreality but it is more often closer to the real world than is an assumption or situation of total certainty. Here the decision must be made considering both strategies or alternatives *and* states of nature, i.e., uncontrollable factors. There is a risk involved, hence the classification of decision-making under risk.

In order to be considered decision-making under risk, a situation must have certain characteristics: (1) Alternative or strategies may be identified and defined. (2) Potential outcomes associated with each alternative or strategy may be identified and defined. (3) The probability of occurrence associated with each identified potential outcome may be established. (4) The value associated with each identified outcome can be known.

In decision-making under risk, definite alternatives exist, each with a set of potential outcomes whose probability of occurrence and value may be known. Thus the job of the executive is to determine the objective of the decision and then to make the decision most likely to achieve that outcome—remembering that the chance of reaching that result is not certain because it is affected by environmental factors of known probability (but still only probability).

Because most decisions are of this type many more occur under conditions other than those of absolute certainty or uncertainty. Most of the work in modern management methods is in this area. This is much of what statistics is about. Also queuing theory and all of the other quantitative techniques using models based on probabilities. Most classic in their approach to decision-making under risk are payoff tables and decision trees. The four characteristics just listed are used as the basic methodology for constructing payoff tables and decision trees.

IV. Decision-Making under Uncertainty

Referring back to the previous example of the weird dice as being decision-making under uncertainty, it might be thought that betting on the results of casting such dice would be absolutely stupid—yet if such a game existed, some people would play and bet on it. Why? The answer to this, of course, depends on many factors: their own personality, whether they gamble for the thrill or for winning or both, what the potential winnings are compared to the possible losses in such a game, how much the player can afford losses, and what the opponent is likely to do in a given situation, for such games become competitive against opponents and not only against odds.

Now it might seem that a situation of this type, where nothing can be known with certainty and where even probabilities cannot be computed, is so erratic and unsystematic that even modern scientific quantitative management could have nothing to offer. If nothing can be known and nothing can be predicted, how can a manager proceed to make a decision?

Fortunately, such situations are not common. Usually something can be discovered: some experience exists; some predictions, no matter how uncertain, can be made. If not however, the manager must still make a decision, so this sort of situation is usually handled in an unscientific manner. The manager has a hunch or a feeling on the subject. This is intuition, a part of the art of management. The usual way to handle such a decision then is to base it on art, since science is apparently of no help.

Surprisingly though, there has been attention paid to such situations of decision-making under uncertainty and two major scientific approaches may help. The first one recognizes that such decisions are often required in competitive situations. The existence of the uncontrollable and unpredictable competition may be the reason for the total uncertainty. If it is a competitive decision-making situation being considered, modern quantitative decision-making theory can help by shifting the emphasis from the unpredictable nature of the situation to the competitive situation itself. Then decisions can be made on the basis of maximizing gains, minimizing losses, or striking a balance between the two, no matter what the opponent does. This is "game theory," previously mentioned in the chapter on gaming with the strong warning to not confuse the two.

The second scientific approach to decision-making under uncertainty involves another sophisticated mathematical approach known as cardinal utility theory. This deals with the worth (utility) of anything to a person compared to what he is likely to risk to obtain it. What would a person do if given a lottery ticket which he could sell now for a million dollars, but which he could hold and have a two out of three chance of winning three million dollars (or nothing) next week. Most people would cash in the ticket and take their million dollars. Yet, in one sense, this is not very rational for the chances of winning three times a million dollars are very high.

Von Neumann and Morgenstern[2] have dealt with this situation and have computed mathematical "N–M utility indices" to help determine when to take such risks and for how much. This is cardinal utility theory, a complex mixture of mathematics and psychology. Consequently, it will not be covered here, although such considerations relating risk of loss to possibility of gain are obviously important to managerial decision-making in the field of health as well as everywhere else.

V. Monte Carlo

Decision-making under risk has already been defined in this chapter as a situation where definite alternatives exist, each with a set of potential outcomes whose probability of occurrence and value may be known. Therefore, quantitative and scientific decision-making methods in this common type of decision-making situation consist of the application of probability theory. The best known of these methods is Monte Carlo which can be defined as *the application of random number probability theory to decision-making under risk.*

Suppose that a situation exists where a decision is necessary and the possible alternatives are very clear. However, there are uncontrollable factors which will affect the outcome. Collecting of sample data shows that the uncontrollable factors occur at random and are predictable in their probability of occurence. Then these probabilities are associated with each alternative by statistical means and the use of random number tables. The likely payoff results of the different alternatives are determined, and these, coupled with the respective probabilities, give the decision-maker the best possible help he can obtain in this situation. The risk is still there but it has been minimized through the use of Monte Carlo.

Random number tables are merely sets of numbers which have been generated at random so that they have no patterns of occurrence within them. Statisticians using such tables can be certain that any number chosen has as much chance of coming up in the table at any place as any other number. They are an important tool in Monte Carlo.

A hospital example of the use of Monte Carlo might be in computing the staffing for a delivery room. This surely is a case of decision-making under risk for the key factor, the admission of women in labor, is not under the control of the decision-maker. However, if sampling shows random arrival of such women and the number of deliveries is known from past data, the probable number of deliveries on each shift may be obtained from random number tables and staffing computed accordingly—with the provision for emergency coverage because this is only based on probability, not absolute certainty. While the risk may have been reduced, it has not been eliminated. As cited in the previous chapter on simulation, this is the method used by Thompson et al.[3] to predict need for physical facilities in a maternity unit.

Taylor[4] used the Monte Carlo method for constructing a model of an epidemic of acute upper respiratory diseases at Simpson Air Force Base in New York, assuming constant and random chance of infection. Then he compared the results of his predictions of number and frequency distribution of cases based on his model against those in the actual epidemic, finding that the predicted and actual number and distribution of cases was very close. Therefore, he suggested that the Monte Carlo method could be used to predict the size and pattern of epidemics and provide resources to combat them. Especially interesting was his observation that when there was a significant difference between predicted and actual data, this could provide a clue to the nature and type of disease. For example, the incubation period or the number of cases which are subclinical in their symptom manifestations might be indicated.

VI. Game Theory

Game theory is based on rational action in an openly competitive situation. You are trying to win—so is your opponent. Only one of you or neither of you can win. Game theory will tell you what to do in each decision based on your own strategy. You may be cautious, assume the worst, and try to minimize your losses no matter what your opponent may do. Game theory can tell you what to do to achieve that. On the other hand, you may be willing to take maximum risk for maximum returns. Game theory can show you how to do that.

Because the mathematics of game theory are complicated and because health administrators rarely find themselves in openly competitive situations, few applications of game theory can be expected in the health field. The mathematics will not be given here. Interested readers are referred to Von Neumann and Morgenstern,[5] the originators of most of game theory, to Luce and Raiffa[6] and to Baumol.[7]

A very simplified hypothetical example of the use of game theory in health administration might give a little better understanding of this decision method. Suppose that a 300-bed non-profit nursing home is overcrowded and is thinking of building a 100-bed addition. The money is available—half from accumulated surplus and half will be borrowed on a mortgage loan.

The issuing of a building permit by the city council to a proprietary corporation to build a new 100-bed nursing home one block away is the first inkling that the administrator and governing board of the non-profit institution have of this possibility. At the same time, the possible addition to the 300-bed institution is common knowledge so the profit-making corporation must be aware of that. The board of the non-profit nursing home has had a survey made which shows that there is a need for 100 more nursing home beds in the area but 200 will be too many with the result being probable operating deficits.

The question is now whether the board should proceed with their plans or not. They have not gone so far that it would be either difficult or embarrassing to turn back. Yet, they are not at all certain the proprietary nursing home will actually be built because twice before similar building permits were issued but never used. They feel an obligation to meet community needs, yet they also feel an obligation to preserve the institution's assets and to "run in the black."

This then is a hypothetical example of an openly competitive situation. The number of patients is limited. Each corporation is faced with the decision of whether to build or not and also, how much to build, for any number of beds up to 100 may be constructed by one or both institutions. Among the financial factors are cost of initial building, depreciation, direct operating expenses, indirect operating expenses, and patient income. Suppose these are all determined for their institution by the administrator and board of the non-profit home on the suppositions that the proprietary institution may build 100 beds, 50 beds or none. Then the non-profit home can consider the same alternatives and arrange them as a payoff matrix in this manner, showing annual surplus or deficit. (Note how this is related to payoff tables except for the addition of the unpredictable, uncontrollable strategy of an opponent.)

Figure 16.1 shows that in spite of not knowing what the proprietary nursing home may do, the scientific approach to making this decision under uncertainty has given the management an assisting tool. It has brought in the advantages of the systems approach. Constructing the table has acquainted the management with the total picture and with the factors involved. Then the possibilities are presented along with the results of each alternative. Now the decision can be made.

Not building at all is the most conservative and "safest" decision, from a purely financial standpoint, of course. No matter what the opponent does, if no beds are built, no money can be lost. Neither can any be gained.

Building one hundred beds has the greatest chance of financial return. If the proprietary home builds no beds, $75,000 a year might be added to surplus on a capital investment of only a million dollars. On the other hand, this strategy has the greatest chance of loss also—a possible deficit of $50,000 a year if the proprietary home builds one hundred beds. There is also a two out of three chance that it will result in a loss.

Building 50 beds is an in-between strategy. It may result in a loss or a surplus—neither as great as with the addition of 100 beds. It may also result in breaking even.

The community needs 100 more nursing home beds. It also needs its capital funds used wisely and its nursing home operated in the black. What the proprietary nursing home may do cannot be predicted nor controlled. What should the administrator and board do?

At this point, the administrator and board may be tempted to try and figure out what the proprietary nursing home may do

Figure 16.1   Payoff Matrix

Proprietary home strategy

	Decision	Build 100 beds	Build 50 beds	Do not build
Non-profit home strategy	Build 100 beds	Deficit: $50,000	Deficit: $25,000	Surplus: $75,000
	Build 50 beds	Deficit: $20,000	No surplus or deficit	Surplus: $30,000
	Do not build	0	0	0

and to "out-guess" them. While certainly the psychology and financial position of the opponent will have a bearing on his strategy, and hence possibly on yours, that is not the idea of game theory. It is not based on guessing; it is based on giving the manager a rational way to maximize his gains, minimize his losses, or strike an in-between strategy *regardless of what the opponent may do*. If what the opponent may do can be known or predicted from his psychology, his financial position, his motives, or his past actions, then this is no longer decision-making under uncertainty. It has a probability dimension and is then the ordinary managerial decision-making under risk.

Since, in this example, what the proprietary nursing home will do cannot be predicted nor controlled in any way, what should the administrator and board of the non-profit institution do? Game theory has laid the alternatives and results before them—*they* must make the choice.

Since administrators and boards usually tend to be conservative (they are administering a public trust), building 100 beds would probably seem too great a risk to them. On the other hand, since they are public spirited and aware of community needs, not building at all would probably not appeal to them either. Torn between these two motivating forces, they will probably go ahead and build 50 beds.

VII. Conclusion

In this chapter, decision-making was presented as occurring under three circumstances: when the result of each alternative is known (certainty), when the result of each alternative is not certain but can be statistically predicted (risk), and when the results of alternatives can beither be known nor predicted (uncertainty).

Two modern decision-making methods were presented in detail with examples: Monte Carlo, for decision-making under risk; and game theory, for decision-making under uncertainty.

People, including managers, do not wish to live under uncertainty. Therefore, they try to push from uncertainty to certainty. If unable to achieve that, at least they strive to move from uncertainty to probability. Modern quantitative systems management has the same objective—to help the manager move from uncertainty to probability to certainty. The total elimination of managerial risk would be considered ideal. Of course, it is recognized that this is not possible but still it remains the goal. In the meantime, modern quantitative systems management will assist the manager wherever he finds himself—under uncertainty, risk, or certainty—by providing tools and methods appropriate to that situation.

Section Six: Conclusion

The major intent of this book has been to provide today's health administrator with an introduction to the administrative techniques, methods and tools available to him in this modern age.

As a background to this, and as an introduction to the subject for those health administrators who may not have had formal instruction in administration, the first section of the book consisted of a review of management theory and principles. Included was a review of many of the findings of the behavioral scientists concerning management as well as a review of managerial decision-making.

This led in section two to a presentation of the systems concept in administration. Systems was defined as the use of the scientific method in management and was presented not as just another school of management thought but as a general comprehensive theory of administration.

The rest of the book consists of a description of various techniques and methods of management—all scientifically derived and hence all part of the systems approach to management.

The application of the systems approach to production functions in the health industry was covered in section three, which included automation, work simplification, and value analysis.

Operations research, which is a decision method involving the use of mathematical models, was the subject of section four. Linear programming, non-linear and dynamic programming, queuing theory, simulation and model building, and gaming were covered in that section.

Less mathematically focused modern administrative decision methods made up section five, including PERT and CPM, payoff tables and decision trees, and decision-making methods for use under risk and uncertainty.

Running throughout this entire book has been the theme that administration is a way of thinking. Modern administration, called systems, is a way of thinking which applies the concepts of the scientific method to administration. It is goal (output) oriented with the two major goals of getting out the organizational product today while at the same time maintaining the organization so that it will continue to function in the future.

That is the basic theme of this book. Modern administration is a way of thinking. All else in this book merely comprises descriptions of techniques and methods of modern administration. But modern thinking and the use of modern techniques and methods are both essential to today's health administrator. So also are his personal qualities, his leadership ability, and his skill in human relations. The modern health administrator must function like an artist. The artist must have the personal artistic ability—he must have a comprehensive and cohesive framework of aesthetic reference to give his work meaning—and he must know, possess, understand, and use the tools and techniques of his art.

So too must today's health administrator have three things—his personal administrative ability, a comprehensive and cohesive administrative framework to hold his administrative work together and to give it meaning, and he must know, possess, understand and use the tools and techniques of his art.

It is unlikely that the modern health administrator will himself need to actually do the things described in this book. Just as he has professional and technical personnel within his organization to carry on their special types of work, so will the health administrator have under him the professional and technical personnel to carry out the special techniques and methods, using special tools like computers, which the administrator and the organization need to carry on their functions.

Just because he will not be doing the work himself does not mean that the health administrator need know nothing about modern quantitative methods. The administrator must be able to understand what these are, their scope and especially their limitations; and he must know the terminology, in order to work with his personnel and associates who will be devoting all of their time to these areas. Further, the modern health administrator must understand modern management techniques and methods to inspire those under him to fully utilize what is available. Yes, and today's health administrator must know about all of this so that he can demand that the advantages of modern quantitative techniques and methods be supplied to him so that he may function as a modern administrator should function in today's space age!

It is realized that few health administrators do have this necessary knowledge. This is to be expected, for administrators are generalists and the material on modern management methods is specialized, scattered, and confusing in terminology and relationships.

That is the reason for this book. To present an introduction to the major modern management techniques and methods which will organize them in such a way as to clarify their relationships to each other and to eliminate confusion in terminology. This has been presented in as simple a way as possible consistent with accuracy and avoiding the dangers of oversimplification.

Before concluding, a few remarks might be appropriate on the subject of how to use the systems concept, and its techniques, methods and tools, without destroying human values in the process. This is an especially appropriate topic in the health field which is dedicated to preserving human life, human well-being, and health without sacrificing human individuality, worth, and dignity.

In this modern computerized age, all of us have many times experienced a mistake made in our credit account, or in placing a mail order, or in extending a magazine subscription. Then the long frustrating negotiations begin to try to correct what is usually a very simple and obvious error. On one side of the contest is you, a mere mortal trying to be logical in your explanations and having to turn out your documents of explanation one at a time, hand-written. On the other side is the company computer, capable of issuing dozens of machine printed letters of a standard type without the handicap of trying to be logical or of even dealing with the issue or problem under dispute. After going through trying to politely straighten out the problem with a half-dozen or so letters, and finally coming to the conclusion that no humans at all work for the company—only pre-programmed computers, the human adversary in this uneven combat finally gives up in disgust and frustration or, horrible to relate, he folds, spindles and mutilates the card sent to him by the computer, thus possibly working off some of his frustrations even if he doesn't solve the problem.

I am certain the reader recognizes this experience. It is bad enough when it happens in one of the circumstances given above. But what if it happens when the issue is concern over the life or well-being of a person or one of their loved ones. And it can happen!

The problem of customer frustration in such cases was the subject of an interesting article by Wnuk.[1] He suggests that such problems of customer relations in computerized operations can be solved by (1) the constant realization of management that problems can happen; (2) making all employees familiar with the computer operations, with its problems, and especially the fact that the computer is only part of the organization and that employees and computer must work together as the total organization; (3) the possible establishment of some type of service individual or department to act as liaison in dealing with special customer problems; (4) an analysis of bills, forms, and form letters to eliminate confusing wording; (5) a plan for educating customers about computer operations, especially if the computer operations has a built-in time delay; and (6) a notation at the bottom of bills, past due account notices, and similar computer generated items, stating that if the bill seems incorrect or if there are any questions, the customer should phone or write directly to a specially designated customer service person, department or point—with address and phone number supplied—instead of merely writing or phoning the company.

An approach to such a special patient service representative at Mount Sinai Hospital, New York City, was reported by Ravich and others.[2] Called an *ombudsman* after the public representatives in Scandanavian countries who represent the ordinary citizens to public officials, this patient service representative has as his or her job solving patient problems, special requests, special needs, issues and complaints, which otherwise go unheeded and unmet in the complexity of the hospital.

But it is not only patients, relatives, and visitors who may run afoul of the impersonality and depersonalizing frustration of dealing with the system or the computer. Cooke[3] writes of the needs of the employee in the computerized hospital. He comments on the human need theories of Maslow and Herzberg (see chapter 2 of this book) and fears that the needs of employees to grow and to attain self-actualization may be inhibited or prevented by the computerizing of the hospital with its emphasis on systems and machines. Especially he warns that this may happen with physicians and nurses who may end up spending less time with patients in a computerized hospital—and yet it is from patient contacts that these professionals obtain their self-actualization and their job satisfaction.

However, Cooke says this need not happen. If the computer systems are designed around human needs—of patients and personnel—and if enough effort is put into special orientation and training programs to teach employees how to properly use and cope with computers and computerized systems—then the computer can free the employees from less satisfying work so that they may go ahead and use this free time to perform more satisfying tasks. Thus, if properly handled, the computer can help employees reach a higher level of job satisfaction than would be possible in a non-computerized hospital.

Notes

Chapter One

1. Theo Haimann, *Professional Management* (Boston: Houghton Mifflin, 1962), p. 1.

2. Dalton E. McFarland, *Management: Principles and Practices*, 2nd ed. (New York: Macmillan, 1964), p.1.

3. Halsey N. Broom and Justin G. Longenecker, *Small Business Management* (Cincinnati: South-Western, 1966), p. 43.

4. Harold Koontz and Cyril O'Donnell, *Principles of Management* (New York: McGraw-Hill, 1964), p. 1.

5. Lawrence A. Appley, "Management the Simple Way," *Personnel*, January 1943, p. 597.

6. Elmore Peterson and E. Grosvenor Plowman, *Business Organization and Management* (Homewood, Ill.: Irwin, 1958), p. 35.

7. *Encyclopaedia of the Social Sciences*, 10 (New York: Macmillan, 1933), 76–77.

8. John F. Mee, Mead-Johnson professor of management, Indiana University. Quoted in George R. Terry, *Principles of Management*, 4th ed. (Homewood, Ill.: Irwin, 1964), p. 48.

9. McFarland, p. 3.

10. Ralph C. Davis, *The Fundamentals of Top Management* (New York: Harper, 1951), p. 6.

11. McFarland, p. 4.

12. Peter Drucker, *The Practice of Management* (New York: Harper, 1954), pp. 8–9.

13. Ernest Dale, from an unpublished address given at a Management Theory Seminar, UCLA, Los Angeles, November 1962, quoted in McFarland, p. 5.

14. Ordway Tead, *The Art of Administration* (New York: McGraw-Hill, 1951).

15. Martin K. Starr, *Management Science* (New York: Macmillan, 1965).

16. Arthur F. Veinott, Jr., *Management Science* (New York: Macmillan, 1964).

17. Ole C. Nord, *Management Science* (Sudbury, Mass.: Management Science Associates, 1964).

18. Daniel Teichroew, *Management Science* (New York: Wiley, 1964).

19. Donald J. Clough, *Concepts in Management Science* (Englewood Cliffs, N.J.: Prentice-Hall, 1963), p. 2.

20. Ralph C. Davis, *Industrial Organization and Management* (New York: Harper, 1956), p. 54.

21. William H. Newman, Charles E. Summer, and E. Kirby Warren, *The Process of Management* (Englewood Cliffs, N.J.: Prentice-Hall, 1967), p. 10.

22. Frederick Harbinson and Charles A. Myers, *Management in the Industrial World* (New York: McGraw-Hill, 1959), p. 8.

23. Broom and Longenecker, p. 43.

24. George R. Terry, *Principles of Management* (Homewood, Ill.: Irwin, 1964), p. 52.

25. Koontz and O'Donnell, p. 1.

26. Herbert G. Hicks, *The Management of Organizations* (New York: McGraw-Hill, 1967), p. 155.

27. Ernest Dale, *Management: Theory and Practice* (New York: McGraw-Hill, 1967), pp. 5–7.

28. V. A. Graicunas, "Relationship in Organization," in *Papers on the Science of Administration*, ed. Luther H. Gulick, Lyndall F. Urwick, and James D. Mooney (New York: Institute of Public Administration, 1937), p. 184.

29. Dale, p. 236.

30. Waino W. Suojanen, "The Span of Control—Fact or Fable?" *Advanced Management*, November 1955, pp. 5–13.

31. W. Warren Haynes and Joseph C. Massie, *Management: Analysis, Concepts and Cases* (Englewood Cliffs, N.J.: Prentice-Hall, 1961), p. 41.

32. William H. Newman, *Administrative Action* (Englewood Cliffs, N.J.: Prentice-Hall, 1963), p. 190.

33. Lyndall F. Urwick, *Elements of Administration* (London: Sir Isaac Pitman, 1947), p. 118.

34. Dale, p. 234.

Chapter Two

1. Ernest Dale, *Management: Theory and Practice* (New York: McGraw-Hill, 1965), p. 242.

2. Andrew Ure, *The Philosophy of Manufactures* (London: Charles Knight, 1835).

3. Chester I. Barnard, *The Functions of the Executive* (Cambridge, Mass.: Harvard University Press, 1938).

4. Fritz Roethlisberger and William J. Dickson, *Management and the Worker* (Cambridge, Mass.: Harvard University Press, 1939).

5. Delbert C. Miller and William H. Form, *Industrial Sociology*, 2nd ed. (New York: Harper and Row, 1964), p. 678.

6. Henry Landsberger, *Hawthorne Revisited* (Ithaca, N.Y.: Cornell University Press, 1960).

7. Roethlisberger and Dickson, *Management and the Worker*.

8. Thomas North Whitehead, *The Industrial Worker*, 2 vols. (Cambridge, Mass.: Harvard University Press, 1938).

9. Paul B. Lawrence and John A. Seiler, *Organizational Behavior and Administration* (Homewood, Ill.: Irwin, 1965), pp. 165–183.

10. William H. Newman, Charles E. Summer, and E. Kirby Warren, *The Process of Management*, 2nd ed. (Englewood Cliffs, N.J.: Prentice-Hall, 1967), p. 179.

11. Cecil J. French, "Correlates of Success in Retail Selling," *American Journal of Sociology*, 66 (1960), 128–134.

12. William F. Whyte, *Human Relations in the Restaurant Industry* (New York: McGraw-Hill, 1948).

13. Chris Argyris, *Diagnosing Human Relations in Organizations: A Case Study of a Hospital* (New Haven: Labor and Management Center, Yale University, 1956).

14. Miller and Form, pp. 245–246.

15. Abraham H. Maslow, "A Preface to Motivation Theory," *Psychosomatic Medicine*, 5 (1943), 85–92.

16. Frederick Herzberg, Bernard Mausner,.and Barbara Block Snyderman, *The Motivation to work* (New York: Wiley, 1959).

17. Robert L. Kahn and Daniel Katz, "Leadership Practices in Relation to Productivity and Morale," in *Group Dynamics, Research and Theory*, ed. Dorwin Cartwright and Alvin Zander (New York: Harper and Row, 1960), pp. 612–628.

18. Keith Davis, *Human Relations at Work* (New York: McGraw-Hill, 1967), p. 37.

19. Ralph M. Stogdill, "Personal Factors Associated with Leadership: A Survey of the Literature," *Journal of Psychology*, 25 (January 1948), 35–71.

20. Alvin W. Gouldner, ed., *Studies in Leadership* (New York: Harper and Row, 1950), pp. 20, 32.

21. Philip B. Applewhite, *Organizational Behavior* (Englewood Cliffs, N.J.: Prentice-Hall, 1965), pp. 111–132.

22. Ralph White and Ronald Lippitt, "Leader Behavior and Member Reaction in Three 'Social Climates,'" in *Group Dynamics*, ed. Dorwin Cartwright and Alvin Zander (Evanston, Ill.: Row, Peterson, 1960), pp. 318–335.

23. Howard Baumgartel, "Leadership Style as a Variable in Research Administration," 2, *Administrative Science Quarterly* (1957), 344–360.

24. Lester Coch and John R. P. French, "Overcoming Resistance to Change," *Human Relations*, 1 (1948), 520–524, 512–532.

25. Rensis Likert, *New Patterns of Management* (New York: McGraw-Hill, 1961), p. 163.

26. Kurt Lewin, "Group Decision and Social Change," in *Readings in Social Psychology*, ed. Eleanor E. Maccoby, Theodore M. Newcomb, and Eugene L. Hartley (New York: Holt, Rinehart and Winston, 1958).

27. D. F. Pennington, Jr., François Haravey, and Bernard M. Bass, "Some Effects of Decision and Discussion on Coalescence, Change and Effectiveness," *Journal of Applied Psychology* (1958), pp. 404–408.

28. George Strauss, "Some Notes on Power Equalization," in *The Social Science of Organizations: Four Perspectives*, ed. Harold J. Leavitt (Englewood Cliffs, N.J.: Prentice-Hall, 1963), p. 62.

29. Chester Barnard, *The Functions of the Executive* (Cambridge, Mass.: Harvard University Press, 1938).

30. Eugene E. Jennings, "The Fallacy of Groupism," *Personnel*, July 1954, pp. 66–71.

31. Harold J. Leavitt, "Unhuman Organizations," *Harvard Business Review*, July-August 1962, pp. 90–98.

32. Herbert G. Hicks, *The Management of Organizations* (New York: McGraw-Hill, 1967), pp. 351–353.

33. Franklin G. Moore, *Management: Organization and Practice* (New York: Harper and Row, 1964), p. 298.

34. Ray E. Brown, *Judgment in Administration* (New York: McGraw-Hill, 1966), p. 77.

35. John Chamberlain, "Rule by Committee," *Wall Street Journal*, 27 December 1956.

36. George R. Terry, *Principles of Management*, 4th ed. (Homewood, Ill.: Irwin, 1964), p. 516.

37. Brown, p. 106.

38. Moore, p. 293.

39. Ernest Dale and Leno C. Michelon, *Modern Management Methods* (Cleveland: World, 1966), p. 67.

40. Aristotle, "Rhetoric," in *The Basic Works of Aristotle*, ed. Richard McKeon (New York: Random House, 1966), p. 1335.

41. Claude Shannon and Warren Weaver, *The Mathematical Theory of Communication* (Urbana, Ill.: University of Illinois Press, 1949), p. 5.

42. David K. Berlo, *The Process of Communication* (New York: Holt, Rinehart and Winston, 1960), pp. 23–38.

43. Joseph H. Foegen, "Should You Tell Them Everything?" *Advanced Management*, November 1955, pp. 28–32.

44. Brown, p. 210.

45. Hicks, p. 319.

46. Richard L. Simpson, "Vertical and Horizontal Communication in Formal Organizations," *Administrative Science Quarterly*, 4 (1959), 188–196.

47. Keith Davis, "Management Communication and the Grapevine," *Harvard Business Review*, September–October 1953, pp. 43–49.

48. Robert M. Hallberg, University of Washington, from a report cited in Miller and Form, *Industrial Sociology*, pp. 276–277.

49. Eugene Jacobson and Stanley E. Seashore, "Communications Practice in Complex Organizations," *Journal of Social Issues*, 7 (Spring, 1951), 37.

50. Harold H. Kelley, "Communication in Experimentally Created Hierarchies," *Human Relations*, 4 (1951), 39–56.

51. Applewhite, p. 95.

52. Justin G. Longenecker, *Principles of Management and Organizational Behavior* (Columbus, Ohio: Charles Merrill, 1964), p. 435.

53. Keith Davis, *Human Relations at Work* (New York: McGraw-Hill, 1962), pp. 250–251.

54. Peter Blau, "Patterns of Interaction among a Group of Officials in a Government Agency," *Human Relations*, 7 (1954), 337–348.

55. Newman et al., p. 238.

Chapter Three

1. Ernest Dale, *Management: Theory and Practice* (New York: McGraw-Hill, 1963), p. 569.

2. Philip B. Applewhite, *Organizational Behavior* (Englewood Cliffs, N.J.: Prentice-Hall, 1965), p. 53.

3. G. L. S. Shackle, in *Uncertainty and Business Decisions: A Symposium*, ed. Charles F. Carter, G. P. Meredith, and G. L. S. Shackle, 2nd ed. (Liverpool, England: Liverpool University Press, 1957), p. 105.

4. Herbert A. Simon, *Administrative Behavior* (New York: Macmillan, 1957).

5. Ray E. Brown, *Judgment in Administration* (New York: McGraw-Hill, 1966), p. 220.

6. Neal Gross, Ward S. Mason, and Alexander W. McEachern, *Explorations in Role Analysis* (New York: Wiley, 1958), p. 281.

7. Delbert C. Miller and Fremont A. Shull, Jr., "The Prediction of Administrative Role Conflict Resolutions," *Administration Science Quarterly*, September 1962, pp. 143–160.

8. Dale, pp. 551–552.

9. George R. Terry, *Principles of Management* (Homewood, Ill.: Irwin, 1964), pp. 113–120.

10. Dalton E. McFarland, *Management: Principles and Practices*, 2nd ed. (New York: Macmillan, 1964), pp. 166–169.

11. Chester Barnard, *The Functions of the Executive* (Cambridge, Mass.: Harvard University Press, 1938), pp. 188–189.

12. Herbert A. Simon, *The New Science of Management Decision* (New York: Harper, 1960), p. 8.

13. Brown, title of chap. 10, p. 200.

14. Erich Fromm, *Man for Himself: An Inquiry into the Psychology of Ethics* (New York: Rinehart, 1947).

15. Ernest Dale, "Planning and Developing the Company Organization Structure," *American Management Association Research Report*, no. 20 (New York, 1952), pp. 42–43.

16. William H. Newman, Charles E. Summer, and E. Kirby Warren, *The Process of Management* (Englewood Cliffs, N.J.: Prentice-Hall, 1967), pp. 338–345.

17. Herbert G. Hicks, *The Management of Organizations* (New York: McGraw-Hill, 1967), pp. 169–171.

18. Frank Barron, "The Disposition towards Originality," *Journal of Abnormal and Social Psychology*, 51 (1955), 478–485.

19. Alex F. Osborn, *Applied Imagination* (New York: Scribners, 1953).

20. Marvin D. Dunnette, John Campbell, and Kay Jaastad, "The Effect of Group Participation on Brain-Storming Effectiveness for Two Industrial Samples," *Journal of Applied Psychology*, 47 (1963), 30–37.

21. Donald W. Taylor, Paul C. Berry, and Clifford H. Block, "Does Group Participation When Using Brainstorming Facilitate or Inhibit Creative Thinking?" *Administrative Science Quarterly*, 3 (1958), 23–47.

22. Newman et al., p. 317.

23. W. Warren Haynes and Joseph L. Massie, *Management: Analysis, Concepts and Cases* (Englewood Cliffs, N.J.: Prentice-Hall, 1961), p. 149.

24. Ernest Dale and Leno C. Michelon, *Modern Management Methods* (Cleveland: World, 1966), pp. 112–113.

25. Stanley Young, *Management: A Systems Analysis* (Glenview, Ill.: Scott, Foresman, 1966), p. 32.

26. John Dewey, *How We Think* (Boston: Heath, 1910), pp. 101–115.

27. Richard A. Johnson, Fremont E. Kast, and James E. Rosenzweig, *The Theory and Management of Systems* (New York: McGraw-Hill, 1963), p. 213.

28. McFarland, p. 170.

29. Peter Drucker, *The Practice of Management* (New York: Harper, 1954), pp. 351–352.

30. Barnard, p. 194.

31. Ordway Tead, *The Art of Administration* (New York: McGraw-Hill, 1951).

32. Terry, pp. 122–124.

33. Brown, p. 220.

Chapter Four

1. Frederick W. Taylor, Testimony before a Special Committee of the United States House of Representatives, 1912. In Frederick W. Taylor "Shop Management," *Scientific Management* (New York: Harper and Row), p. 81.

2. See as an example of his writings, Henri Fayol, *General and Industrial Management*, trans. Constance Storrs (London: Sir Isaac Pitman, 1949), first published in French in 1916.

3. See as an example of his writings, Ralph C. Davis, *The Fundamentals of Top Management* (New York: Harper, 1951).

4. Richard A. Johnson, Fremont E. Kast, and James E. Rosenzweig, *The Theory and Management of Systems* (New York: McGraw-Hill, 1963), pp. 4, 91.

5. Arthur D. Hall, *A Methodology for Systems Engineering* (Princeton: Van Nostrand, 1962), p. 60.

6. Richard B. Kershner, "A Survey of Systems of Engineering Tools and Techniques," in *Operations Research and Systems Engineering*, ed. Charles D. Flagle, William H. Huggins, and Robert H. Roy (Baltimore: Johns Hopkins Press, 1960), p. 140.

7. Ralph E. Gibson, "The Recognition of Systems Engineering," in Flagle, p. 58.

8. John C. Kennedy, "Psychology and Systems Development," in *Psychological Principles in Systems Development*, ed. Robert M. Gagné (New York: Holt, Rinehart and Winston, 1962), p. 18.

9. Ira G. Wilson, *Information, Computers and System Design* (New York: Wiley, 1965), p. x.

10. Ludwig von Bertalanffy, "General Systems Theory: A New Approach to Unity of Science," *Human Biology*, December 1951, pp. 302–361.

11. Donald P. Eckman, ed., *Systems Research and Design: Proceedings of the First Systems Symposium at Case Institute of Technology* (New York: Wiley, 1963). See also Mihajlo D. Mesarovic, ed., *Views on General Systems Theory: Proceedings of the Second Systems Symposium at Case Institute of Technology* (New York: Wiley, 1964).

12. Mihajlo D. Mesarovic, "Foundations for a General Systems Theory," in Mesarovic, *Second Systems Symposium*, pp. 3–4.

13. Kenneth E. Boulding, "General Systems Theory: The Skeleton of Science," *Management Science*, April 1956, pp. 197–208.

14. H. Goode, "A Decision Model for a Fourth-Level Model in the Boulding Sense," in Eckman, p. 106.

15. Bertalanffy, p. 308.

16. D. S. MacArthur and J. J. Heigl, "Strategy in Research," *Transactions of the Eleventh Convention of the American Society for Quality Control* (Milwaukee: American Society for Quality Control, Inc., 1957), pp. 1–18.

17. Stanley Young, *Management: A Systems Analysis* (Glenview, Ill.: Scott, Foresman, 1966), pp. 60, 61.

18. Addison C. Bennett, *Methods Improvement in Hospitals* (Philadelphia: Lippincott, 1964), pp. 15–20.

19. Kenneth E. Boulding, "General Systems as a Point of View," in Mesarovic, *Second Systems Symposium*, p. 25.

20. H. Wallace Sinaiko and E. P. Buckley, "Human Factors in the Design of Systems," in H. Wallace Sinaiko, ed., *Selected Papers on Human Factors in the Design and Use of Control Systems* (New York: Dover, 1961), pp. 3–16.

21. Ward Edwards, "Men and Computers," in Robert M. Gagné, ed., *Psychological Principles in System Development* (New York: Holt, Rinehart and Winston, 1962), pp. 92–96.

22. Alphonse Chapanis, "On Some Relations between Human Engineering, Operations Research and System Engineering," in Eckman, *First Systems Symposium*, pp. 124–166.

23. Robert H. Schaffer, "Managing by Total Objectives," *Management Bulletin No. 52* (New York: American Management Association, 1964).

24. Edward C. Schley, *Management by Results* (New York: McGraw-Hill, 1961).

Chapter Five

1. Mark S. Blumberg, "Hospital Automation: The Needs and the Prospects," *Hospitals*, 1 August 1961, pp. 34–43, 99.

2. Phillip B. Grove, editor-in-chief, *Webster's Third New International Dictionary of the English Language*, unabridged (Springfield, Mass.: G. & C. Merriam, 1961).

3. Malcolm P. Ferguson, "Automation: Its Significance to Management," *Hospital Administration* (Spring 1958), pp. 5–25.

4. Robert M. Smith, "How to Automate a Hospital," *Management Services*, July-August 1966, pp. 48–53.

5. David E. Olsson, "Automating Nurses' Notes," *Hospitals*, 16 June 1967, pp. 64, 69, 70, 74, 76, 78.

6. Henry F. Conrad, "Automation of Building Fund Campaign," *Hospital Accounting*, September 1966, pp. 13–14.

7. Index to 1964 issues, *Hospital Accounting*, December 1964, p. 31.

8. Walter S. Buckingham, Jr., "The Four Major Principles," Robert P. Weeks, ed. *Machines and the Man* (New York: Appleton-Century-Crofts, 1961).

9. Howard R. Bowen and Garth C. Mangum, eds. *Automation and Economic Progress* (Englewood Cliffs, N.J.: Prentice-Hall, 1966).

10. Ferguson, p. 17.

11. E. Todd Wheeler, "Base Line for Evaluating Automatic Equipment: Is it Good for the Patient?" *Hospitals*, 16 September 1962, pp. 42–45.

12. Advertisement, American Sterilizer Company, *Hospitals*, 1 August 1965, p. 434.

13. Jospeh R. Fernandez and Leonard H. Gotler, "Laundry and Linen Service," in Joseph K. Owen, ed., *Modern Concepts of Hospital Administration* (Philadelphia: Saunders, 1962), p. 153.

14. David E. Rothschild, "Laundry Travels Mile-A-Minute in Air," *Hospital Management*, November 1964, pp. 78–79.

15. Vance C. Demong, "Surveillance Systems Guard against Equipment Failure," *Modern Hospital*, July 1965, pp. 142–144.

Chapter Six

1. Gerald Nadler, *Work Simplification* (New York: McGraw-Hill, 1957), p. 1.

2. Charles O. Reynolds, *Work Simplification for Everyone* (Coatsville, Pa.: Pyramid, 1962), p. 4.

3. Clements W. Zinck, *Dynamic Work Simplification* (New York: Reinhold, 1962), p. 3.

4. Robert N. Lehrer, *Work Simplification* (Englewood Cliffs, N.J.: Prentice-Hall, 1957), p. 9.

5. Lehrer, p. 7.

6. Ralph M. Barnes, *Motion and Time Study Design and Measurement of Work* (New York: Wiley, 1963), p. 4.

7. Marvin E. Mundel, *Motion and Time Study* (Englewood Cliffs, N.J.: Prentice-Hall, 1960), p. 27.

8. Ralph C. Davis, *Industrial Organization and Management* (New York: Harper, 1956), p. 294.

9. Davis, p. 252.

10. Irving Abramowitz, *Production Management* (New York: Ronald Press, 1967), p. 67.

11. *Organizing for Effective Systems Planning and Control* (New York: American Management Association, 1956), p. 152.

12. Harold B. Maynard, *Methods—Time Measurement* (New York: McGraw-Hill, 1948), pp. 7–13.

13. Richard M. Crossan, *Master Standard Data* (New York: McGraw-Hill, 1962), p. 31.

14. H. J. Hansen, "Reducing the Work in Work Areas with Time-Measurement Data," *Hospitals*, 16 November 1965, pp. 57–59.

15. Davis, p. 125.

16. Samuel Eilon, *Elements of Production, Planning and Control* (New York: Macmillan, 1962), p. 405.

17. Eilon, p. 406.

18. Davis, p. 434.

19. See Addison C. Bennett, *Methods Improvement in Hospitals* (Philadelphia: Lippincott, 1964), and Harold E. Smalley and John R. Freeman, *Hospital Industrial Engineering* (New York: Reinhold, 1966).

20. Zinck, p. 12.

21. James F. Halpin, *Zero Defects: A New Dimension in Quality Insurance* (New York: McGraw-Hill, 1966).

22. Smalley and Freeman, pp. 16–58.

23. Smalley and Freeman, pp. 59–61.

24. Harold E. Smalley, "A Study of Work Simplification in Hospitals with Emphasis on Economic Implications" (Pittsburgh: Ph.D. diss., University of Pittsburgh, 1957).

25. "Organized Methods Improvement Programs in Hospitals," *Methods Improvement Series No. 1* (Chicago: American Hospital Association, 1958).

26. Karl E. Hansen, "Work Sampling Can Cut Dietary Costs," *Modern Hospital*, May 1963, pp. 86–88.

27. Carl F. Thielman, "Methods Improvement Case Study—Four Departments, One Aim: Find a Better Way," *Hospitals*, 1 June 1961, pp. 40–43.

28. Earl W. Hagberg, "Work Analysis Cut Payroll 14%," *Modern Hospital*, September 1965, pp. 111–113.

Chapter Seven

1. Lawrence D. Miles, *Techniques of Value Analysis and Engineering* (New York: McGraw-Hill, 1961), p. vii.

2. "Purchasing's Part in Cost Reduction," *Purchasing*, June 1955, p. 39.

3. Carlos Fallon, "The All Important Definition," in William D. Falcon, *Value Analysis—Value Engineering* (New York: American Management Association, 1964), p. 10.

4. Miles, p. 1.

5. Lawrence D. Miles, "You Can Slash Costs by 25% with Value Analysis," *Management Methods*, June 1958, pp. 31–37.

6. Miles, p. 14.

7. Miles, p. 17.

8. Publications Committee, American Society of Tool and Manufacturing Engineers, *Value Engineering in Manufacturing* (Englewood Cliffs, N.J.: Prentice-Hall, 1967), p. 217.

9. See Sister Mary Thomas, "Good Organization, Good Records Reduce Maintenance Costs," *Hospitals*, 1 March 1968, pp. 73, 74, 76; Dagmar T. Walch, "Cost Cutting through Group Purchasing, Advance Preparation and Modern Service Methods," *Hospitals*, 1 March 1968, pp. 79, 80, 82; "Improved Washer Concept Reduces Materials Cost, Infection Risk," *Hospitals*, 1 March 1968, p. 84.

10. Miles, p. viii.

11. For example, the 1968 value analysis issue of *Purchasing* dated 16 May 1968 has 358 pages.

12. Ernest Dale and Leno C. Michelon, *Modern Management Methods* (Cleveland: World, 1966), p. 127.

13. J. H. Martin, "Winning Management's Approval for a Value Program," in

Falcon, ed., p. 42.

14. Harold E. Smalley and John R. Freeman, *Hospital Industrial Engineering* (New York: Reinhold, 1966), pp. 102–103.

Chapter Eight

1. Sir Charles Goodeve, "Operational Research," *Nature*, 13 March 1948, p. 377.

2. Herbert A. Simon, *The New Science of Management Decision* (New York: Harper, 1960), p. 15.

3. Ernest Dale and Leno C. Michelon, *Modern Management Methods* (Cleveland: World, 1966), p. 116.

4. Jack D. Rogers, "Perplexities in Economic Analysis for Equipment Decisions," *Advanced Management*, May 1958, p. 31.

5. Herbert G. Hicks, *The Management of Organizations* (New York: McGraw-Hill, 1967), p. 407.

6. Charles B. Allen, "Introduction to Model Building on Account Data," *National Association of Cost Accountants Bulletin*, 36 (June 1955), 1320–1333.

7. Oskar Morgenstern, "Oligopoly, Monopolistic Competition and the Theory of Games," *American Economic Review*, May 1948, p. 12.

8. Ernest Nagel, *The Structure of Science* (New York: Harcourt, Brace and World, 1961), p. 115.

9. Allen, p. 1323.

Chapter Nine

1. Robert O. Ferguson and Lauren F. Sargent, *Linear Programming: Fundamentals and Applications* (New York: McGraw-Hill, 1958), p. 3.

2. Herbert G. Hicks, *The Management of Organizations* (New York: McGraw-Hill, 1967), p. 410.

3. Wassily W. Leontief, *The Structure of the American Economy, 1919–1939* (New York: Oxford University Press, 1951).

4. George B. Dantzig, "Maximization of a Linear Function of Variables Subject to Linear Inequalities," chap. 21 in T. C. Koopman, ed., *Activity Analysis of Production and Allocation*, Cowles Commission Monograph No. 13 (New York: Wiley, 1951).

5. John P. Young, "Information Nexus Guides Decision System," *Modern Hospital*, February 1966, pp. 101–105.

Chapter Ten

1. Richard E. Bellman, *Dynamic Programming* (Princeton: Princeton University Press, 1957).

2. Ibid., p. viii.

3. Ibid.

4. Richard E. Bellman and Stuart E. Dreyfus, *Applied Dynamic Programming* (Princeton: Princeton University Press, 1962).

5. Willard I. Zangwill, *Nonlinear Programming: A Unified Approach* (Englewood Cliffs, N.J.: Prentice-Hall, 1969).

6. Franklin A. Lindsey, *New Techniques for Management Decision Making* (New York: McGraw-Hill, 1958), pp. 42-43.

Chapter Eleven

1. Charles D. Flagle, "Queuing Theory," chap. 14 in Charles D. Flagle, William H. Huggins, and Robert H. Roy, *Operations Research and Systems Engineering* (Baltimore: Johns Hopkins Press, 1960), p. 401.

2. Harold E. Smalley and John R. Freeman, *Hospital Industrial Engineering* (New York: Reinhold, 1966), pp. 342–356.

3. T. J. Norman Bailey, "Waiting Times in Outpatient Clinics," in Smalley and Freeman pp. 345–348. Also published as "Queuing for Medical Care," *Applied Statistics*, November 1954, pp. 137–145.

4. C. Wilson Whitson, "A Queuing Approach to Staffing the Operating Room," in Smalley and Freeman, pp. 348–351. Also published as "An Analysis of the Problems of Scheduling Surgery," *Hospital Management*, April 1965, pp. 58–66, and May 1965, pp. 45–49.

5. W. R. Hudson, "Computer Simulation of a Queuing Process," in Smalley and Freeman, pp. 351–355.

6. John B. Thompson, Oscar Wade Avant, and Ellawyne D. Spiker, "How Queuing Theory Works for the Hospital," *Modern Hospital*, March 1960, pp. 75–78.

7. William J. Williams, Richard P. Kovert, and James D. Steele, "Simulation Modeling of a Teaching Hospital Outpatient Clinic," *Hospitals*, 41 (1 November 1967), 71–75, 128.

8. James R. Stricker, "Queuing Theory Ends Long, Hungry Wait," *Modern Hospital*, September 1966, pp. 178–180, 194.

9. Stricker, p. 180.

Chapter Twelve

1. William J. Schull and Bruce R. Levin, "Monte Carlo Simulation: Some Uses in the Genetic Study of Primitive Man," *Stochastic Models in Medicine and Biology*, ed. John Gurland (Madison, Wis.: University of Wisconsin Press, 1964), p. 180.

2. E. N. Khoury and H. Wayne Nelson, "Simulation in Financial Planning," *Management Services*, March–April 1965, pp. 13–21.

3. H. F. Dickie and E. C. Throndsen, "Manufacturing Systems Simulation," *Factory*, October 1960, pp. 114–117.

4. Warren E. Alberts, "Report to the Eighth AIIE National Conference on Systems Simulation Symposium," *Journal of Industrial Engineering*, November-December 1957, pp. 368–369.

5. Walter C. Giffin, "How Simulation Can Help Analyze Blood Bank System," *Modern Hospital*, November 1962, p. 97.

6. Giffin, pp. 95–97.

7. John D. Thompson, Robert B. Fetter, Clinton S. McIntosh, and Robert J. Pelletier, "Predicting Requirements for Maternity Facilities," *Hospitals*, 16 February 1963, pp. 45–49, 132.

8. Joel Kavet and John D. Thompson, "Computers Can Tell You What Will Happen before It Happens," *Modern Hospital*, December 1967, pp. 102–105.

9. George H. Brooks and Henri L. Beenhakker, "A New Technique for Prediction of Future Hospital Bed Needs," *Hospital Management*, June 1964, pp. 47–50.

10. Marie E. Knickrehm, Thomas R. Hoffman, and Beatrice Donaldson, "Digital Computer Simulations of a Cafeteria Service Line," *Journal of the American Dietetic Association*, September 1963, pp. 203–208.

11. Howard A. Greenwald, "Simulation Training for Senior Hospital Staff," *Hospital* (London), August 1967, pp. 309–312.

12. *Computer Simulation of Hospital Discharges*, series 2, no. 13 (Washington, D.C.: National Center for Health Statistics, U.S. Department of Health, Education, and Welfare, February 1966).

Chapter Thirteen

1. Joel M. Kibbee, Clifford J. Kraft, and Burt Nanus, *Management Games* (New York: Reinhold, 1961), p. 4.

2. G. R. Andlinger, "Business Games—Play One," *Harvard Business Review*, March-April 1958, pp. 115–125.

3. Alfred G. Dale and Charles R. Klasson, *Business Gaming* (Austin: Bureau of Business Research, University of Texas, 1964), p. 4.

4. Paul S. Greenlaw, Lowell W. Herron, and Richard H. Rawdon, *Business Simulation* (Englewood Cliffs, N.J.: Prentice-Hall, 1962), p. 5.

5. George R. Terry, *Principles of Management* (Homewood, Ill.: Irwin, 1964), p. 156.

6. Sam A. Edwards, "Computer Based Hospital Gaming," *Hospitals*, 16 December 1965, pp. 59–60, and *Hospital Resource Management Game*, Medical Field Service School, Brooke Army Medical Center, Fort Sam Houston, Texas, unpub. manual, 1967, p. 31.

7. Greenlaw, pp. 6–7.

8. Kibbee, pp. 46–48.

9. Lois Stewart, "Management Games Today," chap. 11 in Kibbee, p. 176.

10. "Here's a Realistic Way to Play Wholesaler," *Business Week*, 3 September 1960, pp. 108–112.

11. Greenlaw, pp. 729–280.

12. Kibbee, pp. 41–46.

Chapter Fourteen

1. B. J. Hansen, *Practical PERT* (Washington, D.C.: American House, 1965), p. 11.

2. Peter P. Schoderbek, "PERT/Cost: Its Values and Limitations," chap. 41 in *Management Systems*, ed. Peter P. Schoderbek (New York: Wiley, 1963), p. 398.

3. David M. Stires and Maurice M. Murphy, *PERT and CPM* (Boston: Materials Management Institute, 1963), p. 21.

4. Schoderbek, pp. 398–403.

5. "Shortcut for Project Planning," *Business Week*, 7 July 1962, p. 106.

6. Richard E. Beckwith, "A Cost Control Extension of the PERT System," *IEEE Transactions of Engineering Management*, EM–9, December 1962, pp. 147–149.

7. Schoderbek, p. 398.

8. William H. Newman, Charles E. Summer, and E. Kirby Warren, *The Process of Management* (Englewood Cliffs, N.J.: Prentice-Hall, 1967), p. 716.

9. Harry F. Evarts, *Introduction to PERT* (Boston: Allyn and Bacon, 1964), p. 88.

10. Newman et al., pp. 716–717.

11. Francis A. Sando, "Critical Path Is Road to Better Building," *Modern Hospital*,

November 1963, pp. 91–96.

12. Paul F. Nalon and Robert I. Ballinger, Jr., "Critical Path Method of Scheduling and Financing for Hospitals," *Hospital Management*, May 1964, pp. 40–42.

13. James J. O'Brien, "How CPM Can Expedite Your Construction Program," *Hospital Topics*, May 1965, pp. 48–53.

14. Edward H. Noroian, "Critical Path Method Saves Building Time and Dollars," *Modern Hospital*, June 1966, pp. 103–107.

15. Ben Carlisle, "How PERT Simplifies Management of Hospital Programs," *Hospitals*, 16 December 1965, pp. 61–64.

16. Harold E. Smalley and John R. Freeman, *Hospital Industrial Engineering* (New York: Reinhold, 1966).

17. John R. Buchan, "A Critical Path Study of an Emergency Tracheotomy," in Smalley and Freeman, pp. 408–411.

18. Ben W. Latimer, "Minimizing Computer Conversion Time through Network Analysis," in Smalley and Freeman, pp. 412–415.

19. Joseph J. Moder and Cecil R. Phillips, *Project Management with CPM and PERT* (New York: Reinhold, 1964), pp. 5–6.

20. Schoderbek, pp. 398–403.

21. Sando, p. 96.

22. Robert Miller, "How to Plan and Control with PERT," *Harvard Business Review*, March–April 1962, pp. 93–104.

Chapter Fifteen

1. John F. Magee, "Decision Trees for Decision-Making," *Harvard Business Review*, July–August 1964, pp. 126–138. See also Magee, "How to Use Decision Trees in Capital Investment," *Harvard Business Review*, September–October 1964, pp. 79–96.

2. Ernest Dale and Leno C. Michelon, *Modern Management Methods* (Cleveland: World, 1966), pp. 154–164.

3. George J. Brabb, *Introduction to Quantitative Management* (New York: Holt, Rinehart and Winston, 1968), pp. 199–212, 334–335.

4. George R. Wren, "Modern Management Concepts, Tools," *Hospital Topics*, January 1968, pp. 37–42, 48 (Correction in *Hospital Topics*, February 1968, p. 56).

Chapter Sixteen

1. William H. Newman and James P. Logan, *Business Policies and Central Management* (Chicago: Southwestern, 1965), p. 396.

2. John Von Neumann and Oskar Morgenstern, *Theory of Games and Economic Behavior*, 2nd ed. (Princeton: Princeton University Press, 1947), chap. 1 and appendix.

3. John D. Thompson, Robert B. Fetter, Clinton S. McIntosh, and Robert J. Pelletier, "Predicting Requirements for Maternity Facilities," *Hospitals*, 16 February 1963, pp. 45–49, 132.

4. William F. Taylor, "Some Monte Carlo Methods Applied to an Epidemic of Acute Respiratory Disease," *Human Biology*, September 1958, pp. 185–200.

5. Von Neumann and Morgenstern, entire book.

6. R. Ducan Luce and Howard Raiffa, *Games and Decisions* (New York: Wiley, 1957).

7. William J. Baumol, *Economic Theory and Operations Analysis* (Englewood Cliffs, N.J.: Prentice-Hall, 1961), chap. 18.

Conclusion

1. Joseph J. Wnuk, Jr., "The Computer and Public Relations," *Atlanta Economic Review*, July 1966, p. 7.

2. Ruth Ravich, Helen Rehr, and Charles H. Goodrich, "Hospital Ombudsman Smooths Flow of Services and Communication," *Hospitals*, 1 March 1969, pp. 56–61.

3. John E. Cooke, "Needs of the Employee in the Computerized Hospital," *Canadian Hospital*, March 1968, pp. 50–53.

Author Index

Abramowitz, Irving, 109
Alberts, Warren E., 156
Allen, Charles B., 129
Andlinger, G. R., 165
Applewhite, Philip B., 31, 45, 50
Appley, Lawrence A., 3
Argyris, Chris, 25
Aristotle, 40
Avant, Oscar Wade, 147

Bailey, T. J. Norman, 147
Ballinger, Robert I., Jr., 183
Barnard, Chester I., 20, 36, 55, 68
Barnes, Ralph M., 108
Barron, Frank, 63
Bass, Bernard M., 35
Baumgartel, Howard, 31
Baumol, William J., 204
Beckwith, Richard E., 179
Beenhakker, Henri L., 161
Bellman, Richard E., 138, 139
Bennett, Addison C., 85, 111
Berlo, David K., 40
Berry, Paul C., 63
Bertalanffy, Ludwig Von, 80
Blau, Peter, 46
Block, Clifford H., 63
Blumberg, Mark S., 101
Boulding, Kenneth E., 80, 86
Bowen, Howard R., 103
Brabb, George J., 196
Brooks, George H., 161
Broom, Halsey N., 3, 7
Brown, Ray E., 39, 42, 52, 59, 69
Buchan, John R., 185
Buckingham, Walter S., Jr., 102

Buckley, E. P., 90

Campbell, John, 63
Carlisle, Ben, 184
Chamberlain, John, 39
Chapanis, Alphonse, 94
Clough, Donald J., 6
Coch, Lester, 32
Conrad, Henry F., 102
Cooke, John E., 213
Crossan, Richard M., 110

Dale, Alfred G., 165
Dale, Ernest, 5, 7, 11, 13, 19, 40, 50,
    54, 60, 64, 120, 126, 196
Dantzig, George B., 130
Davis, Keith, 30, 43, 46
Davis, Ralph C., 4, 6, 77, 109, 111
Demong, Vance C., 105
Dewey, John, 65
Dickie, H. F., 155
Dickson, William J., 21, 24
Donaldson, Beatrice, 161
Dreyfus, Stuart E., 139
Drucker, Peter, 5, 66
Dunnette, Marvin D., 63

Eckman, Donald P., 80
Edwards, Sam A., 166
Edwards, Ward, 94
Eilon, Samuel, 111
Evarts, Harry F., 180

Fallon, Carlos, 116
Fayol, Henri, 77
Ferguson, Malcolm P., 101, 103

227

Ferguson, Robert O., 130
Fernandez, Joseph R., 104
Fetter, Robert B., 159, 203
Flagle, Charles D., 143
Foegen, Joseph H., 42
Form, William H., 22, 25
Freeman, John R., 111, 113, 122, 147,
    184, 185
French, Cecil J., 25
French, John R. P., 32
Fromm, Erich, 60

Gibson, Ralph E., 79
Giffin, Walter C., 157, 159
Goode, H., 80
Goodeve, Sir Charles, 125
Goodrich, Charles H., 212
Gotler, Leonard H., 104
Gouldner, Alvin W., 30
Graicunas, V. A., 10
Greenlaw, Paul S., 165, 166, 167
Greenwald, Howard A., 162
Gross, Neal, 53
Grove, Phillip B., 101

Hagberg, Earl W., 115
Haimann, Theo, 3
Hall, Arthur D., 79
Hallberg, Robert M., 44
Halpin, James F., 112
Hansen, B. J., 171
Hansen, H. J., 110
Hansen, Karl E., 114
Haravey, Francois, 35
Harbinson, Frederick, 6
Haynes, W. Warren, 12, 64
Heigl, J. J., 83
Herron, Lowell W., 165
Herzberg, Frederick, 29
Hicks, Herbert G., 7, 36, 37, 43, 62,
    128, 130
Hoffman, Thomas R., 161
Hudson, W. R., 147

Jaastad, Kay, 63
Jacobson, Eugene, 45
Jennings, Eugene E., 36
Johnson, Richard A., 66, 79

Kahn, Robert L., 30
Kast, Fremont E., 66, 79

Katz, Daniel, 30
Kavet, Joel, 160
Kelley, Harold H., 45
Kennedy, John C., 79
Kershner, Richard B., 79
Khoury, E. N., 154
Kibbee, Joel M., 164, 166, 168
Klasson, Charles R., 165
Knickrehm, Marie E., 161
Koontz, Harold, 3, 7
Kovert, Richard P., 147
Kraft, Clifford J., 164

Landsberger, Henry, 22
Latimer, Ben W., 185
Lawrence, Paul B., 24
Leavitt, Harold J., 36
Lehrer, Robert N., 107, 108
Leontief, Wassily W., 130
Levin, Bruce R., 154
Lewin, Kurt, 34
Likert, Rensis, 34
Lindsey, Franklin A., 139
Lippitt, Ronald, 31
Logan, James P., 199
Longenecker, Justin G., 3, 7, 46
Luce, R. Ducan, 204

MacArthur, D. S., 83
McEachern, Alexander W., 53
McFarland, Dalton E., 3, 4, 55, 66
McIntosh, Clinton S., 159, 203
Magee, John F., 189, 196
Mangum, Garth C., 103
Martin, J. H., 121
Maslow, Abraham H., 26, 213
Mason, Ward S., 53
Massie, Joseph L., 12, 64
Mausner, Bernard, 29
Maynard, Harold B., 110
Mayo, Elton, 21
Mee, John F., 4
Mesarovic, Mihajlo D., 80
Michelon, Leno C., 40, 64, 120, 126,
    196
Miles, Lawrence D., 116, 117, 119
Miller, Delbert C., 22, 25, 54
Miller, Robert, 187
Moder, Joseph J., 185
Moore, Franklin G., 37, 39, 40
Morgenstern, Oskar, 129, 165, 202, 204

Mundel, Marvin E., 108
Murphy, Maurice M., 172
Myers, Charles A., 6

Nadler, Gerald, 107
Nagel, Ernest, 129
Nalon, Paul F., 183
Nanus, Burt, 164
Nelson, H. Wayne, 154
Neumann, John Von, 202, 204
Newman, William H., 6, 12, 24, 47, 61, 64, 179, 180, 199
Nord, Ole C., 6
Noroian, Edward H., 184

O'Brien, James J., 184
O'Donnell, Cyril, 3, 7
Olsson, David E., 102
Osborn, Alex F., 63

Pelletier, Robert J., 159, 203
Pennington, D. F., Jr., 35
Peterson, Elmore, 3
Phillips, Cecil R., 185
Plowman, E. Grosvenor, 3

Raiffa, Howard, 204
Ravich, Ruth, 212
Rawdon, Richard H., 165
Rehr, Helen, 212
Reynolds, Charles O., 107
Roethlisberger, Fritz, 21, 24
Rogers, Jack D., 128
Rosenzweig, James E., 66, 79
Rothschild, David E., 105

Sando, Francis A., 182, 186
Sargent, Lauren F., 130
Schaffer, Robert H., 97
Schley, Edward C., 97
Schoderbek, Peter P., 172, 177, 179, 186
Schull, William J., 154
Seashore, Stanley E., 45
Seiler, John A., 24
Shackle, G. L. S., 50
Shannon, Claude, 40
Shull, Fremont A., Jr., 54
Simon, Herbert A., 50, 55, 126
Simpson, Richard L., 43
Sinaiko, H. Wallace, 90

Smalley, Harold E., 111, 113, 122, 147, 184, 185
Smith, Robert M., 102
Snyderman, Barbara Block, 29
Spiker, Ellayne D., 147
Starr, Martin K., 6
Steele, James D., 147
Stewart, Lois, 167
Stires, David M., 172
Stogdill, Ralph M., 30
Strauss, George, 36
Stricker, James R., 147, 149
Summer, Charles E., 6, 24, 47, 61, 64, 179, 180
Suojanen, Waino W., 11, 77

Taylor, Donald W., 63
Taylor, Frederick W., 76
Taylor, William F., 203
Tead, Ordway, 6, 69
Teichroew, Daniel, 6
Terry, George R., 7, 39, 55, 69, 165
Thielman, Carl F., 114
Thomas, Sister Mary, 119
Thompson, John B., 147
Thompson, John D., 159, 160, 203
Throndsen, E. C., 155

Ure, Andrew, 20
Urwick, Lyndall F., 12

Veinott, Arthur F., Jr., 6

Warren, E. Kirby, 6, 24, 47, 61, 64, 179, 180
Weaver, Warren, 40
Wheeler, E. Todd, 104
White, Ralph, 31
Whitehead, Thomas North, 24
Whitson, C. Wilson, 147
Whyte, William F., 25
Williams, William J., 147
Wilson, Ira G., 79
Wnuk, Joseph J., Jr., 212
Wren, George R., 196

Young, John P., 132
Young, Stanley, 64, 85

Zangwill, Willard I., 139
Zinck, Clements W., 107, 111

Subject Index

Activity, PERT, 172
Actuating, 7–8
Adaptation systems, 84
Administrative resistance, 42
Authority, 12–13; commensurate with responsibility, 13–14
Automation, 101–106; defined, 101–103

Behavioral science approach to management, 19–49; change, 32–34; communications, 39–48; communications, formal, 41–43; communications, informal, 43–48; human relations, 21–23; informal groups, 24–26; leadership, 30–32; management of change, 32–34; motivation of worker, 26–30; participative management, 34–39; semantics, 40–41; some early behavioral scientists, 20–21; some findings, 23–48; worker motivation, 26–30
Behavioral science school of management, 78
Black box, 83–84
Brain, compared to computer, 93–95
Brainstorming, 63
Break-even analysis, 131
Business games, 164. See also Games
Business simulation, 164

Cardinal utility theory, 201–202
Case-study method, 165
Chain of command, 11, 16
Change, management of, 32–34
Command, chain of, 11, 16
Committees, 36–38, 66; disadvantages of, 38–39

Communication, 39–48; and decision making, 70; downward, 42; formal, 41–43; informal, 43–48; in management, 16; semantics, 40–41; too much, 42; upward, 42
Competitive simulation. See Gaming
Components: machine, 90–92; man as a systems component, 90–92; of a system, 84
Computer: compared to human brain, 93–95; dry, 90; wet, 90
Conflict, and decision making, 53
Control: cost, 111; inventory, 111; production, 110–111; quality, 111; span of, 10–11; systems, 84, 86, 87–90; systems, non-electronic example of, 89; systems, tolerance in, 87
Controlling, 8
Cost control, 111
Cost reduction, 119, 120
CPM, 178–179; characteristics of, 184; cohesive and divisive forces in, 182–183; and PERT, 177. See also PERT
Creative innovation, 16–17
Creative thinking, 63
Creativity: barriers to, 62; in decision-making, 61–63; process, 61; search for, 62; tests for, 63; types of, 62
Critical incident, 165
Critical path, in PERT, 173, 176
Critical path method. See CPM
Customer frustration, 212–213

Decision-makers, types of, 60–61
Decision-making, 50–71, 188–189; as an art, 68–69; the behavioral science

theory, 58; classified, 197–198; creativity in, 61–63; and communications, 70; handling of risk in, 199; improving, 69–71; incorrect ideas about, 70; lowest competent level, 66; marginal theory of, 56–57; mathematical theory of, 58–59; and modern management tools, 70; noncontrollable factors in, 197; and organizational conflict, 53; and personal internal conflict, 53–54, 59–60; probability in, 199; and problem solving, 65, 66; psychological theory of, 58; psychology in, 59–61; the quantitative theory, 58–59; scientific theory of, 57–58; steps in, 64–66; theories of, 56–59; under certainty, 198–199; under risk, 199–200; under uncertainty, 200–202; under risk or uncertainty, 197–207; under risk or uncertainty, game theory, 203–206; under risk or uncertainty, Monte Carlo, 202–203

Decisions: characteristics of, 51–54; classification of, 54–56

Decisions, who should make, 66–68

Decision trees, 192–196; definition of, 195

Delegation, 12–14

Demands, extra on systems, 96–97

Design: Machine, 108–109; physical plant, 109–110; tool, 108–109; systems, 85–87

Designer, of a system, 84

Dynamic decision-making, 164, 167

Dynamic programming, 137–140

Emergency room and queuing theory, 150–151

Employee suggestion systems, 112, 120

Enlightened self-interest, 23

Event, PERT, 172

Exception: management by, 11–12; management by and PERT, 176

Exercise, simulation, 164

Extra demands on systems, 96–97

Feedback, systems, 84, 87

Finances, in management, 16

Flow chart, systems, 85

Frustration, customer, 212–213

Games: business, 164–168; business, two types of, 165; hospital administration, Baylor University, 166; hospital administration, Georgia State University, 166; management, 164; operational use of, 167–168; playing of, 166; what taught, 166. *See also* Gaming

Game theory, 201, 203–206; and gaming, 165

Gaming, 163–168; advantages, 168; definition, 165; disadvantages, 168. *See also* Games

Gantt chart, and PERT, 177

Grapevine, 43–48; executive use of, 47–48

Happiness school of management, 22

Hawthorne experiments, 21–22; criticism of, 22

Herzberg's motivational model, 29–30

Hierarchy of Human Needs, Maslow, 26–29

History of management thought, 75

Human needs, Maslow's hierarchy of, 26–29

Human relations, 21–23; school of management, 77–78; and systems, 95–97

Human values, and systems, 211–213

In-basket exercises, 165

Industrial engineering, 112, 113

Informal groups, 24–26

Innovation, creative, 16–17

Input: systems, 81–82, 85; direct, 82, 85; environmental, 82, 86

Input-output analysis, 130

Inventory control, 111

Job study, 112

Leadership, 17, 30–32

Linear programming, 130–136; advantages of, 133–135; definition, 130; disadvantages of, 135–136; examples, 131–133; history, 130; what is it, 131

Line organization, 14–15

Machine components of a system, 90–92

Machine design, 108–109

Man, as a systems component, 90–92

Management, 1–18; actuating, 7–8; art and science, 6; behavioral science approach, 19–49; behavioral science school of, 78; carrying out functions, 8–17; communications in, 16; controlling, 8; creative innovation in, 16–17; decision-making, 50–71; defined, 3–4; delegation in, 12–14; by exception, 11–12; by exception, and PERT, 176; finances in, 16; formal organization in, 8–11; functions of, 6–8; happiness school of, 22; human relations school of, 77–78; leadership, 17; line and staff organization, 14–15; mathematics in, 127–129; motivation in, 15–16; of change, 32–34; organizational theory of, 77; organizing, 7; participative, 34–39; planning, 7; quantitative, 78; scientific, 75; as a total process, 8, 9; universality of, 4–6; what is it, 3–4

Management games, 164. *See also* Games

Management thought, history of, 75–78

Marginal theory of decision-making, 56–57

Maslow's hierarchy of human needs, 26–29

Mathematical theory of decision-making, 58–59

Mathematics in management, 127–129

Methods improvement, 112

Methods research, 112

Methods study, 112

Models, 129; dynamic programming, 137–140; gaming, 163–168; linear programming, 130–136; non-linear programming, 137–140; queuing theory, 141–152; simulation, 153–162; simulation, types of, 154

Monte Carlo, definition of, 202–203

Morale, worker and productivity, 30

Motivation, 15–16; worker, 26–30; worker, Herzberg's model of, 29–30

Network, PERT, 172

Non-linear programming, 137–140

Operation analysis, 112

Operations research, 123–129; definition of, 126–127; history of, 125–126

Operator of a system, 84

OR. *See* Operations research

Organization, formal, 8–11

Organizational balance, 11

Organizational theory of management, 77

Organizing, 7

Output, systems, 83, 85

Overcommunication, 42

Owen, Robert, 20

Participative management, 34–39

Payoff tables, 188–192, 196; definition of, 189

PERT, 171–187; activity, 172; advantages of, 183–184; computing time in, 173; and CPM, 177; and CPM, cohesive and divisive forces in, 182–183; critical path, 173, 176; criticisms of, 187; definition, 171–173, 176; event, 172; and Gantt chart, 177; health example, 180–185; history, 176–178; and management by exception, 176; methodology, 176; misuse of, 186–187; network, 172; slack, 173; time, 173; weaknesses, 186; what it is, 171–176. *See also* CPM

PERT-COST, 179–180

Physical plant design, 109–110

Planning, 7

Plant layout, 109

Poisson distribution, 149

Poisson function, 146–147

Policies, 11

Probability in decision-making, 199

Procedures, 11

Process, systems, 83, 86

Production: automation, 101–106; modern management in, 99–122; value analysis, 116–122; work simplification, 107–115

Production control, 110–111

Productivity and worker morale, 30

Program evaluation and review technique. *See* PERT

Psychological theory of decision-making, 58

Psychology in decision-making, 59–61

Quality control, 111
Quantitative management, 78
Quantitative methods, 127
Quantitative techniques, 127
Queuing theory, 141–152; characteristics, 143–146; definition, 143;
and the emergency room, 150–151;
general theory, 143; health applications, 147–151; hospital applications
of, 149; Poisson distribution not
necessary in, 149; Poisson function
in, 146–147

Random number tables explained, 202
Resistance, administrative, 42
Responsibility, 12–13
Risk in decision-making, 199
Role-playing, 165
Rules, 11
Rumors, 45

Scientific approach to management.
See Systems
Scientific management, 75
Scientific method, 65–66
Scientific theory of decision-making,
57–58
Self-interest, enlightened, 23
Semantics, 40–41
Short chain of command, 11
Simplex method, 130
Simulation, 153–162; advantages,
156–159; business, 164; definition,
153; disadvantages, 159; and gaming,
163; health examples, 159–162; how
used, 155–156; models, types of, 154;
necessary conditions, 155; reasons to
use, 156–157; steps in, 155; what is
it, 153–155. *See also* Gaming
Simulation exercise, 164
Slack in PERT, 173
Span of Control, 10–11
Staff organization, 14–15
Stochastic, 190

Subsystem, 85
Suggestion systems, employee, 112, 120
"Sweetening" of reports, 42
Systems, 73–98; adaptation, 84; black
box, 83–84; closed, defined, 80;
components, 84, 90–95; components,
machine, 90–92; components, man
as a, 90–92; control, 84, 86, 87–90;
control, non-electronic example of,
89; control, tolerance in, 87; definitions, 79–80; design, 85–87; designer,
84; direct input, 82, 85; environmental
input, 82, 86; extra demands on,
96–97; feedback, 84, 87; flow chart,
85; general theory of, 80; and human
relations, 95–97; and human values,
211–213; input, 81–82, 85, 86;
open, defined, 80; operator, 84;
output, 83; process, 83, 86; subsystem, 85

Taylor, Frederick W., 19, 20, 75
Terrill, Thomas E., on PERT, 186
Time and motion studies, 108, 120
Time in PERT, 173
Tolerance, in systems control, 87
Tool design, 108–109

Universality of management, 4–6

Value analysis, 115–122; compared with
work simplification, 122; definition,
116–117, 120; health field applications, 118–119; obtaining professional assistance for, 121–122;
organization of, 121
Values, human and systems, 211–213

Worker morale and productivity, 30
Worker motivation, 26–30
Work measurement, 112
Work simplification, 107–115; defined,
107
Work standardization, 110

Zero defects, 112